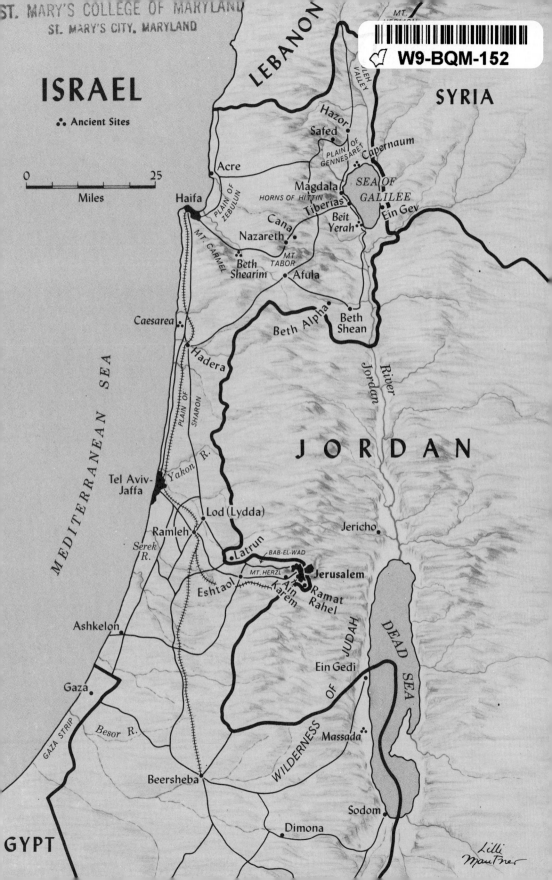

ISRAEL

∴ Ancient Sites

0   25
Miles

LEBANON

SYRIA

MT. HERMON

HULEH VALLEY

Hazor

Safed

PLAIN OF GENNESARET

Acre

Capernaum

Magdala

SEA OF GALILEE

HORNS OF HITTIN

Tiberias

Ein Gev

Haifa

PLAIN OF ZEBULUN

Cana

Beit Yerah

MT. CARMEL

Nazareth

MT. TABOR

Beth Shearim

Afula

Caesarea

Beth Alpha

Beth Shean

MEDITERRANEAN SEA

Hadera

Jordan River

J O R D A N

PLAIN OF SHARON

Yakon R.

Tel Aviv-Jaffa

Lod (Lydda)

Jericho

Ramleh

Serek R.

Latrun

BAB-EL-WAD

MT. HERZL

Jerusalem

Eshtaol

Ain Karem

Ramat Rahel

Ashkelon

WILDERNESS OF JUDAH

DEAD SEA

Ein Gedi

Gaza

GAZA STRIP

Besor R.

Massada

Beersheba

Sodom

Dimona

GYPT

Lilli Mautner

The Splendor of Israel

Books by Robert Payne

THE SPLENDOR OF ISRAEL

THE SPLENDOR OF GREECE

THE SPLENDOR OF PERSIA

THE SHEPHERD

THE WHITE RAJAHS OF SARAWAK

THE GOLD OF TROY

THE HOLY FIRE

THE HOLY SWORD

THE WHITE PONY

FOREVER CHINA

The

Harper & Row,

Splendor of Israel

by Robert Payne

Publishers · New York, Evanston, and London

LIBRARY OF CONGRESS CATALOG CARD NUMBER: 63-10607

I-T

TO THE HAPPY MEMORY OF PHILIP BALL

Contents

x

Illustrations

These illustrations will be found following page 128:

Porphyry statue at Caesarea

Herodian capital at Ashkelon

Winged Victory at Ashkelon

Hazor. The Dragon's Teeth
　　Government Press Office, Tel Aviv

Beth Shearim. The Catacombs
　　Government Press Office, Tel Aviv

Beth Shean. The Roman theater in foreground, and the fortified Tel in background
　　Government Press Office, Tel Aviv

Capernaum. The synagogue

Massada

These illustrations will be found following page 160:

The Tremore at Nazareth

A goddess from the Painted Tomb at Ashkelon
　　Government Press Office, Tel Aviv

Bread and Fishes mosaic from Tabgha
　　Government Press Office, Tel Aviv

A nymph from the Painted Tomb at Ashkelon

Peacock mosaic from Tabgha
　　Government Press Office, Tel Aviv

The Cenaculum on Mount Zion
　　Israel Government Tourist Office

Courtyard in the Church of John the Baptist at Ain Karem

Mount Tabor
　　Government Press Office, Tel Aviv

The Sea of Galilee
　　Government Press Office, Tel Aviv

Cana
　　Government Press Office, Tel Aviv

The photographs are by the author unless otherwise stated.

ACKNOWLEDGMENTS

I am most grateful for the generous help given to me during two visits to Israel by Shaul Arie, Giora Bartov, Sam Becker, David Landor, Meron Medzini and Lionel Pyetan, and for the many kindnesses of Theodore Kollek, Chief of the Prime Minister's Office.

The Splendor of Israel

Jerusalem

When you leave the coast and go up to Jerusalem, you are in splendid company. For thousands upon thousands of years men and women have made the same journey and seen the same familiar landmarks. The ancient Hebrews came along this road, bringing the first fruits to the Temple. The Egyptians came, and marauders from the Philistine cities in the southwest, and the Assyrians with their long spears, and the Persians with their battle standards topped with golden apples; and then came the Greeks, the Romans, the Arabs, the Seljuks, the Crusaders, the Mamelukes, the Ottoman Turks and the British. The Sages said that nine-tenths of the world's beauty was to be found in Jerusalem, but this beauty was paid for with nine-tenths of the world's suffering. From the beginning of recorded history there have been incessant wars along the road, and for almost as long a time pilgrims have come to gaze at the holy places. On this road there is scarcely a stone which has not been kissed, or a clod of earth which has not been soaked in blood. Swords and prayers are the road's companions.

The ghosts linger and throw their shadows on the road which winds across the plain and climbs the steep Judean mountains. It is a wild road, which seems to have cut loose from the ordinary life of mankind, so pounded by prayers and blood and legends that it resembles nothing so much as a shadowed highway of the imagination:

1

not real, only to be guessed at, having its existence in the furthest reaches of the human spirit and in the wilderness of the human heart.

When the first pilgrims came to the Holy Land in the Middle Ages, eager to touch the holy relics and to stand in the paths of holiness, they followed very much the same road which we travel today. Usually the pilgrim ship put to shore at Jaffa, a bowshot from the modern city of Tel Aviv. Here they found the great church with ten altars erected by St. Louis, and for a fee they might inspect the authentic bones of the whale which had swallowed Jonah. From Jaffa they would make their way by slow caravan to Lydda, fortified by Joshua, with the head of St. George the dragon-slayer lying beneath the altar of his church, and here again for a fee they might be permitted to examine the relics of the dragon. At a rather higher fee, they might obtain one of the hairs from the head of St. George. Then on to Ramleh, the ancient Arimathea, which for four hundred years was the capital of Palestine until the Crusaders wrested it from the Arabs. Ramleh had its tower of the forty martyrs, and the legends of St. Joseph and St. Nicodemus. There was also, according to Sir John Mandeville, "a fair church of our Lady, where our Lord appeared to her in the likeness that betokeneth the Trinity." Beyond Ramleh lay the Vale of Ajalon, where Joshua fought the five kings and bade the sun and moon be still, and here, if the pilgrim was lucky and carried the right credentials, he would rest for the night in the Fortress of the Good Thief, the *Castellum boni latronis,* or at nearby Emmaus. Already in the span of a single day the pilgrim would have encountered a whale, a dragon, the head of a saint, and six or seven holy sites directly or remotely associated with the Crucifixion and the Resurrection. But the main drama of the journey was yet to come.

The modern traveler in Israel cannot stay at Emmaus or Latrun, where the good thief was believed to have been born, for these are blocked off by the armistice lines, Latrun being a heavily defended Jordanian outpost. Here he departs from the ancient pilgrim road, but never for more than a few miles. The road swings to the southeast and rounds the bend of the Jordanian salient through Eshtaol, which was Samson's camping ground, and so to Bab-el-Wad, the Gate of the Valley, where the long climb begins. We speak of going up to

Jerusalem, but until this point there is only a slow rise through orchards and vineyards. The lowlands shine yellow in the sun, the water sprinklers are glittering, there are neat fields which might, for their luxuriance, be in the south of France. Suddenly the highway turns sharply into the hills, and there is a raw excitement in the air, the sense of a drama unfolding, pines and cypresses crowding the slopes and forming a kind of curtain. When this green curtain lifts, the drama will begin with a savage and unsuspected intensity.

For three or four miles there is the illusion of traveling along a winding mountain road that might be in California or in the Black Forest. The pines and cypresses cling close to the road. Here and there the boulders show through the trees, and rusted barbed wires spring out of the earth. Then there are rough cairns which may be boundary posts but are more likely to be memorials for dead soldiers, and some of the larger cairns have names inscribed on them. Then suddenly at the turning of the road, which seems to be losing itself in a green fairyland, for the forest lies close and the shadows move within it—there are four smashed armored cars. There are bullet marks on them, they have lost their wheels, and they lie where they fell. They have been painted red to preserve them from rust, and some bear their original numbers. They are hideous and startling. They sprawl there like obscene skeletons, like the carapaces of animals that died so long ago that we no longer remember their names. At that turning of the road, under those pines, the appearance of the wrecked armored cars has the effect of an hallucination. The fairy tale has turned into nightmare. The cars seem to be bleeding.

I know no war memorials so effective as these cars lying by the roadside: so empty, so devoid of any ordinary meaning, and yet so deliberate and so threatening. No statue in bronze can speak so loudly of war's terrors. The haphazard way in which they lie there, some overturned, others on their sides, echoes the insanity of war. They are like giants encountered in the magic forest, all the more dangerous because they are dead.

Along the winding road more armored cars appear. There are altogether about a dozen of these cars on the way to Jerusalem, and all are terrifying. They are Israeli cars lost during the bitter fighting in

1948, when the Jordanians almost succeeded in cutting the new "Burma Road" which enabled a trickle of supplies to reach embattled Jerusalem.

First the flowering lowlands, then the green forest, then the lonely heights.

For as suddenly as one enters the forest, there is an end to it. There is almost no warning. Suddenly the curtain rises on what for the unsuspecting traveler is the most dramatic spectacle that Israel has to offer. The shadowy forest is over, the heavens open out, and there is no longer any earth—only a titanic ground swell of naked rocks shaped like enormous skulls all gray and ocher and parchment-colored, stretching, it seems, to infinity. It is as though the earth had exploded in a multitude of volcanic bubbles, which became petrified at the moment when they were about to burst. That prodigious naked landscape, boiling under the sun, is the Judean wilderness.

In the sun's intense glare these billows seem to sway and reel; they crowd ominously together; an army marching over them would appear like an army of ants. They have a savage and unrelenting life of their own, like swollen tongues clamoring to speak: the voice is choked at the source. Skulls or tongues, they have enough of the elements of human life to be strangely familiar; one has seen these plains of bubbles before, but God knows where. Compared to this wilderness, the deserts of Arabia are consolingly gentle, for in the deserts at least even under the most pitiless sun there is the knowledge that one could crawl in a straight line towards the nearest oasis. Here there are no straight lines. Here there are only the round tops of mountains and the ash-colored canyons, the precipitous slope down into the wadis, where in winter the flash floods roar.

But not now; not in summer when no rain ever falls. Now the eroded rocks with their honeycombed surfaces pitilessly reflect the sun's fury. The light boils in the air, for all these domes and bubbles reflect the sun's rays as from curving mirrors, and the light glancing off one mountain clashes visibly with the light glancing off another. It is an effect comparable with the strange behavior of light over the island of Delos, which is magnified by reflections from all the islands around it, so that high in the air the light comes to a dazzling focus.

So here again the light boils and spills over, but it is not the crystalline light of Greece. The shimmering gold in the air comes from the dust of the Negev, and from the Dead Sea, and from Arabia. For much the same reason the traveler in Peking is amazed to see the sky flowing liquid gold, laden with the sands of the Gobi.

The skies over the Judean wilderness are a rich golden-blue, never at rest. It is the color of majesty, so ornate a color that it seems almost artificial, as the frozen and petrified billows seem artificial. Once seen, that continual flashing, that glinting as of angels' wings high in the air, is unforgettable. Having seen it, you no longer wonder why the prophets entered the wilderness and came out again with revelations of God's presence.

In the pure air of Greece, among those sharp-sided mountains, it is not difficult to imagine the gods walking on the mountaintops, stepping easily from one to another; but there are no gods walking casually over the mountains of Judea. Here there is only the intense trembling glare, the sense of a splendor beyond human comprehension, the gold and the blue at war with one another. Here on any summer day God's face shines visibly in the heavens.

After the Judean wilderness even Jerusalem comes as an anticlimax.

For Jerusalem is a small city, like a child's toy lost in the immensity of the wilderness. The old city is like a square fortress crowning one of the bare, scalded hills, and the new city leaps along the valleys and over the neighboring hills like a vine which pushes out at random; and while both cities have their own grandeur, nothing made by human hands can equal the grandeur of the wilderness.

The pilgrims in the Middle Ages followed a road which runs parallel to the present road, just inside Jordanian territory. They came at last to the heights of Mizpah, where the Prophet Samuel was born, where King Saul was elected to his high office amid cries of "God save the king!" and where the Prophet Jeremiah lived with a small group of companions who had escaped exile to Babylon after the destruction of the first Temple. Here the pilgrims caught their first sight of the holy city, calling it Montjoie, "for it gives joy to the pilgrims' hearts, being the place where they first set eyes on Jerusalem." Arriving at Montjoie Richard the Lion-Heart fell on his knees and hid his face in his hands, refusing to look upon the city which had fallen into Arab hands, crying out: "Lord God, I pray that I may never see the holy city if I may not rescue it from the hands of Thine enemies." But such self-denial was rare. Most pilgrims, Jews and Christians alike, fell on their knees and intoned the Psalm: "I was glad when they said unto me, Let us go into the house of the Lord."

THE GOLDEN WALLS

When in 1917 the young and erudite Ronald Storrs was appointed military governor of Jerusalem, being the first Englishman to occupy the seat of Pontius Pilate, he permitted himself certain dictatorial privileges. He renamed the streets to his own liking, ordered new tiles for the decaying façade of the Dome of the Rock, rebuilt the Tower of David, knocked down a peculiarly horrible Turkish clock tower which stood on the Jaffa Gate, revived the art of glass blowing, and issued a proclamation commanding that all new buildings should be built or faced with the local sandstone. Not all his street names have been retained, but the ordinance in favor of the local sandstone remains on the statute books. Storrs made many contributions to Jerusalem, but this proclamation issued under his seal in the early weeks of his governorship was the most beneficial and the most enduring.

Jerusalem sandstone has a beautiful color that weathers well. There are many shades of it, from yellowish-gray through pink-gold to russet-gold and a deep reddish-gold. It is a solid and noble stone, rather rough, with little delicacy about it, and therefore admirably suited for building fortress walls and crenelated towers and imposing modern buildings. You cannot build a cottage with it successfully any more than you can armor-plate a rowing boat. It suggests power and endurance, and for good reason. Out of this stone are formed the immense, tumultuous waves of the wilderness which surround the city on all sides.

That stone, weathered for five centuries, forms the wall of the old city. It is a more yellow stone than most, and there are some hours in the afternoon when it shines like bars of gold. But nearly all the buildings in the new city are made of the same stone. Even the smallest buildings acquire dignity from the texture of the stone, and even the very large modernistic buildings like the new synagogue on King George V Avenue remains interesting simply by virtue of the quality of the stone; if they were in concrete they would be unendurable. And when concrete is used, as in the strange egg-shaped synagogue on the Hebrew University campus, the effect is tragic. The pale white of concrete seems to shrivel and grow limp in that golden-blue air. White becomes an outrage when the eyes are accustomed to richer colors. Recently the Dome of the Rock has been plated with pure gold. The golden dome seems to draw all its richness from the surrounding stone, and the effect is magical.

I never went into the old city, for the Jordanians in their fury against the Jews have barred the passage at the Mandelbaum Gate, and will let no one enter. Their loss is Israel's gain, for while the Church of the Holy Sepulcher, Gethsemane and the Wailing Wall remain in forbidden territory, there are more than enough holy sites to visit on the Israeli side of the frontier. Above all, there is Mount Zion, clinging to the corner of the old wall, and after the sacred sites there is the entire new city to explore, spilling over the hills and dramatically beautiful in its own right, with its population gathered from all the ends of the earth, intoxicated with its new freedom and the sense of danger. There is almost no part of the modern city which is not within rifle range from the Jordanians on their ancient walls.

The new city, then, gives the appearance of being wide-open to attack, of being in love with its openness, its fragility, gathering strength from its weakness. This apparent weakness, however, is only an illusion. Even the sprawling of the streets and the haphazard design are illusory. These streets, which at first suggest wild vines climbing over the rock, are more like the branches of an oak thrusting powerfully according to a logic of their own. The longer you stay in the new city, the more you become aware of its hidden strength.

The old city has its fortress walls, its ramparts and great fortified gates; they must have been formidable when they were built by

Suleyman the Magnificent, but they look like museum pieces now, and would crumble at the first touch of a battering ram or a small tank. The real strength is in the new city, the vast oak tree with its roots deep in the rock.

The main artery of the new city is the long avenue named after King George V, because it was in his reign that the Balfour Declaration favoring a Jewish state in Palestine was given to the world. The avenue follows the contours of the ridge facing old Jerusalem. Here are the house of parliament, the vast Yeshurun Synagogue, the Jewish Agency building and the seat of the Chief Rabbinate. Most of these buildings have the scale and dimensions of fortresses dominating the valley below, and looking tranquilly towards the enemy on the opposite heights. The King David Hotel and the Y.M.C.A. stand a little lower down the slope like sentinels commanding the approaches. The Jewish Agency building was the headquarters of the Jewish military governor of Jerusalem during the fighting in 1948, but any one of the other buildings could have served the same purpose.

The new Jerusalem is powerful, and has been made to last. It is not something which can be leveled to the ground with a broadside of six-inch guns. If it has no obvious shape, if it leaps from hill to hill, if it seems to be in danger of expanding all the way down to the seacoast, this too is a sign of its strength. Near the campus of Hebrew University vast new buildings are going up, and they will eventually form the government quarter of the city. Jerusalem has many lines of defense.

If one speaks of defense lines and battles, it is because war is in the air, and it could hardly be otherwise as long as the new city occupies a salient deep into Jordanian territory. The armies are on the alert. Military trucks are seen on all the roads. And since there are whole sections of the city which still show the scars of war, with barricades still standing, one can easily imagine that the war is still going on. At night I found myself instinctively searching the sky for enemy airplanes. But the sky was silent, immensely high, running with purple wine, the stars like silver grape-clusters hanging within reach. At night the city is silent, for men go to bed early to awake with the dawn.

While Jerusalem is conscious of being in the front lines, it is also conscious of its traditions going back to the remote past. It is still David's city, and David was lover and poet and king as well as warrior. Men walk sedately in Jerusalem. There is none of the head-long hurry one encounters in Tel Aviv. There are no great avenues filled with sumptuous shops, no attempt towards an outward ele-gance. It cultivates the atmosphere of a university town. There are ruined churches still entangled in barbed wire, and bombed-out sites which no one has had time to restore, but the work of government and scholarship goes on as though the enemy were a hundred miles away. To live in Jerusalem is to possess a quiet pride, and there is even some scorn for Haifa and Tel Aviv, which were scarcely touched by the war.

It would seem that the best come to Jerusalem. The Tel Aviv face tends to fat, and the Tel Aviv clothes tend to be smart; Hollywood and Miami have left their imprint. In Jerusalem men are careless of clothes and wear open-neck shirts and care little for appearances. The girls dress without extravagance. The mood is calm, a little somber, not given to ostentation, quietly self-assured. Wages are low. There are theaters and cinemas and art galleries, there is even a ferris wheel outlined with electric lights at the bottom of the municipal gardens, but there is no feeling that people are desperately searching for enter-tainment. They are self-contained, and a surprising number of them are young: the average age must be about thirty. In five minutes, in any of the main streets, you will see Jews from Persia, India, Morocco, Argentina, Yemen, Europe and America. Jerusalem is the melting pot. All colors, all races are represented, and all are Jews.

Jerusalem is a fortress. So it has been, and so it will always be. The forward defenses are scattered among the hills, as they were in the time of King Jehoiakim, whose southern bastion has recently been discovered by archaeologists in nearby Ramat Rahel, a hilltop with one of the world's most spectacular views. From there you look out across a valley to Bethlehem and the red-roofed Church of the Nativity, and not far away stands a white and gleaming mountain shaped like an extinct volcano: Herod made it into a fortress palace, and on the summit he was buried in a gold coffin studded with jewels. The mountains of Moab lie far to the east, the honey-colored wall of Jerusalem rise to the north, and the modern city sweeps around to the west. From that hilltop, near the ruins of a Judean fortress of the eighth century B.C. and of a Byzantine church, all of Jerusalem and the land around it seem to lie at your feet. The frontier is only two hundred yards away.

AT HERZL'S TOMB

In the Judean hills, not far from Jerusalem, and on the road to Ain Karem, where John the Baptist was born, there stands the square block of polished black marble which commemorates Theodor Herzl, the founder of Zionism, who in 1898 prophesied that the state of Israel would come into existence in fifty years. He lies beneath that immense marble tomb. On one side, written in a peculiarly vivid and powerful Hebrew script, there is his name.

There is no date of death, no date of birth, nothing about him. No text from the Old Testament decorates the tomb, as it decorates so many of the memorials in Israel. No star or shield of David, no Menorah, no Ark of the Covenant, is depicted on the tomb. There is only the immense black stone and the great name. So, in the Middle Ages, might men commemorate the death of a great prince.

The tomb stands on the summit of the hill, with Jerusalem in the distance dusky yellow and gold, very beautiful. There is an impression of height, of wind-swept spaces, of being between the desert and the sown. The site has been chosen with exquisite care.

Today and for many years to come Herzl, who began life as an obscure Hungarian playwright, will continue to haunt Jerusalem. His portrait—always the same portrait—hangs in all the public buildings. Yet this portrait is scarcely fair to him; he is shown in profile, frowning, heavily-bearded, lost in deep meditation. It is the portrait of a faintly sinister prophet, dark and saturnine. In fact, he was red-cheeked, with deep-set eyes which often glowed with laughter, and in his elegance he resembled a guardsman or a man about town rather than a prophet. He was vain of his good looks, and was perfectly aware of the power of his flashing eyes.

He was born with many gifts. He could have been a poet or a novelist or a journalist or a playwright with a European reputation, but he wrote his plays too easily and his one surviving novel is not a novel at all; it is a visionary account, in minute detail, of a Jewish state in Palestine as it would appear about the year 1962. Nor was there anything original in his book *The Jewish State*, which he completed when he was thirty-six; others before him had proclaimed that the Jewish state needed to be founded, preferably in Palestine. What was original in him was his vision of the New Jerusalem, which he saw in such clear outline that he almost believed in its existence. His greatest gift was nothing less than the gift of prophecy.

Once he had conceived of the idea of the New Jerusalem, he painted it in such rich colors that it became credible even to those who had no sympathy with it. For centuries the Jews had dreamed of returning to Jerusalem. "Next year in Jerusalem" was a common greeting, which had lost its meaning by repetition. Herzl proclaimed: "Jerusalem this year, now, this very moment." He drew a picture of a modern Jerusalem lying outside the walls of the sacred city. A modern gleaming metropolis with wide avenues, boulevards, parks, tree-shaded streets, recreation centers, electric streetcars. As for the old city, it would be conserved as a monument to the past with hospices for the pilgrims of all the denominations which regarded Jerusalem as a holy city, but there would be no private dwellings. There would be hospitals and clinics and a great Peace Palace. Whenever a disaster occurred anywhere in the world, the Peace Palace would respond immediately with help. The victims of floods, earthquakes, famine, drought and epidemics would have only to turn to the Peace Palace to know that they were being cared for. It would be the United Nations, the World Health Organization, and UNESCO, the largest and most powerful center of humanitarian activity on earth.

So he dreamed, and though the Peace Palace was never erected in Jerusalem, his vision of the new city outside the walls, rising on the encircling hills, came about very much as he predicted it. He wrote his description of Jerusalem in 1898 when only about forty thousand Jews were living there, many of them in squalor.

In those days, at the beginning of the century, the Valley of Esdraelon was little more than marshes and swampland. It was owned largely by absentee Turkish and Arab landlords, and seemed destined to become a kind of permanent graveyard. The scattering of Arab peasants who lived there called it "the Gateway to Hell." Herzl, in one of the visionary passages of his novel *Old-New Land*, described it as a great flowering plain thickly sown with wheat, oats, maize, hops and tobacco, with cows and sheep grazing in the meadows, and trim villages and homesteads dotted about the valley and crowding the hillsides. So it became, but no one except Herzl had ever guessed there would be this flowering.

When Herzl published his novel in 1902, Haifa was little more than a village lying at the foot of Mount Carmel, with a population of perhaps ten thousand people. He never visited the town, though he caught a passing glance of it from the sea. In his imagination the village became a city towering up the entire length of Mount Carmel, and spreading all the way to Acre. There was a superb port with great piers and jetties, and vessels of all nations lay at anchor under the sheltering mountains. For some reason he imagined this teeming city very silent, with almost no noise in the streets. He wrote:

> Brilliant Oriental robes mingled with the sober costumes of the Occident, but the latter predominated. There were many Chinese, Persians and Arabs, but the city itself seemed thoroughly European. One might easily imagine oneself in a large Italian port. The brilliant blue of sky and sea were reminiscent of the Riviera, but the buildings were much cleaner and more modern, and the streets less noisy. The quiet was due largely to the dignified behavior of the many Orientals which precluded the raising of their voices, but also to the absence of any draught animals. There was no hoofbeat of horses, no crackling of whips, no rumbling of wheels. The roads were as smooth as the sidewalks, and the automobiles drove past silently on rubber wheels.

Again and again in his diaries, where the best of his writing is preserved, he sketches out some detail of the Jewish state which has proved to be amazingly accurate. He sketched out its constitution, labor laws, social welfare, education, town-planning. He wanted entire communities transplanted in the Jewish state, and they must be kept together; this too has been done. He wanted a public works system, and he insisted that the new state should follow the middle road between capitalism and collectivism. He wanted a limit set to the growth of the towns, and each town must live on the produce of the surrounding fields. He made vast plans for irrigation, and wrote happily about the wealth that would come from the potash of the Dead Sea. Sometimes he was overwhelmed by the sheer ebullience of his imagination, as when he dashed off in his diary: "The high priests will wear impressive robes. The cuirassiers will wear yellow trousers and white tunics. The officers will have silver breastplates." But there are not many statements like this. The diary is largely a sober examination of his own triumphs and defeats, and a continuing exploration of the nature of the Jewish state.

But when he was writing, the Jewish state belonged to the distant future. He was a statesman without a state, a prophet without a country. He bearded the powerful Jewish multimillionaires, Baron Maurice de Hirsch and Baron Edmond de Rothschild, and made them listen to his plan for settling the Jews on the soil. He inaugurated a series of Zionist Conferences, and laid down a program for establishing a home for the Jewish people which would be secured by public law. He believed the home should be in Palestine, then under the rule of the Sultan of Turkey, "the sick man of Europe," who sometimes gave the impression that he would cheerfully sacrifice Palestine in payment of an astronomical purchase price. Many Jews preferred assimilation in their adopted countries to the adventure of setting up a Jewish state. Herzl thundered against them, accusing them of timidity and cowardice. At various times he thought he would be able to establish the Jewish state in the arid El Arish area of northern Sinai, in Mozambique, Tripoli or the Congo, but all these ventures failed. The prize was always Palestine.

With his commanding presence, his social graces, his missionary zeal, he was able to engage the interest of kings and princes and European statesmen. The German Emperor and the Sultan of Turkey listened to long speeches on the need for building a Jewish state and its advantages to the rest of the world. His interviews with the Sultan were curiously disturbing, for Herzl had the impression that he was talking to a marionette and it was beyond his power to know who was pulling the strings. Sultan Abdul Hamid II was a small, shabby man with long yellow teeth, the hooked nose of a Punchinello, and ears that stuck out from the side of his head, thus protecting his fez from falling down and completely covering his face. He listened politely to everything Herzl said, made vast promises, and never kept them. It was the same wherever Herzl went. The Kaiser made a ceremonial tour of the Holy Land, and Herzl succeeded in interviewing him in Constantinople and Jerusalem. The Kaiser promised to approach the Sultan on behalf of a chartered company of Jewish farmers in Palestine, but nothing came of it. Herzl visited Russia and had an audience with the Premier, von Plehve, who had given the order for the massacre of the Jews in Russia. He visited London and gave evidence before a Royal Commission inquiring into the troubles caused by the alien immigrants in East London, and his pleas for the building of a Jewish state were listened to attentively by the imaginative Colonial Secretary, Joseph Chamberlain. Thereafter the British became sometimes the willing allies, sometimes the determined enemies, of Zionism, always inextricably involved with it. Herzl even discussed Zionism with Pope Pius X and King Victor Emmanuel III, who remarked that the Jews had waited a long time to return to the Promised Land and might therefore be a little more patient and wait another hundred years.

Herzl was in no mood for waiting. He exhausted himself with endless interviews, speeches and travels in search of sympathetic audiences. Sometimes he would fall into profound fits of depression, but these were rare. He was a politician fighting for the existence of a country which had not existed since A.D. 70, and he was continually crying out against the politicians who got in his way. He wanted no professional politicians in the Jewish state. He wrote in his diary: "A crop of professional politicians must be prevented at all costs. I must study this problem in due course, and with the utmost care." He never had time to study the problem. His life was too full, too urgent, for the study of peripheral problems. For many years he had known he was suffering from heart disease. In the summer of 1904 he died suddenly, at the age of forty-four. He had asked that his body should be buried in Vienna, "to remain there until the Jewish people carry my remains to Palestine."

On August 16, 1949, his coffin was flown from Vienna to Israel, and on the next day he was buried on the hill which bears his name, facing Jerusalem from the west. Military honors were paid to him, and airplanes flew over the grave. He had left his testament to the Jewish people. It was a very simple one, and read: "So build your state that the stranger shall feel contented among you."

The black marble tomb on the wind-swept hill is the fulfillment of a dream. The passing clouds are mirrored on the highly polished surface, and the bold letters gleam like fire. It is right that he should have a tomb of such grandeur, for without him the Jewish state would never have come into existence.

THE MINISTER OF FOREIGN AFFAIRS

She sat there among the flowers, wearing a brown dress, her hands folded on her lap, and if you did not know who she was, you would have said she was a doctor or a surgeon, who had only that minute stepped out of the hospital. Her voice was low, the eyes were calm and probing, and there was no trace of worry on the strong face. When she spoke about her own life, she was quietly dispassionate, almost as though her life had been lived by someone else. And when she spoke about Israel, then again she was dispassionate, but in a different way; for Israel meant so much to her that she dared not introduce passion into the debate which she had carried on with herself all her life.

She spoke of her childhood in the family of deeply religious Russian Jews who had emigrated to America and how, very early, she had been fired with Herzl's vision of a Jewish state. So, in 1921, she came to Palestine and worked in a *kibbuts* not far from Nazareth. It was a wretched time for the workers on those small farms. There were Arab raids, and no one dared go out at night. It was swampy land, and there were times when everyone on the *kibbuts* suffered from malaria, and many died. All over Palestine there were these small groups of dedicated Jews living on the land, and scarcely surviving. "Sometimes I wonder how we survived at all," she said. "We seemed to be living on our faith, on nothing else. We were thin and ill most of the time, and we were surrounded by enemies. We belonged to the movement called Labor Zionism, and somehow this gave us strength to endure. We were Zionists, and we knew that our salvation came through work on the land. We were socialists, and we regarded communal work as the highest good. But in those days the state of Israel was still far away—we thought it might come about in three or four generations, and we wondered whether our children would live to see it."

She spoke of Herzl as though he were still a living presence in Israel. His calm prophecies even now bewildered her. That he should have prophesied the coming into existence of the Jewish state to the exact year was bewildering enough, but there were all the other prophecies in his novel *Old-New Land* which had come to fulfillment. "I have lived to see the restoration of the Jews," Herzl wrote in 1902, his imagination spinning across nearly fifty years of the future, "and I should like to pave the way for the restoration of the Negroes." "The Negroes and the Jews suffered in the same way," she was saying, "and so there is an understanding between them. Every day our scientists are becoming more and more helpful in providing assistance to Negroes who come to study in Israel. We understand them, and they understand us. But how could Herzl have known that the Negroes and the Jews would gain their independence about the same time?"

She talked of her life during the time of the British Mandate in Palestine: the clandestine years when many of the Jewish leaders were under arrest or in hiding, and sometimes vital decisions had to be made by her because there was no one else available to make them. She spoke of those years gravely and quietly, and sometimes she wondered whether it might have been possible for the state of Israel to emerge without bloodshed, without the bitter fighting against the Arabs and the British. "There might have been another beginning," she said. "It might have been completely peaceful, with one of the members of the royal family solemnly presenting us with our independence, and it might have been better that way. We shall never know."

She was proud that she had been one of the thirty-seven signers of the Declaration of Independence of the State of Israel in 1948. She had signed her name: *Golda Meirsohn.* For brevity's sake she had since lost the last syllable of her name.

As she looked back, everything about her life seemed to flow naturally, inevitably, out of the deeply religious childhood. Politics was only another aspect of her religion. For her Israel's existence was a fact which was essentially religious, bathed in the light of divinity. Intelligence reports piled on her desk, Nasser threatened and blustered, the Soviet Union sent massive supplies of guns, tanks and airplanes to Egypt, but she remained calm and unyielding, fortified by the strength which came from her religion.

She sat there among the flowers with her hands folded on her lap, and one thought of Deborah commanding the armies to victory.

> *They fought from heaven; the stars in their courses fought against Sisera. The river of Kishon swept them away, the ancient river, the river of Kishon. Oh, my soul, thou hast trodden down strength.*

The Place of Splendor

One can wander through the streets and alleyways of Jerusalem and out into the Judean hills with almost no sense of the passing of time. Morning comes, and then afternoon, and all that has happened is that the light has shifted a little on the golden stone. Time vanishes, and becomes space, becomes stone and air. There is almost no sense that great events are taking place, for they have already taken place. Abraham has come and gone, Christ has been taken down from the Cross, and life goes on as though in the shadow of events which happened so long ago that they have passed out of history into legend. There has been so much history that in the end there is no history.

So you may find yourself stumbling upon a ruined wall erected in some wasteland, and wonder whether it was built by Herod or by Moslem conquerors, only to learn that it was a barricade erected by Israeli soldiers only a few years ago. You can sit among the broken stones and tombs where the priests of the Sanhedrin were once buried and look across the bare hills to the peak of Mizpah, the Crusaders' Montjoie, and there are no buildings and no pathways in sight, only the burnt soaring hills, and you know with certainty that Samuel and David and Solomon and all the prophets saw the same sight. There is a windmill on the rising land facing Mount Zion, and this too in its proportions and perfect appropriateness seems as though it has come down through the ages, until you learn that it was built by Sir Moses Montefiore, an English philanthropist, only a hundred years ago. So it is everywhere in Jerusalem: the dates are almost meaningless, and everything is the same age as Jerusalem stone.

From one of the flat roofs of the Church of Notre Dame de France you can look over the ancient walled city of Jerusalem. There below you, forming a perfect square, are the great walls built by Suleyman the Magnificent, with the Dome of the Rock only a little way away. The onion-colored cupola of the Church of the Holy Sepulchre is almost within a stone's throw, and Gethsemane is a splash of green olive trees almost within reach. One had thought of the ancient city as standing on the summit of a mountain dominating the landscape, but it is not so, for the hills look down on it. Even from the Church of Notre Dame de France it seems to be lying quietly in a valley. It looks old and worn, shaken by so many storms that it is close to crumbling. Age has darkened it, and you find yourself wondering how many more storms the ancient city can survive.

Jerusalem is a place of splendor, and it can grip your heart more powerfully than Athens or Rome. There are no spectacular views, no crowded Forum filled with the debris of ruined temples, no Parthenon rides majestically over the city. What is spectacular is the landscape, the fierce hills, the golden-blue sky, the endless variations in the color of the rich stone, the sense of holiness which hovers over both the ancient and the new cities with an exquisite impartiality. Holiness, indeed, seems to rise from the stone and fall from the sky: it is in the air you breathe and in the food you eat. How it came to be there is a mystery upon which theologians may happily ponder, but its presence is not subject to argument. "Ye shall be holy, for I, the Lord your God, am holy," acquires ample meaning when you have wandered over the Jerusalem hills.

A man traveling to Rome or Athens suffers a sea change and is never quite the same afterwards. So it is in Jerusalem: some extra sense organ seems to spring suddenly into existence. It is not only that a man coming to Jerusalem will forever afterwards possess a deep affection for bare rocks and golden stone, but he will have fallen into the enchantment of holiness from which there is no escape, nor are there any words unless they are the songs of David with which he can relate the experience. In the Middle Ages the pilgrims gave to Jerusalem the name of Hierosolyma. Those gentle and useful syllables are closer to the Hebrew than the savage-sounding Jerusalem. The Jews speak of Yerushalayim, which somehow describes the city as well as the experience of living in it.

Take a man from Haifa or Tel Aviv and settle him in Jerusalem, and he will change his character within a month. He will grow roots in the barren rock faster than he ever grew them in the softer earth by the seashore. He will become graver, quieter, kindlier, even though the enemy is only a few yards away, even though the danger is much greater than in his own city. Outwardly nothing may happen for a few weeks. He will wear the same face and put on the same clothes, but the essential element will be transformed. There is little or no mystery in the transformation. A man coming from a remote village in the south of France is changed in the same way when he arrives in Paris. Usually one can recognize a man from Jerusalem by the fact that he knows few answers but asks the right questions. He is civilized, though he may not have read many books. He does not need books, for he has absorbed from the air of Jerusalem nearly all he needs to know.

So it is with the Jews returning from their long exile: the best come to Jerusalem and stay there. The rootless become rooted, the timid become as audacious as lions. In the clear, high air intelligence grows sharper and the imagination acquires stronger wings. In the hills of the wilderness even the impossible becomes commonplace or at least very close to attainment. In those hills it is even possible to believe that the world will one day be at peace.

At one time I had thought of sketching some portraits of the men of Jerusalem. There would be profiles of students and scholars and poets and engineers and judges and generals. There would be the grave and wise Moshe Silberg, a judge who looks like a poet, and the equally grave and wise Yehoshafat Harkavi, who looks even more like a poet though he was once Chief of Military Intelligence.

There would be a brief sketch of Moshe Dayan, who lost an eye in a foray while leading some British troops into Syria and went on to become the conqueror of Sinai; he wears a dangerous piratical air as he presides over the Ministry of Agriculture. Then there would be David Shaltiel, who commanded the Israeli Army in Jerusalem during the worst days of the war of independence, having learned to fight in the French Foreign Legion. There would be Moshe Sharett with his nimble brain and quiet courtliness, the only man beside Ben-Gurion who has been Prime Minister of Israel. There would be perhaps twenty more, in order to give a rounded picture. In this way perhaps it might have been possible to describe the peculiar quality of the men of Jerusalem. Instead I have described briefly two men who by common consent stand above the rest. They are at poles apart, but Jerusalem is their flesh and their blood.

DAVID BEN-GURION

There are few men in the world who can claim to be the father of their country, and there is only one living man who can claim to have revived a nation which vanished two thousand years ago. Israel is very largely the work of Ben-Gurion. He mapped out the strategy which brought it into being, organized its defenses, stamped it with his own character and inspired it with his beliefs. The country's political structure, the organization of the army, the determination to conquer the desert, the campaign to bring more and more immigrants—all these things derive directly from him. Wherever you travel in Israel, you find evidence of his ideas, his theories, his implacable desire to give the Jews a place in the sun. It is not only that he is more responsible than any other man for the creation of the state, but the state is almost unthinkable without his guiding presence. So much springs from him that you sometimes find yourself wondering where Ben-Gurion ends and Israel begins.

In Israel he is called "B-G" or "the old man," and there is reserved for him the special affection which is given only to legends. Strong men stammer in his presence, and school children have been known to become tongue-tied when the small man with the halo of silky white hair appears. Because he is a legend, he is no longer judged according to ordinary human laws. When he speaks, history speaks through him. He wears the weight of history lightly, even though he is perfectly aware of the place he has carved for himself, and he is sometimes appalled by the reverence in which he is held. Inevitably his character is complex, riddled with the contradictions which make for greatness. He is proud and humble, learned and ignorant, deeply religious and contemptuous of religion, at times completely conscious of his powers and at other times so unconscious of them that he will immerse himself for days on end in his library as though in search of the real sustenance of his life, while the work of the government has to go on without him. His roots are in the nineteenth-century socialist movements in eastern Europe, but sometimes he appears as a man in advance of his own time. He gives an impression of astonishing directness and single-minded purpose, but beneath the austere and sensitive mask he presents to the world there are unresolved conflicts and fierce battles are being waged.

From a very early age he had a sense of mission, the desire to lead the Jews to the Promised Land. His father, a lawyer in a small town near Warsaw, encouraged him. His childhood was happy, and he was fourteen or fifteen when he showed remarkable powers of oratory. Very soon he was a Labor Zionist, one of those who believed that Zion would belong to the Jews only if they exerted their physical strength as settlers in the land, living their communal lives in complete dedication. He embraced Herzl's vision of the Jewish state, but with an important difference. He saw the state with the eyes of an eastern European socialist, and from the very beginning he knew it would have to be fought for.

Even in the old days, when he lived in a communal settlement at Sedjera in Galilee, he was an omnivorous reader, learning as much from books as from people. He had little formal education. Modern Israelis will tell you that he betrays the inconsistencies and excitements of the self-taught mind, but that is to misunderstand his character. The inconsistencies were there from the beginning; and his excitement in the face of new ideas is the tribute he pays to them.

In the last few years he has been a voracious student of Zen Buddhism, a subject which interested him ever since he visited Burma and spent many hours discussing oriental philosophy with the Burmese premier, U Nu. Over many years he has been absorbed in Greek philosophy, especially in Plato, whom he first read in a Russian translation when he was seventeen. For a large part of his life the Bible and Plato have been his constant companions. Self-taught he may be, but the mind was trained and honed to a razor sharpness from the time of his adolescence. He knew where he was going.

He did not, of course, know that he would become Prime Minister of Israel. What he knew with complete certainty was that if the state ever became viable in his lifetime, he would be one of those who would help to bring it into being. Relentlessly he studied a subject which is not included in the curriculum of a university: the making of the Jewish state. In his writings there is nothing so revealing as his constant preoccupation with the sources of power. What he was after was quite simply a Jewish state resourceful and powerful enough to survive. He became the technician of the revolt. He studied Clausewitz and Thucydides' *History of the Peloponnesian War*, which close friends say he read eight times, in the years between 1945 and the battle for the Jewish state. He said once that his whole life was a preparation for battle, and it was no more than the truth.

Today, ruddy and vigorous still, he remains a fighter. Age is beginning to mark his features and the famous white halo is thinning out to the consistency of spun silk, but the set of the jaw is as determined as ever. At first when you enter his office in the new government building in the Judean hills, seeing him as though at the far end of a corridor, you are struck by his resemblance to a benignant and slightly tousled owl peering at you from the top of a large black desk where everything is arranged in orderly piles. But when he emerges in front of the desk, small and compact, an enormous head, brown eyes blazing in the sunlight pouring through the wide windows, he resembles a sinewy farmer, hard-muscled and determined that his acres should bring forth fruit, and the owl vanishes. He has the wariness, the intransigence, the deep faith of a farmer who knows every inch of the land, and who will fight for it against all enemies and against all the catastrophes which nature elects to send down on it.

Like many others I had thought of him as the philosopher king, the ruler who is continually guided by philosophical principles, but he was quick to dispel the illusion. He leaned forward across the desk, the white hair flaming, and said quietly, "You cannot learn about the art of government from Plato. The Greek city states have vanished and we live in another world altogether. We live in a new world, with new political laws, and there has been a great break with the past. Think of the Second World War, and what that meant, and of the emergence of Africa in the last fifteen years, and what that means. Plato was a great poet and a superb artist, but he was no systematic philosopher, and his theories of government are obsolete. He had no conception of democracy, no idea how it works. He envisaged rule by an elite, but this is intolerable to us."

As he spoke, he made vigorous chopping movements with his hands, slicing up Plato and all the ancient philosophers who had proved so useless in their researches on the art of government.

"We have a new world, and we are faced with new problems undreamed of in the past," he went on, and it was clear that he thoroughly enjoyed the new dangerous world which he had helped to bring into existence. He talked, as Golda Meir had done, of emerging Africa and the vast potentialities of the Negroes, who were coming into their freedom, and then returned to Plato.

"Of course, I respect Plato, and I suppose I have been reading him most of my life. I was seventeen when I first read him in a Russian translation, and some time later I read him in English, but in those days he meant very little to me. Later I learned Greek, and realized with a shock what a profound difference there was between Plato in translation and in the original; and it was only then that I realized what a profound artist he was. I read him for pleasure. It seems to me that Plato very often reports the words of Socrates accurately, and the *Apology* rings true—Plato could hardly have invented that superb defense—and most of the early dialogues seem to me authentic Socrates, but this is a matter for scholars to debate among them-

David Ben-Gurion

Golda Meir

Yigael Yadin

Martin Buber

selves. For me it is simply pleasure. We are Jews, and we have had some painful quarrels with the Greeks in the past." He was referring to the wars between the Jews and the successors of Alexander the Great when they occupied Palestine, but as he spoke of them, they seemed to be wars which took place within living memory. "Still," he went on, "the Greeks have deeply affected our thinking, and many Greek words have been taken over into Hebrew. We learned from them, but our philosophy is not theirs. Philo of Alexandria was a Jewish philosopher who wrote in Greek, but he remains Jewish to the core. Jewish thinking also influenced Greek philosophy." He spoke tenderly of Philo, and evidently had a great affection for him. Philo had attempted to marry Greek thought with the philosophy of the Bible, and to some smaller or larger extent the Prime Minister had followed in his footsteps. Then he said sharply, "There was a time when the Jews were saturated with Greek thought, but it was a very brief time and it passed a long time ago. Now we are on our own."

He said, "Plato was a superb poet, and we should not ask more of him."

I asked him whether he had ever written poetry.

"Yes, when I was sixteen or seventeen. Then I gave it up, and I have never written a line since."

"Why not?"

He shrugged his shoulders.

"I had other things to attend to. I had no gift for it, no liking for it. I never read poetry."

"Not even modern poetry?"

"No, I never read poetry with pleasure. I don't understand it."

Like Plato he seemed to be a little afraid of the poets for the harm they could do. He wanted facts, precise colors, sharp outlines. The edges of poetry dissolve into fantasy, and he had set his mind against fantasy from a very early age.

But surely there were elements of fantasy in being the Prime Minister of a state which for two thousand years had vanished from the map. Extraordinary things were continually happening to him. A few weeks previously he had entered Hebrew University, unannounced, to take his seat among the students at a philosophy seminar, which was being addressed by a German authority on Plato. He had simply wanted to attend the seminar like any other student, but it had not happened like that. Heads were craned, the professor became nervous, the audience grew restless in the presence of the living legend, and in the midst of the confusion the lights went out. Such things were continually happening. To be a legend is to be poetry walking, but the temper of his mind is such that he despises the legend-making machinery of men's minds, perhaps because the Bible contains enough legends to last a lifetime.

I asked him whether he intended to write a testament to the Jewish people, a summary of his plans for the new-born state as short and clear perhaps as the Gettysburg address, but he shook his head vigorously.

"Why should I?" he asked. "What good would it do? Our plans are known. They are all stated in the Bible, which was true for us in the past, is true now, and will be true in the future. We are the people of the Book."

The white hands made short chopping movements. He leaned over the desk and touched the small, worn pocket Bible, which he carried with him everywhere and which lay now on top of an immense Concordance.

"It's all there!" he said again and again, as though puzzled that anyone could ever have thought of Israel without remembering that it had sprung fully formed from the Bible. "It's all there! Everything we need in addition to science we find in the Bible. We have no need to look anywhere else!"

Of the overwhelming importance he attached to the Bible there could be no doubt, but generations of scholars have interpreted it according to their lights. It seemed to me that one could read into it almost anything one pleased. Almost, the Bible had vanished under the weight of its interpreters. How, for example, did the modern Jews regard the Covenant with Abraham? Were the Jews the Chosen People? Were they alone in being chosen?

"No," he said. "They were not chosen by God, for it is impossible for a people to be chosen. The Jews chose God. The particular distinction of the Jews is that they made the choice, and this we learn from the last chapter of the Book of Joshua, where it is written that the choice was given to them. 'Joshua said unto the people, Ye are witnesses against yourselves that ye have chosen you the Lord to serve him. And they said, We are witnesses.' So they chose God, and they were alone in choosing Him. And this is as it should be, for God, being the symbol of justice, cannot discriminate between people, but the people can discriminate."

So he spoke while the heavy November sunlight drifted through the windows, and sometimes a secretary would come and lay papers on his desk, but he paid no attention to them. He liked talking about the Bible, and he talked well. He wore a white open-neck shirt which balanced the white flame of his hair, and sometimes he would throw back his head and laugh happily: it was an innocent laugh, like a child's. He talked of Nehru and Mao Tse-tung, but they seemed to be shadowy figures who existed on the frontiers of his imagination, remote and insubstantial, behaving according to laws beyond his comprehension. The Far East intrigued him, but he was not at home in it. Gradually the conversation would come round to the Bible, to Plato, to the *kibbutsim* and the state of Israel.

He said of Jesus, "I believe Jesus spoke in Hebrew, not in Aramaic. Take the words *Eli eli lama sabachthani*, which He spoke on the Cross. All these are Hebrew words, and only one of them— *sabachthani*—could also be Aramaic. I believe Jesus grew up in the Jewish tradition of his time, and it is not surprising therefore that He spoke and thought in Hebrew. All through the New Testament I find the evidence of purely Jewish thought. In St. Paul, too, we find characteristic Jewish ideas. In the thirteenth chapter of the First Epistle to the Corinthians, which I regard as the greatest of the epistles, St. Paul speaks of *agape*, which has been translated 'charity,' but what he means is something of course much greater than charity —he is talking about love, and it is very close to the Hebrew concept of *chesed*, which is mercy and intellectual love, and more than both of these. When I read the New Testament, especially Matthew, I have to translate them from the Greek into Hebrew to understand them. The Greek is not very good Greek, but it becomes good Hebrew when translated back. All this disposes me to believe that Jesus and the apostles were men who spoke, thought, and acted according to Hebrew tradition."

Later he discussed the prodigious vigor which sometimes manifests itself in new nations only to disintegrate within two or three generations. The Arab historian Ibn Khaldun had attempted to analyze that vigor, which he called *assabiya,* and to trace its decline. There was no doubt about the vigor of Israel, but could it endure? What would happen if Israel became relatively wealthy, or if there was peace with the surrounding states? The Prime Minister thought for a moment, and then counted off on his fingers the saving graces which protected Israel from any loss of its primitive vigor.

"It is true," he said, "that nations lose their primitive force, but for a long time to come we shall have advantages in safeguarding our vigor. In the first place we are still surrounded by enemies and we are still being besieged. Then there is the Negev, which will challenge the best efforts of our young men. Then there are the new immigrants coming from all over the world. We are still in a state of becoming, and very far from being decadent. We have our own word for *assabiya.* We call it *khalutziot.* It means vision and dedication, and we have this vision, this dedication."

A moment later he said, "And then there is the Bible, and this too must be taken into consideration. Our strength is in the Bible. By the power of the Bible the past lives through us, though we are not living in the past. Everyone who wants to understand Israel must read the Bible—it is all there!"

Two days later there was a Bible meeting at the Prime Minister's house. These meetings take place twice a month, and are attended by scholars from all over Israel. About thirty people sat round a long table, listening to the exposition of a text and afterwards joining in the general debate. On this occasion they were debating the meaning of two words in Deuteronomy. They were mysterious words, which had evidently changed their meanings over the passage of years, and experts in Akkadian and Babylonian discussed them at length. Oranges and tea were served. It was a bright room with yellow walls and flowered curtains, the light beating up from the long white tablecloth. These experts all behaved like college students at a seminar: they were continually whispering and exchanging notes, and at any moment one expected the college bell to ring to announce the end of the class.

So the hours went by, while Moshe Silberg of the Supreme Court presided over the deliberations, and the Prime Minister nodded approvingly and took careful notes and consulted the Bible. Yigael Yadin spoke for the archaeologists, and the experts in Akkadian and Babylonian courteously pointed out the errors of those who knew only ancient Hebrew. From time to time one of the heavy-set bodyguards attached to the Prime Minister's office would pour tea or pass the biscuits around, while I dozed and listened to the sounds of Hebrew spoken in soft Sephardic accents, understanding scarcely a word, admiring the bald heads shining in the lamplight, while the crosscurrents of argument swirled round me. On a shelf, not far away, there was a small bronze statue of Pericles next to a miniature model of a *davidovka*, the loud-booming mortar which was the chief weapon of the Israelis in their war against the Arabs. Pericles and armaments! They stood well together on the shelf, and I suspect they were not brought together unintentionally.

At last Mrs. Ben-Gurion appeared, and this was the signal for the meeting to end, for she was determined that her husband should not grow tired. The Bibles were closed, and the scholars moved out into the street to continue their debate under the stars. One by one the lights in the Prime Minister's house went out.

MARTIN BUBER

Recently, when the great philosopher Martin Buber sent a message to the Prime Minister's office, asking for an urgent appointment, the Prime Minister replied that he would himself go to Buber's house "because you are older than I am." They discussed whether Eichmann should be hanged, and while Buber employed all his considerable art of persuasion to prove that the hanging would be a mistake, the Prime Minister pointed out that no other action was possible. Buber appealed to philosophy and morality, to the ultimate absurdity of hanging the monster responsible for so many crimes. He asked what good the hanging would do, for the evil had been done, and nothing would bring back the six million dead. Why compound the evil? Why take a life, when that life no longer has any meaning? So they debated like two titans wrestling for the soul of Israel, and Buber, the philosopher, must have known he would be defeated by the man of action.

Yet Buber is still a force to be reckoned with. At eighty-four, still in good health, with ruddy cheeks and shining eyes, with his long beard gleaming like ripples of frost, he looks and talks like a prophet upholding the spiritual law against the ruses of expediency. His Israel is not Ben-Gurion's Israel, and the two Israels are in fact irreconcilable. Buber demands that Israel should become a "metaphysical state," which derives its power from God alone; he is more concerned with the spiritual development of its citizens than with power politics, which he regards as an unmitigated evil. Why a large standing army? Why nuclear reactors? Why so much insistence on the social community and so little on the spiritual community? In a famous essay he has spoken of the present rulers of Israel as collectors who have somehow inherited the coronation robe of an ancient kingdom, but there is no one to wear the robe. By a miracle the state has been brought into existence, but there has been no accompanying miracle of faith. What he wants above everything else is a state dedicated to the moral law, wielding the power of the spirit, and he believes perhaps rightly that Israel is not viable unless it is pervaded by faith.

Though he is a deeply troubled man, you would not guess it if you saw him. Like Ben-Gurion he is small and compact, completely in command of himself. He has a firm handshake and his eyes twinkle under bushy eyebrows. Born in Vienna, he has the instinctive graces of the Viennese, and there hovers around him something of the atmosphere of the nineteenth century. He speaks English slowly in a beautifully clear and well-modulated voice, gesturing frequently with his hands, which might be the hands of a young man, so white they are, and so powerful. In his study there is little furniture: a desk, a few chairs, a few books. There are wide spaces to permit leisurely perambulations along the uncluttered floor.

That evening he spoke about Socrates and Plato with a strange and happy intimacy. He knew them well, had entered into their lives and thoughts, and saw their relevance to the present time. When he spoke of them, they seemed to enter the room and stand by his side. The room was dark with a single lamp burning, and the ghosts wandered in the shadows.

For some reason he found himself speaking of the time when Plato was arrested in Sicily and sold into slavery, and it amused him to ponder the act of sale. He wondered how much was paid for the world's greatest philosopher—probably only a few pennies. He wondered, too, how Plato reacted to being a slave, and what porridge he fed on, and what thoughts passed through his head when he saw himself shackled and led away. Plato had been invited to create the moral state in Sicily, but the only result was that he suffered a tyrant's vengeance. He said, "The philosophers have no place in history, and so it has been from the very beginning. Can you name one political figure in history who paid the slightest attention to great thoughts? No one ever listened to Plato or Isaiah, no one ever took their advice in creating a state, and if you ask yourself why philosophy and the life of the spirit have been so ineffective in society, then you are forced to conclude that the spirit works very slowly, while society continually changes and explores new methods. Many, many generations have to pass before the spirit can do its work."

Just as Ben-Gurion kept coming back to the Bible, so Buber, after long forays and wanderings among his own thoughts, kept returning to the life of the spirit. Why was it so slow and faltering? Why did it seem to come limping far behind? Once an extraordinary thing happened. He waved his hands and pointed to the darkness of the air, and I could have sworn a small silver object about the size of an apple emerged from his finger tips. "The spirit is everywhere," he said. "How can they possibly believe it is absent? For surely the spirit is wherever God is, and God is everywhere. Yet God works slowly. They speak of the spirit as though it were almost inexistent, but in fact it is the world of reality." And then a little later, "In all the centuries since Plato we have advanced only a little way, and sometimes I wonder whether we have advanced at all."

He went on, "The spirit endures, but it is terribly slow. Almost, one could despair of it. But I refuse to despair. I am a follower of the famous Rabbi Nachman who seriously suggested an addition to the Mosaic Law. It was not enough, he thought, that men should not kill or commit adultery or any of the other crimes engraved on the tablets. He said there should be an eleventh law—*Thou shalt not despair!* This is a law which I firmly believe and firmly obey."

The conversation turned to the vast numbers of paperbacks of fine quality appearing in America. I thought these books had produced a revolution in the minds of young Americans, but he was not convinced and waved a reproving finger.

"What have these books done?" he asked. "Have they really changed the lives of Americans? Have they led to political action? Is there more faith, more awareness of spiritual things now that these books have become available? The seed goes into the ground and is corrupted and then ripens, and all this takes time—a great deal of time. Many centuries pass before the seed flowers. You are too hopeful if you believe these books will have any effect in a single generation. You must learn patience."

"But Americans are always impatient—"

"So they are, but they have to learn patience like the rest of us."

He was amused when I suggested that it was intolerable that one should have to pay for books. They should be free, as matches are in America.

"Nonsense," he said. "The laborer is worthy of his hire. Books should and must be paid for, so that the authors can live. The important thing is not that the books should have a price on them, but that the authors should have their independence. After all, vast sums were paid for the manuscripts of Plato. Should the manuscripts of Plato have been free?"

For some reason we found ourselves talking about the strange statue depicting an ape gazing at a skull which Lenin kept on his table in the Kremlin. I said I thought the statue answered to some terrible destructive force in Lenin's soul.

"No," he said, "I see it as something else altogether. I see it as despair. Just despair. I met him in Zurich in 1915, and I felt even then that he was given over with despair. There was simply nothing one could do with such a man."

Then he talked of the essay he was writing on Thoreau and his feeling of deep affection for the man who earned a bare living by making pencils. He regarded Thoreau as one of those rare philosophers who have exerted pressure on the world by his manifesto on Civil Disobedience. Would there were more! Would there were a hundred or a thousand more! He said, "If only thirty or forty men of good will could get together and talk quietly about the nature of the state in the modern age, we might find a solution. It is not necessary that they should be philosophers. It is only necessary that they should want to find a solution, for it is not impossible that a solution exists. If only we could learn to say things clearly, then we would understand what has to be done."

Mount Zion

When I was a child, Mount Zion seemed to me a place of unparalleled splendor, with blue crystal walls and angels standing guard at the gates. It was high as a mountain, shimmering in the jeweled light of heaven. Only the good went there, so we were told in Sunday school, and since we believed we were good and thoroughly deserving, we sang lustily about the glory of the place; and sometimes we wondered why the holy mountain was also called the city of David, whose chief claim to our affections was that he had killed Goliath with a sling shot. We knew that David, Jesus and God walked through those shining streets. We knew that the sun never set on it. There it was, high in the air, gleaming like cascades of rubies and diamonds, infinitely far away and very near, and eminently desirable.

> Hail, holy Zion, the seat of God,
> Hail, holy bliss, the heart's awakening . . .

So we sang, while the thin-lipped Sunday school teachers beat time with their hands and our faces turned red as apples as we roared a welcome to the golden gates, the crystalline walls, the towers gleaming like pearls. The vision faded as soon as we left the Sunday school, and by Monday morning it was no more than a faint ghostly luminescence, and by Tuesday it had vanished altogether. But every Sunday afternoon, as regular as clockwork, there would come the beguiling vision of the celestial city.

34

I never thought I would set foot on Mount Zion, or walk through its shady streets. I never thought it would be so empty of life and so full of legends. The real, the palpable Mount Zion soars up from the Valley of Hinnom to the southwest corner of the walled city of Jerusalem; no angels guard its gates, and there are no blue crystal walls. Today the slopes are barren except for the winding steps. On the summit you can walk amid the wild lavender, under the cypresses and Aleppo pines and the wild pepper trees, through ancient arcades and up the worn steps which lead to roofs overlooking the old city, with the golden Dome of the Rock no more than a bowshot away. From there you see the crenelated walls of the old city of Jerusalem from above, as they stretch into the distance. The city seems to be asleep; Mount Zion too is sleeping. But it is an uneasy sleep. Mount Zion was captured by Israeli forces in 1948, and the Jordanians have never relished the thought of an Israeli position so close to the walls of Jerusalem. Occasionally there is the crack of rifle fire. The traveler is warned to be careful.

But even now the bullet-riddled and dangerous summit of Mount Zion is a place of enchantment, haunted by a past as ancient as Israel. Here, huddled close together among the shady trees, are the tomb of David, the room of the Last Supper and the crypt where the Virgin Mary fell asleep.

KING DAVID'S TOMB

The Rabbi Benjamin of Tudela, a careful chronicler who rarely wrote down anything he disbelieved, visited Jerusalem in A.D. 1163 in the course of the travels which would eventually take him to the borders of China. He had a habit of making exhaustive inquiries about the origins of things, and when he learned that the royal tombs of the Kings of Israel had been discovered only a few years before, he asked a friendly rabbi to tell him all the details. This rabbi had talked with the laborers who made the discovery and with the Bishop of the Church of Holy Zion, for the tombs had been found on church property. The Church of Holy Zion was no ordinary church, for it enclosed the room of the Last Supper and bore the title "*Mater Omniarum Ecclesiarum*," "The Mother of all the Churches."

The learned rabbi wrote down the story as he heard it with all its obvious exaggerations and its oddly convincing details. This is the story:

Fifteen years ago one of the walls of the church on Mount Zion fell down, and the Bishop thereupon ordered one of the members of his staff to repair it. Accordingly this priest arranged for stones to be brought from the original wall of Zion, and twenty workmen were hired at a given wage to break up the stones which had formed the foundations of the walls of Zion.

Now it happened that two of the workmen were close friends, and one day they regaled themselves with a feast and returned late to work. The foreman upbraided them for being so slow in their work, but they answered that they could still perform a day's labor, and in future they would work while the other laborers were taking their meals. So they went on breaking up the stones.

Then it happened that while they were breaking up stones, they came upon one which covered the mouth of a cave, and they decided to enter the cave and search for treasure. Soon they found themselves in a large hall supported by pillars encrusted with gold and silver, the pillars being made of marble, and there was a table bearing a golden scepter and crown. This was the sepulcher of David, King of Israel. To the left stood the sepulcher of King Solomon, very similar to the other, and then they saw all the sepulchers of all the Kings of Judah who had been buried there. Then they saw locked chests, of which the contents were unknown. They were on the point of going further when a blast of wind like a storm issued from the mouth of the cave, so strong that it threw them down and rendered them almost lifeless. There they lay until evening, when another wind rushed forth, from which they heard a voice like that of a man crying aloud, saying, "Get thee hence from this place, for God does not desire to show it to any man."

At this the men rushed away full of fear, and went to the Bishop to report what had happened to them. The Bishop summoned into his presence Rabbi Abraham el Constantini, a pious ascetic, one of the mourners of the destruction of Jerusalem, and he commanded the two laborers to repeat their story. The Rabbi thereupon told the Bishop that they had indeed discovered the sepulchers of the house of David and of the Kings of Judah.

On the following morning the laborers were sent for again. They were found lying in their beds, trembling with fear; and they declared they dared not enter the cave again, for it was not God's will to discover it to any man. Then the Bishop ordered the place to be walled up, to conceal it from the eyes of men, and so it has remained to this day.

The man who told me the story is Rabbi Abraham.

There are of course some strange omissions in the story. The Rabbi Abraham never seems to have entered the cave, we never learn the names of the workmen, nor the reason why the Bishop ordered the cave to be walled up again. Rabbi Abraham was a well-known astrologer, and he may have enjoyed mystifications. But Benjamin of Tudela was convinced that the story was true, or at least had some basis of fact.

The odd, the charming thing is that something like this may very well have happened. To this day there is an ancient sepulcher in a rock-hewn chamber just below the Chapel of the Holy Ghost, where the Christians believe the Last Supper took place. The enormous stone sarcophagus may date from the time of the Israelite Kings. It was evidently made for someone of importance, and its dimensions are sufficiently regal to suggest that it might be the tomb of David, known to have been buried on Mount Zion. The Biblical sources do not say exactly where he was buried. They say simply that "David slept with his fathers, and was buried in the city of David." But when David first attacked Jerusalem, he took the stronghold of Zion. "And David dwelt in the fort and called it the city of David."

Archaeologists are not convinced that the present Mount Zion corresponds to the Zion of King David's time, or even of King Herod's time, and they are more inclined to seek for the royal tomb on Mount Ophel. Strange and wonderful stories were told about the tomb. Josephus tells how it was twice opened, first by the High Priest Hyrcanus who removed treasure to the value of three thousand talents, and then by King Herod who removed the remainder of the treasure. "It occurred to Herod," says Josephus, "to make a more careful search of the tomb, even as far as the very bodies of David and Solomon, but the two guards he sent in were struck dead by a flame that issued out of the tomb, and Herod, visibly frightened, thereupon caused a propitiatory monument of marble to be erected outside the tomb at great expense." The site of the royal tomb seems to have been well known in the time of Jesus, for on the day of Pentecost St. Peter spoke of the tomb as being "with us to this day." It is just possible that he was speaking of a tomb which was only a few yards away.

Why then did the Bishop of the Church of Holy Zion wall up the cave? There were perhaps many compelling reasons, the most important being his fear that the Jews and Moslems would claim the church property as a holy site. To the Moslems David was a *khalifa*, a messenger of God, all the more to be worshiped because he was a valiant warrior and swordsmith, the reputed inventor of coats of mail. To the Jews David was the superb exemplar, the anointed king who had brought Jerusalem into the power of Israel and driven her enemies out of the land. No; it was far better to keep the discovery secret, to demand an oath of secrecy from all those who had known about it, and then to forget the matter.

But it was not of course so easily forgotten by the Jews, who continued to read Benjamin of Tudela long after he had passed from the scene. They remembered the story with all its ghostly improvisations, the voices speaking out of the storm, the shimmering scepters and crowns lying on the tombs. Exactly eight hundred years later, with the coming to birth of the state of Israel, they were permitted to worship at the legendary tomb of David.

Today we see a single tomb of massive proportions cut out of the living rock, reached through a long arcade painted in green and blue and ornamented with Armenian tiles, and this tomb is indissolubly connected with the story related by Benjamin of Tudela. Here, under the heavy-arched aisles of a long-disused Crusader church, pious Jews chant to David the Psalms which were first sung by him, and on the festivals associated with David priests blow on rams' horns and processions climb up Mount Zion to offer him reverence.

Candles glow around the dark tomb, catching the light of the gold threads on the heavy embroideries flung over the tomb and the glittering Torah crowns which stand in a long row above it. There were sixteen crowns on the day I went there. They shone wonderfully against the smoke-stained walls.

There is a story, widely believed but perhaps apocryphal, that when the Israeli forces captured Mount Zion in the spring of 1948, David

Ben-Gurion wept with gratitude and said, "Up to this moment we had a state, but now we also have a soul." Men who are close to David Ben-Gurion are inclined to dismiss the story on the grounds that he has never been known to weep and he would not regard the possession of the tomb of David as a matter of great importance. Men had been killed on the mountain during the attack; no tomb, however venerable, would have been worth a young man's life.

Operation Mount Zion was part of a deliberate plan to force the Zion Gate and reclaim the Jewish quarter of the old city. It was a daring night attack undertaken by volunteers, with a purely military purpose. Inevitably legends arose. It was remembered that during the time of the destruction of the Second Temple in A.D. 70, the defenders had sometimes escaped to freedom through underground tunnels which led out of Mount Zion. Then for centuries the Jews of the Diaspora had consoled themselves with the slogan: "On Zion we fell; on Zion we shall rise again." I heard stories that the attackers had used these same underground tunnels, and suddenly emerged on the top of Mount Zion, armed with dynamite and hand grenades, and they made short havoc of the Jordanian guard posts, fulfilling the ancient prophecy. But when I asked General David Shaltiel, who was military commander of Jerusalem at the time, whether the Israeli Army had used the underground passages on Mount Zion, he laughed. It had not happened like that. His soldiers had simply stormed the mountain, and nothing would have been gained by using the underground passages blocked with rockfalls. Without benefit of these legendary tunnels they had captured the stronghold.

Yet Jerusalem is honeycombed with tunnels, and you can see the entrances of some of them in that rather desolate garden which must be crossed before you reach the tomb of David. The archaeologists have dug deep into the earth and revealed the cavernous openings; and now the pits are fenced in to prevent the unwary from falling into them. And here and there on that stony garden you come upon heavy blocks of worked stone which once formed the walls of the Church of Holy Zion, forgotten now, though it was once a place of pilgrimage. A roughly painted sign says: TO THE CENACULUM. It does not sound very inviting. It sounds like a Roman ruin or perhaps another sepulcher. Even when you know that *cenaculum* means "a dining room," it does not immediately proclaim that it is a place of any importance. What is the tomb of David doing next to a dining room? Why trouble to climb Mount Zion for a tomb and a room? It is worth the trouble, for in that room, according to a very ancient tradition, the Last Supper was held.

THE UPPER ROOM

And he sendeth forth two of his disciples, and saith unto them: Go ye into the city, and there shall meet you a man bearing a pitcher of water: follow him. And wheresoever he shall go in, say ye to the goodman of the house, The Master saith, Where is the guestchamber where I shall eat the passover with my disciples? And he will show you a large upper room furnished and prepared: there make ready for us.

There are people who go about the world happily collecting relics. They are moved by the sight of the little piece of bone in the museum of the Duomo in Florence which bears the label, "From the thigh of Abraham," and by the rough black gown in the Ognissanti which proclaims itself to be the gown worn by St. Francis when his breast was pierced by the heavenly light, and there is a large hole where the light burned through the cloth. I am enchanted when I come across vials of the Virgin's milk, and the many nails of the Cross, and I see no reason to sorrow over the extent of human credulity. It is simply that men are made that way. We would give a good deal for a lock of Keats's hair or Shakespeare's quill pen. We pay fantastic prices for paintings by Rembrandt, even when the paintings are not very good. We treasure the signature, the sense that Rembrandt has touched the canvas, the numinous power which seems to emanate from the painting. And though in recent days we have learned to look coldly at the relics of saints, knowing how many Syrians were busily engaged in their manufacture during the Middle Ages, there are still many relics that can take our breath away.

The *cenaculum* is a relic, a very large and imposing one, very airy and full of light, possessing considerably more authenticity than most of the relics in Christendom. The early Christians believed it was "the large upper room furnished and prepared," where the Supper was held, and Judas betrayed, and Jesus said, "I am the true vine, and my Father the husbandman," and changed the world. We do not know why they believed this, why they were so sure that it was on Mount Zion, but there is no escaping the fact that they did. They also believed that many other events of incalculable importance to the faith took place in the Upper Room.

I went to the room many times while I was in Jerusalem, and never saw anyone else there. I suspect that it has fallen into disrepute, and I find this puzzling. The Virgin's milk, the bone of Abraham, the nails of the Cross seem to me to belong to the wildest improvisations of the human imagination, but the *cenaculum* belongs to another order of things altogether. Here is authentic history.

The tradition that the room of the Last Supper was on Mount Zion goes back to the second century. According to a fourth-century saint, Epiphanius, a church was established there shortly after the Crucifixion and to his certain knowledge services were being held in the room when the Emperor Hadrian entered Jerusalem in A.D. 135. It was, he says, in "the quarter of Zion which survived the destruction of the city," meaning the destruction of Jerusalem in A.D. 70. It is not improbable that some houses survived the destruction, especially in the southwestern corner where there was least fighting and burning. Josephus gives an appalling account of the pillage, rape, torture and butchery which attended the last days of Jerusalem, and it is true that he says that only a few towers and pieces of wall were left standing as a warning, while all the houses were leveled. But it would have taken fifty years to destroy Jerusalem inchmeal.

There are other reasons for placing trust in Epiphanius. The room of the Last Supper is one of the few relics which the early Christians are likely to have cherished and preserved. They did not dwell, as we do, on the Crucifixion. They dwelt on the love feast and the promise of the Kingdom, affirmed during the Last Supper, and for them no place could have been holier than the place where He said, "Take, eat: this is my body."

Around A.D. 440 a certain Bishop Maximus built the Church of

Holy Zion on the primitive sanctuary. On the wooden dome there was a painting of the Last Supper. There were two churches, one above the other. In the lower church Jesus was believed to have washed the feet of the apostles. The Upper Room was called "the hall of mysteries." There was an altar, and the Crown of Thorns hung down from the roof. This was the church which bore the title of "Mother of All the Churches." It stood outside the new wall built by Hadrian on the ruins of Jerusalem.

In time the holy relics began to accumulate in the basilica, and we learn that the spear and the pillar of scourging were already being shown to pilgrims in the fourth century, and not long afterwards they were shown the table at which the Last Supper had taken place, and the precise place where Jesus was sitting was indicated by a tablet let into the wall. Not only was the Upper Room celebrated for the Last Supper. Here, it was believed, Jesus first showed himself to the apostles after the Resurrection; here Thomas doubted until he thrust his hand into the wound; and here the Holy Ghost descended at the Pentecost. For this reason the Upper Room was sometimes called the Chapel of the Holy Ghost. Sometimes it was known by the simpler and gentler name of Galilee.

On its unprotected scrap outside the walls the basilica was always in danger. About the year A.D. 450 the Empress Eudocia, the wife of Theodosius II, ordered repairs to the wall which included a new section enclosing Mount Zion and adding it to the city. Safe within the containing wall, with its painted dome and high bell tower, the basilica remained unharmed until A.D. 614, when the Persians conquered Jerusalem. Then it was burned, to be rebuilt again a few years later when the Byzantines reconquered the city. It survived the Arab conquest, and Arculf, coming to Jerusalem in A.D. 680, found it in fair shape. On the mosaic map of Palestine discovered at Medeba and dating from the seventh century, there is a bird's-eye view of Jerusalem made up of brilliant green, orange, red, white and black *tesserae*. The Church of Holy Zion appears as an imposing building with red roof tiles and a lemon-green façade.

The Arab conquerors, though without enthusiasm, permitted the Christian churches to remain, and there were continual pilgrimages especially to the Church of the Holy Sepulcher and to Mount Zion. There were occasional Moslem riots, and Yahya of Antioch records that the church was set on fire in A.D. 966 by mobs who seem to have been more determined upon plunder than destruction, for the church was soon repaired. But some forty years later, when the strange blue-eyed Caliph al-Hakim came to the throne, the church suffered more seriously. The mother of al-Hakim was the sister of the Patriarch of Jerusalem, and a devout Christian. In one of his sudden rages against his mother and against all Christendom, the Caliph ordered the destruction of the Church of the Holy Sepulcher, which was leveled to the ground, and most of the other churches were severely damaged. The Church of Holy Zion was sacked and fired, but apparently the shell remained, for when the Crusaders first came to Jerusalem, marching their siege engines up the slopes of Mount Zion to the consternation of the Moslems, there was still a church there; and writing only a few years after the First Crusade the anonymous author of the *Gesta Francorum* points to the place where "Our Lord ate the Last Supper with his disciples before his Passion and filled them with the Holy Ghost" and says the church on this spot was "built by Solomon." He meant perhaps no more than that in its splendor and adornments it was worthy of Solomon. In fact, it was built by Godfrey of Bouillon on the foundations of the earlier church. He built it well, with a tiled roof and two slender bell towers; and in the Crusader map known as the *Plan of Cambrai*, drawn about A.D. 1150, it appears very clearly, standing in proud isolation outside the city walls.

So it remained through the centuries, surviving all wars and catastrophes, especially beloved by the pilgrims whose first glimpse of Jerusalem was sometimes the lofty church on the high mountain. In sight of it they would swing their legs off their donkeys, kneel to the ground and pray. Jerusalem was lost to the Crusaders, but the Moslems usually permitted the pilgrims to enter freely. And when in A.D. 1219 Sultan al Muazzam, fearing he would have to surrender Jerusalem to the Christians, decided upon a scorched-earth policy, destroying towers, walls and churches at his leisure, and sending his soldiers to loot the city, even then, according to the chroniclers of the time, the Holy Sepulcher and the Chapel of the Holy Ghost were spared.

The church which was "the Mother of All the Churches" survives to this day, or rather there is still a large fragment of it left standing. It is true that it no longer wears the aspect of a church. No services are held there, no altar lights glimmer in the Chapel of the Holy Ghost, no pilgrims come to pray. The church—what remains of the church—can easily be overlooked, and few people today realize how great a role it played in the imaginations of the people of the Middle Ages, when the bells ringing out from the Church of the Holy Sepulcher would be taken up by the bells of the Church of the Holy Ghost, and all of Jerusalem would lie hushed in the sound of bells.

In 1483 Friar Felix Fabri made a pilgrimage to Jerusalem. The first glimpse of Zion shining in its splendor was enough to make him tremble at the knees, and he climbed the mountain in a state bordering on delirium. He was one of the lucky pilgrims invited to stay in the dormitory of the Franciscan friars next door to the church. They were the guardians of the holy mountain, and they had in fact been guarding it continually for a hundred and forty years, ever since Queen Sancha, the wife of Robert of Anjou, King of Naples, paid 32,000 ducats to the Sultan of Egypt for the right to let them stay there. They were good friars, living in true poverty, although surrounded by a vast treasure of golden monstrances and reliquaries. Philip the Good, Duke of Burgundy, had left them a small legacy, together with some fabulous tapestries woven in gold and showing scenes of the life and death of Christ for the decoration of the church. They were famous for their wine, but this was their only luxury. They depended on the alms of pilgrims.

Friar Felix felt profoundly at home among the Franciscans and the five Italian ladies who lived according to the Third Rule of St. Francis in a small house nearby. They washed his clothes and scapular, and performed other services of mercy. The dormitory was small and cramped, but the friars were cheerful companions. The great Church of Holy Zion was no longer the glittering thing it had been when Godfrey of Bouillon rebuilt it; the walls stood, the chapel of the Last Supper was still in place, but the wooden roof had fallen in, or had been burned in a fire, and the friars had neither the money nor the skill to repair it. The church was a handsome shell, and so it appears on the wonderfully detailed bird's-eye view of Jerusalem drawn in that same year by Ethard Rewich, which later appeared in the *Peregrinatio in Terram Sanctam* of Bernhard von Breydenbach. There is a stairway leading to the upper room from outside the walls. The beautiful bell towers have vanished, but the church wears a remarkable air of solidity, like a fortress.

Friar Felix enjoyed walking up and down the slopes of the mountain with the Franciscans, who liked to point out the other sacred places in the neighborhood. There, near the bottom of the mountain, Isaiah had been executed, Stephen had been stoned, Peter had hidden in a cavern, and Bathsheba had bathed in full sight of David looking out of the palace window, which could not have been very far from the room of the Last Supper. On a broad, sun-warmed wall set on the edge of a steep slope he would look from the Church of Holy Zion to the Mount of Olives and the gleaming Dome of the Rock, with the whole of Jerusalem and most of the surrounding valleys within his gaze. It was, he thought, the best view of Jerusalem, and in the intervals of wandering over the city he would make plans for staying there, not in the crowded dormitory of the Franciscans, but on a small plot of land of his own on the slope of the mountain among the ruins of abandoned chapels, and there he would plant gardens, vineyards and orchards to his heart's content; and then he would remember that Mount Zion had always been in an exposed situation and it would be dangerous to stay there alone, and he would think of the comforts of his native Germany. He would lie on the wall, dreaming his life away like a ripe apple in the sun, and then he would take his book and go down the mountain and read under the shadow of the gnarled tree which marked the place where Isaiah had died.

Friar Felix was one of the last to report on the Church of Holy Zion, for it existed as a church for only a few more years. In 1521 the Sultan of Turkey, Suleyman the Magnificent, drove the Knights of St. John from the island of Rhodes, so putting to an end the long story of the Crusades. No longer could the Christians in Jerusalem expect protection. Two years later he issued an edict ordering the Franciscans out of the Church of Holy Zion. For a little while longer they were permitted to retain the room of the Last Supper. The French ambassador intervened, every effort was made to retain the church, but at last in 1551 they were expelled. They never returned. From that summer day when they left the upper room to the present it has remained a mosque.

The room of the Last Supper still stands, very much as the Crusaders left it. You enter it now through what was a former window, climbing the steps which lead from the arched hallway below, where Jesus is said to have washed the feet of His disciples, but this hallway is deserted now and no one would guess that it was once regarded as a holy place. A clerk sits at a wooden table, offering to issue certificates to prove you have climbed Mount Zion, and all the weariness of the ages is on him. Languidly he points to the door which leads to an upper room. It might be a kitchen door. You push it open, climb a few stairs, and you are in the room of the Last Supper.

It is not a very large room, but the high vaulted arches give an impression of spaciousness. The stone-flagged floor, the brilliant porphyry columns, the heavy capitals carved with grapes and wheat ears signifying the wine and bread of the Last Supper suggest a vanished elegance. The plaster is flaking off the ceiling with the fine ogival vaulting, and there are bullet holes here and there. The sunlight pours through brilliant emerald windows, now cracked, with inscriptions from the Koran written over them. It might be the dining room of a Norman castle except for these green windows and the white marble mihrab, the Moslem prayer niche, standing against the wall. There is an air of peace and seclusion, and no sounds come from outside.

In this quiet room the mihrab with its delicate carving and the jeweled light through the two windows seem oddly appropriate; they do no harm, and they add the necessary dimension of color. The porphyry columns are short, out of proportion to the vaulting, and in medieval times the floor was probably lower than it is now and the columns were therefore longer. There is no altar, but a small broken column of veined marble, less than two feet high and standing against the wall, is said to mark the place where Jesus sat during the Last Supper. Around this room and this column the silence laps interminably.

From the *cenaculum* a winding stone stairway leads to the flat roof overlooking the old city. From here the gold Dome of the Rock seems almost within reach, and the ancient city lies at your feet. Faintly from below comes the sound of students chanting the Psalms before the tomb of David.

THE SLEEP OF THE VIRGIN

Legends have a life of their own and a prodigious power of proliferation. They do not obey the normal laws of history, and sometimes they are more real to us than our daily lives. Visions, nightmares, the greatest flights of the human imagination have gone into their making: and much pity, and some squalor. We rarely know when they are born, and the ghosts of legends linger long after their deaths.

We can watch the legend-making process at work in the Middle Ages, when the tide of tradition ran high and men were more disposed to believe than they are now that holiness resides in places where holy acts were performed. The Church of the Holy Sepulcher was the traditional site of the Crucifixion and the Resurrection; the tomb and Golgotha lie close together within its walls. But men were not content with these simplicities. They came to believe that on this very spot nearly all the great and legendary events of history had taken place. There Adam died; there Abraham was blessed by Melchizedek, and brought Isaac to be sacrificed; there the brazen serpent was set up; and there all things would have their final consummation.

So with Mount Zion. It was not enough that this was the holy mountain of David and contained the house of the Last Supper. Very soon the legends proliferated by a strange process of association. At first they were content to believe that the disciples had returned to the Upper Room after the Crucifixion, and there the Risen Christ had shown Himself, and there Thomas had doubted, and there the pentecostal flames had descended. But gradually, like the ripples of a pool when a stone is flung into it, the original enchantment gave birth to an ever-widening circle of enchantments. The spring at the foot of the mountain became the Virgin's spring, where Mary had bathed, and Bathsheba before her. On these slopes Stephen had been stoned. Here, too, Peter had heard the cockcrow, an event of sufficient importance to justify the building of the Church of St. Peter in Gallicante, or St. Peter of Cockcrow. The house of Caiaphas stood on the heights of the mountain; this, too, became a church. Not far away stood the house where Jesus was scourged and crowned with thorns: another church. The grotto where Peter wept became a chapel. The place where the apostles had divided after leaving the Upper Room was pointed out, together with the exact spot where Mary stood as she watched them go. And here, most marvelous of all, was the underground chamber where Mary fell into her last sleep. On this spot the Empress Helena built the Church of the Dormition, the Sleep of the Virgin.

What is delightful, and a little baffling, is the prodigality of it all. Every rock, every stone on the holy mountain was given its appropriate share of legend. Every well, every tree, every ruined wall was given a portion of the magnificence, as though the mountain were a mosaic made up of countless events in the story of Jesus. Crowning and towering over all these events was the Last Supper commemorated in the Chapel of the Holy Ghost with the table still in place, with its golden tapestries, with the Spear and the Crown of Thorns.

We cannot explain these things away simply by pointing to the compendious power of associations. The medieval mind warmed itself in the fire of legends, but it was also an eminently practical mind. If, as they believed, the Upper Room belonged to St. James, the brother of St. John, then what more likely than that Mary had taken refuge in this house after the Crucifixion? What more likely than that she had died there? What was more logical than to associate Mary with the Last Supper in this way? Caiaphas and Peter, too, must have their appropriate setting, for if the holy mountain resembled a mosaic of events, it also resembled a crown studded with jeweled legends; and some of the jewels shone brightly, others darkly, and all were bathed in the hidden light of God.

The medieval mind spun a web of probability around the mountain, but it did much more. A pilgrim might hack off a piece of the pillar of scourging or of the table of the Last Supper, but he would do this without irreverence: simply because the tangible shapes and colors of things brought him closer to the mystery. To see the very grotto where the Virgin died was to see the dying Virgin, in some mysterious way to partake of her death. To touch those walls, to climb down the narrow steps, was to make a leap through time into a legendary eternity. The pilgrims were absorbed in the drama of Jesus, and felt themselves to be at once actors and spectators, being instantaneously sinners and men blessed with holiness. Also they saw what they wanted to see.

In the Church of the Dormition, built on the site of a fourth-century basilica, there is a gilt statue of the Virgin lying beneath a canopy on which Jesus appears, summoning her to heaven with the words: "Arise, my love, my fair one, and come away." The statue lies in the crypt beneath a church richly decorated in mosaics, and if there is very little to commend in the mosaics, which resemble the most sentimental colored illustrations in cheap Bibles, at least there is a continual flashing of gold in the air and a sense of spaciousness. The crypt is another matter, for the statue of the Virgin lying on her deathbed is strangely haunting when seen in the light of rare candles. The shadows wheel across the sleeping face, the hands are folded, the long gown vanishes into the surrounding darkness. According to doctrine, it was from this place or somewhere very close that the Assumption took place. The air and heaven opened to receive her bodily. Here, briefly, the laws of nature were suspended to permit her to escape from the earth into the company of heaven.

The exact site has long been forgotten, but for centuries the pious were shown in the northwest corner of the basilica of the Dormition the stone on which the Virgin lay down to die, and long after the basilica was destroyed and the ruins became a rubble-strewn field, a stone marked with a cross was believed to be the site. Henry Maundrell, coming to Jerusalem in 1697, saw only the rubble, for he speaks of seeing the *cenaculum*, "which is now a mosque and not to be seen by Christians," and nearby there was a well which marked the place where the apostles divided from one another, "and close by the well are the ruins of a house in which the blessed Virgin is supposed to have breathed her last." At the end of the nineteenth century this rubble-strewn field was bought by Kaiser Wilhelm II from the Sultan of Turkey and given into the care of the Catholics of Germany. From that strange traffic between emperors the present church and abbey owe their origin.

I spoke to the Benedictine monk who has charge of the crypt, a grave man with an apple-red face and a silky black beard of majestic proportions.

"We do not know where the blessed Virgin died," he said. "We never found the stone which marked the site in the Middle Ages, but we are still searching for it. All we know is that she died very near here—very near here—" He said the words caressingly, and then turned on a lamp which lit up a distant altar showing the dove descending in golden rays against a blood-red sky. He smiled and said, "See, now the Virgin is ascending to heaven." And, in fact, in this light the Virgin seemed to be no longer sleeping, but awake and joyful.

We talked of the fighting which had taken place inside the church and the bullet marks in the golden mosaic above the crypt, and then he went on to talk of the *cenaculum*, which still wears the look of a mosque. Though it could be reached by a short walk under the cypresses from the Church of the Dormition, it remained wholly outside Christian jurisdiction.

He said, "By order of the Armistice Commission all the mosques in use in 1948 must remain mosques, even when they are on the Israeli side and no one visits them, and it is the same on the Jordan side. The synagogues remain synagogues, though no Jew can visit them. And though this means that the buildings will fall into ruins, it is for the best. Many churches have fallen into ruins, and that is God's will. We do not complain because the Mother of all the Churches is abandoned and the mihrab stands there. All this is for the sake of peace, and for the sake of peace all things must be endured."

Then he turned off the light over the altar and said, "The Virgin sleeps again."

Tel Aviv

Even now there is some mystery about the name Tel Aviv, though the city has been in existence for more than fifty years and all the documents concerning the name of the city have survived. The mystery begins with Theodor Herzl and his extraordinary novel *Old-New Land,* which was written in German and given to his friend Nahum Sokolow to translate into Hebrew. Sokolow at the time was busily writing a story about the revolt of Bar Kokba and the destruction of the last remnants of Jewish military power in Palestine. He was a man of a more nervous and excitable temperament than Herzl. He was a scholar and a poet, absorbed in the tragedies of Jewish history and a firm supporter of the Zionist movement. He wrote a letter to Herzl in 1902 discussing the title the novel should bear in Hebrew, and suggested there should be the same number of syllables as *Old-New Land,* but there should be an attempt to discover a more evocative title, one which would sound like the name of a place in Palestine.

Sokolow's suggestion was a perfectly sensible one: three syllables forming a place name "with Biblical-Palestinian overtones." Thereupon he chose the three syllables "Tel Aviv," explaining that *Tel* meant "ruins," *Aviv* meant "spring," and the combination meant "a ruin surviving into a new spring," *"Eine Ruine, die einer neuer Frühlung erlebt."* In his view the ancient ruins surviving into a new springtime suggested a more or less exact equivalent of *Old-New Land.*

51

Sokolow was delighted with his discovery, which may have owed something to a reference in Ezekiel to an obscure town in Babylonia where some of the Jews of the Captivity were living in the time of the prophet, for he says: "Then I came to them of the captivity at Tel-Aviv." But nothing at all is known about this town, and there were more pertinent reasons for choosing the name.

Sokolow's explanation of the meaning of Tel Aviv is a very odd one. He says that *Tel* means "ruins," and he must have known that this was far from being an accurate translation. *Tel* means "a hill" or "a mound," under which ruins may or may not be found. Today Tel Aviv is usually translated as "the hill of spring," but that was not the intention of the man who first put the syllables together. Remembering perhaps the destruction brought upon the land by the revolutionary armies of Bar Kokba, he wanted to suggest the tragedy of the ruined past and the renewal of Israel in the springtime of Zionism. Herzl raised no objection to the suggested title, and in any event he was faced with a *fait accompli,* for the book was already in the press. The Hebrew translation was published in Warsaw in 1902 under the title of *Tel Aviv*. The fame of the three syllables was only just beginning.

Seven years later some of the Jewish inhabitants of Jaffa, weary of living among the Arabs, formed a committee to select the site for a new town nearby. The new town was to be entirely Jewish, ruled by Jews for Jews, drawing its inspiration from the Bible: "I shall build thee and thou shalt be built." Only enough money was available to buy thirty-two acres near the sea to the north of Jaffa, above the railroad lines. Under the leadership of Meir Dizengoff, sixty families, comprising about two hundred and fifty people, marched out and solemnly took possession of a patch of rolling sand dunes which no one else wanted: they were infested with lizards and snakes, and jackals prowled the dunes at night.

A fading photograph of the inauguration ceremony has survived. In the foreground, standing close together, are some of the sixty families wearing their best clothes, the women wearing the heavy, voluminous garments fashionable at the time, the men in bowler hats. About twenty feet away stands Meir Dizengoff in white trousers and double-

breasted jacket, his feet apart, as he addresses the small crowd, proclaiming that all dangers can be overcome and in time they may
expect to see a town with perhaps 25,000 inhabitants. Soon they were
drawing lots and marking out claims along the length of the single
street, called after Herzl. Then for weeks and months and years they
went to work under the broiling sun, leveling the ground, living in
tents shaped like Indian wigwams, gradually building the small cottages which lined the street. At first there was only one wheelbarrow,
and this was used by all the families in turn. And when they had
finished building the cottages, they set about building a school, also
called after Herzl, who would probably have preferred to call it the
"Old-New School," for it was the Altneuschule in Prague which first
suggested the title of his novel. Characteristically, the builders of Tel
Aviv put the greater part of the available wealth into the building of
the school, which was modeled after a medieval drawing of the
Temple at Jerusalem with turrets and crenelated walls and an imposing façade, but in fact it bore very little resemblance to the Temple; it
looked like a British fort in the Northwest frontier of India. The
Herzliya Gymnasium was the first Jewish high school built in Palestine, and the Telavivians were notably proud of it. When it was
destroyed in 1959 to make way for a block of modern flats, the newspapers had leading articles which read like the obituaries of famous
statesmen and generals.

Tel Aviv grew and grew. There were occasional setbacks, but Herzl
Street continued to throw out branches, and these in turn threw out
more branches until they reached very close to Jaffa. In the spring of
1917 the Turkish governor, Jemal Pasha, ordered all the Jews removed
from the town, but they were back soon after the British conquered it
later in the same year. In 1921, twelve years after it was founded, it cut
itself adrift from Jaffa, elected its own mayor, and acquired its own
coat of arms, a fortress-like lighthouse spreading its beams far and
wide, with the motto from Jeremiah, "I shall build thee and thou
shalt be built," words which had been spoken over the derelict sands
at the very beginning of the enterprise. It had been a small suburb of
Jaffa. Soon Jaffa became the suburb of Tel Aviv.

Today Tel Aviv is the largest completely Jewish city in the world, with a population of nearly four hundred thousand. It is a sprawling, pale yellowish, angular city, which seems to have no settled character. Passing through the town shortly after World War I, Ronald Storrs said he thought the architecture had been added after the building, and this is still largely true. Jerusalem demands an unyielding affection. Haifa, carved out of Mount Carmel, like a white flower embracing a mountain, has enough character for five cities of its size. Every village in Israel has a character supremely its own; and even the huddles of goat-hair tents in the Negev have a deliberate design and purpose. Tel Aviv has been called "the plunging neckline of Israel," but such statements avoid the issue. How devoutly one wishes that Tel Aviv had the shadowy mystery of a plunging neckline. Instead, it has an oddly sterile appearance, as though about to be packed in cellophane and kept in some kind of metropolitan refrigerator.

Driving around Tel Aviv, I used to feel nonplused when some peculiarly objectionable apartment house was pointed out as an example of modern architecture at its best, while the few remaining crumbling gray houses of the original settlers were described with contempt. At least the old houses, though cracking at the seams, possessed character. The hotels on the seashore are uniformly grandiose and ugly in their streamlined, black marble luxuriance. It is Miami Beach all over again, and one Miami Beach is enough for one universe.

Happily Tel Aviv in its turn is producing new suburbs, and these have been designed with greater care and dignity. At Ramat Aviv a new workers' colony is springing up; the houses are built on stilts and provided with brilliantly colored panels. The buildings sit well in the landscape. They have not the insufferable crowded smartness of Tel Aviv, they do not flaunt their luxury. The air flows between them, and they belong to the landscape. The new University of Tel Aviv will soon be rising in the nearby sand dunes, and with luck it will have the quiet luxurious air of belonging to the landscape.

In Israel nearly all the large towns are like twin stars, being two towns with wholly separate histories lying close together. So there are the old and new cities of Jerusalem, and modern Haifa lies close to ancient Acre, and new Kiryat Natzrat stands on the hills above Nazareth, and while Tiberias hugs the lake shore a new town called Kiryat Shemuel spreads over the hills above it. In much the same way Tel Aviv is continually reminded of its modernity by the presence of Jaffa, which has some claim to be the oldest city on that coast. Pliny says it came into existence forty years before the Flood. What is certain is that it was old when Athens was young. It was the seaport of Jerusalem in the time of King Solomon, and through its port came the cedars of Lebanon offered by King Hiram of Tyre for the embellishment of the Temple. There is a pleasant Jewish legend which tells how "all the silver, gold and precious stones which perished in shipwrecks will rise and flow into Jaffa, to be delivered as a ransom for the righteous at the time of the coming of the Messiah."

But today there is no hint of wealth in Jaffa, which bears the scars of too many wars. There was bitter fighting in Jaffa between the Arabs and the Jews in 1948, and sometimes, as you wander through the crumbling ruins of the city still inhabited by Arabs, you have the feeling that the fighting ended only yesterday. In the narrow alleyways and on the broad brow of the hill there is an air of desolation. It is like a place that has been cursed, and you flee from it gladly.

Beyond Jaffa lies the Plain of Sharon, a place which has been abundantly blessed.

Caesarea

In the hot summer afternoon, when you could scarcely breathe for the heat, the Plain of Sharon lay freshly green. There had been no rain since April, and there would be none again until November, but all through the summer and into the fall there would be that luscious carpet of green, with only here and there a stretch of uncultivated desert. When the winter rains came, then it would be even more green and luscious than before.

"Sharon" means "forest," and there was a time not long ago when all this land between the sea and the dusty reddish hills of Samaria was a wild straggling forest set amid marshlands, the haunt of wild beasts. Strabo called it "a vast woodland," and Josephus called it simply "the forest," as though there were no other in the world. The Crusaders knew it well and complained bitterly of having to fight animals as well as enemies as they plunged through the forests, and because the memories of the Crusaders lingered, it became Tasso's enchanted forest, *la selva encantada*, in the long epic he wrote on the delivery of Jerusalem by the Crusaders. For Napoleon too it was dense woodland, and on eighteenth-century French maps appears as the "forest of Miski." There were still woodlands here when Allenby's army fought its way along the coast to Haifa; the retreating Turks left a trail of tree stumps. It was the beginning of the end. Soon most of the remaining trees were cut down, and the marshes drained. The

56

traveler, peering out of the window of the Tel Aviv–Haifa train, sees gleaming farmlands, citrus orchards, neat white houses and broad motor roads: as fresh and unhistorical, it seems, as any new settlement in California. No one would guess how many armies had fought their way along the coast, or how many men had died in the vast malaria-breeding swamps, or how many trees were cut down in the last forty years. Sharon, the dark forest, has become a flowering orchard.

Not that it is altogether orchard; there are still patches of scrub and desert where the asps and vipers linger, coming out at night to leave their sinuous trails in the dust. Wild animals still occasionally appear, and eagles hover in the sky. Though the land has been reclaimed, there is always the knowledge that the forest may reappear. It needs only another war to set it moving again.

This narrow plain was always a highway of history. In spite of swamps and forests, the armies swept up and down, for the Plain of Sharon is the bridge between Asia and Africa. There were no harbors along the coast; therefore the sea was a barrier, keeping at bay the enemies from the west. The enemies came mostly from the east and the south, until first Alexander and then the Crusaders came from the north. Uncounted battles have been fought on the red earth of the plain.

Here, midway between Tel Aviv and Haifa, stood the great city of Caesarea with its artificial harbor built by Herod the Great. It stands there still, though most of it remains hidden under the drifting sands, where only rushes and lentisk grow. Once it was the largest city in Judea, its chief port and marshaling yard, the seat of the governor. "*Caesarea Judaeae caput est*," says Tacitus simply; but if it was the head, it was also the heart, the center of all directed activity, the place where all the nations came together. Here Herod lived in state, and Pontius Pilate kept his official residence, and Peter converted Cornelius, a centurion, and Paul was imprisoned. Here the early Fathers of the Church built their great library; here Origen lived, and Pamphilus, and Eusebius, who compiled from among the books in the vast library the first history of the youthful Church. Here the Genoese Crusaders found the green crystal chalice, the *sacro catino*, which it pleased them to call the Holy Grail. Here St. Louis of France built a prodigious fortress with moats and drawbridges; the fortress remains. But though Caesarea has been occupied successively by Byzantines, Arabs, Crusaders, Syrians, Kurds and Turks, it is still Herod's city. He has left his stamp on it, and his stamp prevails.

Josephus, who alone provides us with a detailed account of the building of the city, was considerably puzzled by the choice of the site, which had little to commend it. There seemed to be no reason why Herod should have chosen this strip of land rather than another. It is true that there was a small anchorage called Strato's Tower, but there were many other small and dangerous anchorages along the shore. Herod came to Strato's Tower and announced that he would build a port as large as Piraeus, then the largest port in the Mediterranean, and he kept his word.

He was twelve years building it. Enormous blocks of limestone were lowered into twenty fathoms of water to form a breakwater and a quay. The sea wall was two hundred feet wide, and furnished with towers. Warehouses and lodgings for seamen were built in alcoves along the landward end of the great wall. A vast and complicated drainage system, operated by tidal power, cleaned the city, and the public buildings included a theater, an amphitheater and a hippodrome which could seat twenty thousand people. Here is Josephus's description of Herod's city:

> The entrance to the harbor faced north, because in these latitudes the north wind is the most favorable of all. At the harbor mouth rose three colossal statues on either side, supported on pillars; and the pillars on the left of the ships entering the harbor were supported by a massive tower, those on the right by two upright blocks of stone clamped together, even higher than the tower on the other side. Adjoining the harbor were houses, also of limestone, and the streets of the city, laid at equal distances apart, led to the harbor. On rising ground facing the harbor mouth stood Caesar's temple, of exceptional size and beauty; it contained a colossal statue of the Emperor, not inferior to Olympian Zeus, which served as a model, and there was another statue dedicated to Rome comparable with the Hera of Argos. Herod dedicated the city to the province, the harbor to those who sailed the seas, and to Caesar went the glory of the new creation: therefore he gave it the name of Caesarea.

Josephus's account reads like the work of an eyewitness, who has actually landed on the mole and seen the harbor crowded with shipping, and the gleaming white temples and palaces rising behind it. The account breathes authority, and the buildings he mentioned have all left their traces; only the mole, as he described it, presents difficulties and remains something of a conundrum to the archaeologists who have examined the harbor from the air and from the sea bed. We still do not know the exact site of the harbor, but we can draw up a plan of Herod's city almost to the last street.

Herod the Great came of Arab stock, with little Jewish blood in his veins. Handsome, robust, intensely athletic, possessed of an astonishing flair of self-dramatization, he was incapable of half-measures. He built Caesarea for eternity: the city was intended to rival Rome, as the harbor rivaled and perhaps excelled the harbor of Athens. That geometer's city, with its circular harbor and absolutely straight streets, was to be his civic triumph, while the Temple he built in Jerusalem testified to the triumph of the religion which he ornamented, though he had no faith.

The evil genius of Herod laid a heavy burden on the Jews. His wars, his fortresses, his great cities and the gifts which he squandered on his allies led ultimately to the impoverishment of the Jewish nation. Singlehandedly, he opened the way for Roman military domination in Judea. In time Caesarea became the hammer which destroyed the Jews of Palestine. It is just possible that this was his intention.

THE HEADLESS STATUES

A hundred yards from the walls of the fortress built by St. Louis, in open fields overgrown with wild thistles, among suspicious-looking hummocks and mounds which testify to the presence of buildings still unexcavated, stand below the level of the earth two enormous headless statues, whether of Roman gods or emperors no one knows. One is of dark and gleaming porphyry, purple-red. The other is carved from a single block of white marble, which has been cut in two at the level of his waist. The statues belong to different periods, for the porphyry one must date from the end of the fourth century A.D., and the marble one must be at least a hundred years earlier. That two statues of different periods should be brought together, facing each other, is not remarkable. What is remarkable is that they have been set up in what was clearly a Byzantine building of about the sixth century. Israeli archaeologists are inclined to believe that these two statues were pillaged from Roman temples to decorate a Byzantine cattle market.

Everything about Caesarea suggests a timeless quiet, the wars forgotten. In the tranquil air there is only the rustling of the wild thistles. In the places where Herod walked and the ancient Fathers of the Church pondered the mysteries of faith, time has come to a stop. Here all ages become equal and contemporary, and therefore no one should be surprised to discover objects from different ages lying side by side. But these headless statues have a rare appropriateness. Grave and majestic, they have about them something of the power of agelessness, belonging to no time or place, enthroned deep below the earth, headless and armless, incapable of thought or action, but possessing a strange purposefulness. They reign with Buddha-like calm, inspiring no fear. Once they must have looked out upon the world with commanding aspect, their arms raised in benediction or in gestures of demonstration, but all this has been removed from them. What remains is the abstract shape of power.

When the Moslems sacked Caesarea in A.D. 1291, they left it a desert. For six hundred years the ruined city remained uninhabited except for occasional nomads. The Turks established a small settlement of Bosnians, who erected the squat and ugly minaret which still stands near the harbor, but they seem to have stayed only a little while. The first to settle permanently since the time of the Crusaders were the young Jews of the Sedot Yam *kibbuts* who arrived there in 1937. One day in the spring of 1951 they were clearing the fields east of the Crusader fortress when they uncovered the shoulders of the porphyry statue. Surprised, they sent off to Jerusalem for help. During the summer the second statue was found, and in the following months columns, walls, troughs, clay pipes, mosaic pavements and inscriptions came to light. The archaeologists are still puzzled by one of the mosaic inscriptions which refers to a hitherto unknown governor of Caesarea. It reads: "Under the Governor Flavius Entolius the mayor Flavius Strategius built out of public funds the wall, the steps, and the apse in the tenth indiction. In a good hour." No one is quite sure what the inscription means, but it suggests that the mayor, living in a Christian community, but possessing antiquarian tastes, had looted the statues from a pagan building and set them up in the cattle market in his own honor. There seems to be no doubt from the shape of the troughs and the clay pipes that this was the cattle market. As for the statues, they probably came from the temple of Hadrian, which may have been somewhere in the vicinity. The odd thing is that the statues had already lost their heads before they were set up in the Byzantine market place.

Caesarea is full of these puzzles. Nothing is quite in the place where it would be expected. A considerable part of the Crusader fortress has been uncovered, but there is as yet no sign of the chapel which must have existed there, if only because a fortress built by St. Louis would inevitably have a sumptuous chapel with stained-glass windows. A small and admirably constructed theater has been discovered with an inscription testifying to the fact that the theater was dedicated by Pontius Pilate. It was built facing the sea, and modern audiences are uncomfortably blinded by the sea's glare. Josephus describes the theater accurately, saying that "it is conveniently situated for a prospect of the sea." But who wants to be blinded by that subtropical glare when watching a play? Most puzzling of all are the two headless statues sitting deep in the trench carved out of a field of thistles.

THE PROFESSOR

I knew the Professor well from his books, for he has written at great length on the archaeology of the Holy Land. There were countless papers under his signature in the *Israel Exploration Journal*, a five-volume survey of Palestine appeared only a few years ago, and he had also written a scholarly commentary on the Medeba mosaic, that tantalizing and fragmentary map of Palestine and Egypt, found in the ruins of an ancient Byzantine church. He wrote with great authority and with a pleasant addiction to mountains of footnotes. Because he was the pure scholar, I imagined him old and frail, with a skull cap, a face of parchment and a thin beard.

The man who came out of the sea at Caesarea, rising like Aphrodite from the foam, did not at first resemble a great scholar. He looked, in fact, like a walrus. He was fat and jolly, his great voice boomed and echoed off the walls of the citadel, as he stamped about in the sand and shook the water off his body. He had a round red face, a straggling mustache, heavy shoulders, a powerful body. When he stamped, you expected an earthquake or a bolt of lightning. Dripping, he advanced up to the small hut which served as a combined dressing room and storehouse for the excavations north of the Crusader city which were being conducted by the oddly named Department for the Preservation of Landscape and Antiquities of the Prime Minister's Office.

It was a large and cavernous shed under the shadow of the Bosnian minaret, fitted with long rows of shelves where the potsherds were laid out, as though they were so many tomatoes ripening in the dark. The Professor stood outside in the sun, wringing the water out of his ears, blowing it out of his nose, stamping his feet and making the appropriate garumphing noises. In the intervals of peals of laughter, while he toweled himself, and wrung the water out of his mustache, he talked about mosaics.

They were his chief love, and sooner or later in his writings he always came back to them.

"We've just found two feet," he said. "Think of that! Two feet, rather big ones, outlined in mosaics on the floor of what is certainly a synagogue. Now what the devil do you think two mosaic feet are doing there?"

I told him that it was the habit of American film stars to leave the imprints of their hands and feet in concrete outside a theater in Hollywood. Probably it was something like that.

"Rubbish! We never had any American film stars in our synagogues in the fourth century A.D. It's inconceivable that anyone wanted to immortalize his feet. Besides, they are men's feet—"

"How many of them?"

"We have found two in Caesarea. And two is quite enough, thank you. If there were more, we would go out of our minds. As it is, we are perilously close to it. It's against anything we can conceive, everything we know about the period. It's not the first time it has happened —they found two feet in a mosaic in the Negev. If you find one pair of feet, you can dismiss it as a local aberration, but if you find two pairs of feet, you have to accept the possibility that it was the accepted custom. There were no inscriptions, nothing to tell us what the feet are doing there. They are not, as far as we know, where anyone would normally stand to deliver a sermon, and they were certainly not near the Holy of Holies. Furthermore, we have no tradition about two feet. There's nothing in the writings of the sages to suggest that anyone cared a hoot about two feet."

I said something about the possibility that the two feet meant that this was where people were meant to remove their shoes.

"Oh dear, no, it's nothing as simple as that. That wouldn't be playing fair. Besides, we're not like the Arabs, we don't go barefoot into the synagogue. Then, too, it is unlikely that they represent the feet of actual people. There's nothing to suggest that some great sage once stood there and they wanted to preserve his memory. If there had been anything like that, they would have written his name."

He was going into the storeroom to change his clothes.

"Just think about it, if you please," he said over his shoulder. "Two feet, and what the devil were they doing there? I'll expect an answer when I come out."

While the Professor dressed, a young archaeology student from Kentucky took over. He had a long, lean, sunburned face and a dry, casual, Kentucky manner. It was obvious that he worshiped the Professor. This was the first season he had spent digging in Israel, and he was hopelessly in love with the work, though he would sometimes sigh over Israeli food. He was having dreams of well-cooked steaks and blueberry pie. He said, "They're not really feet. They're sandals with straps on them. There is another pair of sandals in a synagogue in Beersheba. That makes two pairs of sandals, and not the slightest clue about what they are doing there."

"What does the Professor really think?"

"He doesn't know. He thinks it means, 'Shake the dust off your sandals before you enter the synagogue,' but he's not entirely satisfied with this explanation."

The student went into the storeroom and came out with some of the recently excavated treasures—some coins from a hoard of about four thousand found underneath a synagogue. They were all bronze coins, and the latest dated from the reign of Gallus Caesar, who came to the throne in A.D. 351. During his reign a fierce Jewish revolt was quelled. Gallus gave orders to massacre the Jews and burn down their synagogues, and this synagogue in Caesarea had evidently been burned, for there were traces of fire-blackened earth and cinders. Later a new synagogue had been built on the foundations of the earlier one, but no one had suspected the existence of the hoard of coins among the ashes. It was the largest hoard of coins ever discovered in Israel, but since the coins were of bronze, it was by no means the most valuable.

Then he brought out a small clay head, dark purple-red, no larger than a palm, the head of a man with a pointed beard and an expression of great power and assurance. It looked vaguely Assyrian. It might have been the portrait of a prince or a high priest.

"What is it?"

"We don't know. It's like the sandals. We've looked up all the books and all the reports of other excavations at Caesarea, but nothing like it has been found before. In the end the Professor will track it down—he always does!"

By this time the Professor had returned, dressed in a neat blue suit, his cherubic face with the straggling mustache outlined with a wonderful halo of tousled hair.

"Well, have you thought about the two feet?" he asked.

"Yes."

"What conclusions did you come to?"

"I suppose they are angels' feet."

"Rubbish."

"Then I give up."

"So do I. That's the trouble with mosaics—too many problems. Have you seen the mosaic at Beth Alpha? There it is, with the date and the names of the craftsmen who made it, and until we find others like it, we still won't know how that particular design came into existence. Normally we can trace the influences, study the texts written in the mosaics, come to conclusions. But the mosaic at Beth Alpha is utterly unlike anything known. And heaven knows what the new excavations will bring! Only a few years ago no one believed we would ever find representational figures in the mosaics of the synagogues. Now we find them everywhere. Only two or three months ago we found near the hot springs at Tiberias, one of the sacred cities of the Jews, a magnificent mosaic depicting the chariot of the sun. We are growing accustomed to these chariots—they are turning up everywhere—but this one is so Greek that you would not be surprised to find it in Athens. We still don't know what it was doing in the synagogue at Tiberias. It's all mystery!"

"Like the feet?"

"Yes, like the feet!" he said, and he threw back his head and roared with laughter.

A few moments later he locked the storeroom door and went off, for the day's work was done. It was evening now, and the blue shadows were descending over the ruins. Not a stone's throw away were the columns of a palace dating from Herodian times, and a little way beyond it lay the ruins of a fourth-century church which the historian Eusebius must have attended, and not far away was a Roman arch, and there was a collection of Roman statues in an enclosure nearby. At Caesarea you can walk ten yards and travel through ten centuries. Here the civilizations are piled one upon another, and each has left its own vast, indelible trace. Acre has only a Turkish mosque and a Crusader keep. Caesarea has everything.

Above all, Ceasarea has the romance of its lonely, abandoned position by the seashore. Strangely, a golf course has been built nearby, but there is no crowding the ancient walls with modern buildings. Hadera, the nearest town, is a good twenty minutes away. For a little while longer Caesarea will sleep its deep sleep interrupted only by the archaeologists, who can only shore up the ruins and reveal a few of its treasures. There are still acres upon acres of Caesarea which no archaeologists have yet penetrated, though the evidence of those buried streets is clearly indicated by aerial photographs. "We have turned up only the corner," an archaeologist told me in Jerusalem. "I envy those who will come after us, for they will be able to see Caesarea in all its glory."

Only about a quarter of the Crusader city has been excavated, and perhaps only a hundredth of the Roman city has been unearthed. The Byzantine city lies beneath the hummocks of earth around the two headless statues, and far beyond. In the time of Herod and Pontius Pilate this seacoast was the most densely populated part of Judea. Now there are only the huge walls, the waving grasses, the dunes, and the deep blue sea.

We left Caesarea in the gray dusk, while the starlings were flying madly among the ruined turrets of the Crusader fort. There was still light enough to see the mosaic floor of a church which once stood high above the sea, overlooking the harbor. To reach the mosaics you must climb ankle-deep in sand; on the summit there are perhaps fifty birds and animals playfully enclosed in circles of leaves. There were pelicans and bears and lions, there were ducks with red beaks and pink flamingos all posturing gaily behind a wire fence; and there was not one which did not look like a child's toy. The playfulness of the Byzantine artists was in happy contrast with the formidable power of the Herodian walls lying below.

By building Caesarea Herod gave hostages to Rome; this city became the hammer, the focal point of Roman influence in Palestine. Through the streets now covered with sand marched the Roman legions on their way to Jerusalem, burning and pillaging as they went. When they had destroyed all they could lay their hands on, the great port lost its importance. Already in Byzantine times the city was scarcely more than a large straggling village; and when the Crusaders came and built their own fortress, it had a garrison of perhaps five hundred men who were permanently resident. The Arabs destroyed Caesarea. Then for centuries there were only a few fishermen's huts among the ruins.

Today you can still trace the long aqueduct which brought sweet water to the wells of Caesarea, though most of it is covered with sand. But close to the city the supporting arches of the aqueduct can still be seen. In the twilight it looks like an immense serpent sloughing off its interminable coils.

Haifa

They were close enough now to make out the details. In the road-stead between Acre and the foot of Mount Carmel huge liners rode at anchor, and beyond the liners could be seen the charming contours of the bay and the mountain. At the northern end there was Acre with its harsh oriental beauty, with its grey castle walls and cupolas and minarets spearing the morning sky, and from Acre to the top of the mountain there were those thousands of white houses and the mountain itself was capped with magnificent buildings.

When Herzl wrote these words in 1902, there was scarcely a single house on Mount Carmel and no liners had ever put into the bay. But the memory of Mount Carmel, seen only briefly from a ship's rail, haunted him as no other landscape had ever haunted him. Of Jerusalem he always spoke somberly, as of a place so ancient that it should be kept as a museum or under glass, and neither Paris nor Rome nor any of the other cities he visited and discussed in his letters drew from him the excitement he reserved for this small town which sheltered at the foot of a green mountain.

In Herzl's day the harbor of Haifa had long since been silted up with sand, and the streets, according to a contemporary traveler, were "filthy and wretched beyond description." A colony of German Templars had settled there in the sixties of the last century, outnumbering the pitifully small group of Jewish merchants and the Arabs who sometimes pastured their sheep and goats on the slopes of the moun-

68

tain. The Templars cultivated the narrow plain near the seashore; there were olive fields, small orchards and occasional palm trees, a few shops, a few lanes of houses huddled together. Herzl saw the thickly wooded mountain turning into a modern city gleaming in the sunset, all stone and marble. He saw great avenues ringing the mountain, and vast public squares "shaded by palms which served as lamp-posts at night, with clusters of lamps hanging from them like glass fruit." He believed Haifa would become a great metropolis "with the safest and most convenient harbor in the Mediterranean." All this he saw with his prophetic eyes, after seeing with his ordinary eyes a dismal village on the seacoast. It is always a mystery when prophecies are fulfilled.

Today, when you arrive in Haifa and see that white mountain which only sixty years ago was the haunt of leopards and hyenas, you wonder whether such things are possible. Haifa has the look of an old city. It is well anchored on its mountain, and does not have the bright, new, chromium-plated look of Tel Aviv. It has grown organically, spreading up the mountainside according to the natural laws of growth. At first it grew very slowly, cautiously, throwing up small shoots along the lower ranges of the mountain. The Jewish immigrants arriving from Germany in the 1930s forced the pace a little, so that already by the time of World War II most of the mountain was covered with houses. Now the whole mountain has become a city, which is beginning to spread over the neighboring mountains. Whole new settlements have beeen built on the top of Carmel, and there is no knowing when the process will stop.

Haifa even today is still very largely a German-Jewish city. The people go about with the methodical, practical air of German Jews. There is no nonsense about them. In all other towns in Israel life comes to a virtual stop on the Sabbath. In Haifa on the Sabbath the buses are kept running, ships enter the dock, the funicular railway still operates. It is the largest and best-equipped seaport in Israel, with the only deep-water harbor, and it is determined that nothing shall impede the flow of trade. Significantly it has acquired a reputation for quiet, unobtrusive scholarship, and has more bookshops per street than any other town in Israel. I found ten bookshops in three blocks on Herzl Street, and this may well be the world's record. The pride of

Haifa is the technological institute known as the Technion, originally built in 1912 on the slopes of the mountain, now in a pine forest on top of the mountain, with a magnificent view of the great bay and the houses clustered along the white slopes.

Where there are new hotels and gleaming white modern buildings there were once hermit caves and quiet sanctuaries in the woods. For centuries Carmel was sacred to Baal Hadad, the ancient god of the Canaanites, who was Lord of the Heavens, Maker of Thunder and Rain, and of Fertility; and when the prophet Elijah called upon the priests of Baal to summon down fire upon the sacred bull, he was, in order to destroy them, deliberately taunting them with their own sacred symbols—the holy fire, the holy bull. If it had not been for Elijah, Baal Hadad might have become the ruling god of the Near East. Jehovah conquered, but Baal Hadad never entirely disappeared. He haunted the topmost crags of the mountain, a mysterious and powerful force whose fame reverberated across the Mediterranean. Vespasian sacrified to the god when revolving in his mind his secret hopes of empire. Tacitus tells the story of how Vespasian came to Carmel and heard what he wanted to hear:

> Between Syria and Judea is Carmel—the name given to a mountain and to a god. Here there is no image of the god nor any temple: the traditions of antiquity prescribe only the altar and its sacred associations.
>
> Vespasian came here to offer sacrifices and ponder his secret ambitions. Basilides was the priest, and after repeatedly inspecting the entrails he said: "Vespasian, whatever you desire, whether it is to build a house or to enlarge your estates or to increase the number of your slaves, all these will be given to you. To you shall be given a vast palace, boundless territories, multitudes of men."
>
> These obscure auguries were soon spread among the populace, and various attempts were made to interpret them. Indeed, little else was spoken about by the common people; and in Vespasian's presence they discussed the auguries all the more freely because men have more to say to men who desire great things.

Tacitus is not always reliable when he speaks about the Jews—he had some theories about them which must be among the most inaccurate ever recorded—but here he was speaking about matters which he may easily have learned from members of Vespasian's entourage. The account rings true. Vespasian went on to seize the empire and to become the scourge of the Jews. A few months later Jerusalem fell and Judea became a small province under Roman rule.

But it is not for such stories that we remember Carmel. We remember the mountain chiefly because with Hermon and Tabor it possesses a particular holiness and a particular beauty. "Thine head upon thee is like Carmel, and the hair of thy head like purple," wrote the author of the *Song of Songs*. The prophet Isaiah speaks of "the excellency of Carmel and Sharon, they shall see the glory of the Lord." That the green forests on the mountain should wither, and its fruits perish, is his darkest image of desolation. For the ancient Hebrews, Carmel is the emblem of the earth's ripeness and blessedness, for while the rest of the country changed to the yellow of death during the heat of summer, Carmel, luxuriating in its heavy dews, remained unfailingly green. The green has nearly vanished and the forest has turned into stone, but somehow the city still suggests ripeness.

Like the new city of Jerusalem, Haifa has all the advantages of ancient traditions and up-to-the-minute modernity. Elijah and Elisha are almost physical presences; there are still pilgrimages to Elijah's smoke-blackened cave. Yet sometimes the prophetical voices acquire ironical overtones. "Feed Thy people with Thy rod, the flock of Thine inheritance, which dwell solitarily in the forest in the midst of Carmel," said the prophet Micah. But "the forest in the midst of Carmel" has vanished, and no one can dwell solitarily on the mountain.

As though the possession of a holy mountain, a beautiful bay, a rich harbor and a teeming modern city were not enough, Haifa also possesses Acre as a suburb. This is rather like having an enormous mansion with an exquisite Oriental summerhouse at the bottom of the garden. Acre is the ancient Ptolemaïs, once endowed by the luxury-loving Emperor Ptolemy II Philadelphus with marble colonnades, libraries and gymnasiums. St. Paul landed there when he went up to Jerusalem for the last time, saluting the brethren then staying in the town, and spending a day with them. Under the Crusaders it became St. Jean d'Acre, and was held by them for a hundred and eighty-two years except for a two-year period when it fell to Saladin. There, finally, in May, 1291, exactly a hundred years after it had been wrested from Saladin by Richard the Lion-Heart, the Moslems took the walls by storm and in a single day killed thirty thousand of the defenders. On that day ended the Latin Kingdom in the Holy Land.

Wandering through Acre today, you would hardly dream that it was ever a city of importance. The small gray donkeys wind through shadowy streets where the jutting eaves keep out the sun. There are streets so dark you can barely see the faces of passers-by at noon, and so narrow that even the donkeys must go in single file. There is the smell of spices. You might be in some small town in Persia or Malaya, so pervasive is the atmosphere of the Orient. Then suddenly, you find yourself looking down from street level at a vast Crusader church sunk deep in the earth and still being excavated, with huge columns like roots which have never seen the sun. At such moments, very briefly, you become aware of the power wielded by the Crusaders.

THE HOUSE OF HORROR

Not far from Acre, along the coastal road, an enormous yellow building faces the sea. Here the air is sweet, for there are orange groves all round, and the plains are well watered, very green even at the height of summer. A long Turkish aqueduct, biscuit-colored, runs along the road, and through the arches you can see green fields, tall cypresses, red-roofed houses, silvery water towers. The yellow building might be a school or a theater, except for the fact that there is no town or village nearby. I thought it might be a very large and well-equipped government experimental station until it occurred to me that no government would build in such a modern style, with such deliberate art in the making of the building. In fact, the yellow building was a house of horror.

The history of this house begins in 1949 when a small handful of survivors from the ghettos of Poland and Lithuania settled here on the Plain of Acre and founded a *kibbuts* which they called *Lohamei Hagetáot*, meaning "The Fighters of the Ghettos." They had brought with them a few pathetic relics and souvenirs of the fighting inside the ghettos and the subsequent partisan campaigns. At first it was to be a very small museum housed in one of the buildings on the *kibbuts*, but gradually the concept widened to include relics, archives and photographs concerning the entire history of the extermination of the Jews by the Nazis. It would be a memorial to the six million dead. It would say what had to be said, commemorate what had to be commemorated. It would be, as well as human hands could make it, an eternal monument to a senseless and intolerable crime.

Inside, the yellow building gives an impression of extraordinary spaciousness. The rooms are palatial, very high, very broad, with their dark polished floors and well-proportioned windows. One large room contains a scale model of a concentration camp with its wretched huts and tall watchtowers; the model is half the size of the room. There are blown-up photographs along the walls, here and in all the other rooms. There are scraps of uniform, slabs of the black bread fed to the prisoners, proclamations, orders. Mostly there are these blown-up and grainy photographs reproduced from books and newspapers. We see the Jews herded into cattle trucks, or walking about the ghettos of Warsaw wearing the yellow badge of David, or assembling in the concentration camps. It is a world of black and white, without depth, without dimension, soundless and strangely impersonal. They might be stills from an old movie. It is only with a great effort that one can bring oneself to feel that these photographs represent events that actually happened, that this bath chamber or this smokestack formed part of a terrifying engine of destruction, and that these people looking out calmly from the faded photographs are in agony.

What was shocking was the sense of unreality, the appalling ineffectiveness of these photographs hanging in these palatial rooms. The photographs lied: they left out everything of importance. Just as it was impossible to suffer with these ghostly people in the photographs, so it was impossible to feel any emotion in front of the loaf of bread, resembling a black cinder, which stood in a glass case. No doubt a ghetto fighter had carried it with him during long and dangerous wanderings; this was his prize, the pathetic treasure he had stolen from the flames, but in the context of the holocaust the black cinder remained meaningless. So, too, with the torn shreds of clothing, the toys left by the children, the hanks of hair. The horror, the urgency had gone. Instead of bringing us closer to the concentration camps and the incinerators, the exhibition did precisely the reverse by removing them into the limbo of shadowy photographs.

I asked my companion, a Jew who had fought in the British Army and in the war against the Arabs, what he thought of the museum.

His reaction was completely unexpected.

"What I hate most," he said quietly, "is that everything is written in Hebrew. It's our damned parochialism. Why don't they have it in German and English and half a dozen languages? Why have a museum about the extermination of the European Jews, with only Jews being able to read the captions?"

I asked him what he thought of the photographs. He shrugged his shoulders.

"They are not there," he said with a ghostly half-smile.

"How are they not there?"

"Because they say nothing, and might just as well not be there!"

This was true: the horror was not in the concentration camps; it was in the vacuity of the museum which had failed to accomplish its purpose.

Perhaps it is inevitable. Perhaps the scale of the German massacres was so great that it will be forever impossible to erect a monument which will suggest the immensity of the tragedy. These photographs were mostly taken by Storm Troopers with Brownies, but even a great photographer would probably fail to record the savagery and sorrow of the concentration camps in their full dimensions. It is a task for the artist, not the photographer. And through the centuries the artist has nearly always failed. He has painted victorious generals on horseback and depicted battle scenes, usually unrelated to any battle known by any serving soldier, and he has carved abstract designs intended to suggest suffering. But the suffering of the Jews under the Germans went beyond anything conceivable by the human imagination. Only very rarely has it been hinted at in words. Here for example is an account by a German engineer, Hermann Graebe, who saw the Jews being led to the slaughter pits at Dubno in the Ukraine:

I walked around the mound and stood in front of a tremendous grave. People were closely wedged together and lying on top of each other so that only their heads were visible. Nearly all had blood running over their shoulders from their heads. Some of the people who had been shot were still moving. Some were lifting their arms and turning their heads to show that they were still alive. The pit was already two-thirds full. I estimated that it already contained about a thousand people. I looked for the man who did the shooting. He was an SS man who sat at the edge of the narrow end of the pit, his feet dangling into the pit. He had a tommy-gun on his knees and was smoking a cigarette. The people, completely naked, went down some steps which were cut in the clay wall of the pit and clambered over the heads of the people lying there, to the place to which the SS man directed them. Some caressed those who were still alive and spoke to them in low voices.[1]

It seemed to me that where photographs, sculpture and painting have failed, words sometimes succeeded in suggesting the full measure of the horror. Hermann Graebe's words have no cadence of violence, and are all the more effective for their quietness. Strangely, the scene resembles a painting. There are no voices, no rattle of the tommy gun, no screams of the dying, almost no movement takes place; the sacrifice occurs in a dreadful silence. Only at the very end do we hear the authentic note of human sympathy rising above all the world's tragedies. *Some caressed those who were still alive and spoke to them in low voices.*

We went out into the strong sunlight with the odd feeling we have when, having seen an exhibition of abstract paintings, we find ourselves bemused for a few moments by a world which resolutely refuses to become an abstraction. The abstract world of the concentration camps had vanished, and in its place there was the green and living world of Israel. A truck passed, loaded with red-cheeked schoolchildren. Green orange groves stretched on every side, and the birds were singing.

"Did you notice the name they have given the house?" my friend said. "It is 'Lest We Forget.' The trouble is that we have already forgotten."

The truth is that a new generation is springing up which has al-

[1] Testimony of Hermann Graebe, *Nuremberg Trials*: Judgement, p. 52.

most forgotten the massacres: they seem to have happened long ago, in another age, on another earth. The young workers on the *kibbutsim*, brimming with health, have little time or inclination to think of the wounds suffered by the Jews in their long history. Their thoughts are of the future.

Some months later, wandering among the Judean hills, I came upon one memorial which almost succeeds in conveying the tragedy and man's pathetic memory of it. It is a low building set on one of those rounded mountaintops southwest of Jerusalem, and there is nothing except a stark, bare chamber shaped like a low tent with walls made of rust-colored boulders from the shores of the sea of Galilee set into concrete. The iron gates of the chamber are covered with great hammered thorns and shapeless metal splinters, the floors are the gray of charcoal. In one corner, in a cup shaped like a thorn tree, a blue gas flame rises palely. On the ominous gray floor, in no discernible pattern, are set the white names of the extermination camps: Dachau, Auschwitz, Treblinka, Babi Yar, Mauthausen, Bergen-Belsen, and many more.

There is about this cavernlike hall a sense of death's naked power, of a horror from which there is no escape. There is no alleviation: only the horror expressed in the gas flame, the smooth gray floor, the great rust-colored boulders lifted from the volcanic slopes of Galilee which seem to hem you in, and to keep you there in the gray darkness of the place. Under the gas flame lie the ashes of the dead, but even if they were not there, one would be aware of death's presence. Somehow, by some miracle, out of twisted metal plates and gray mosaics and weather-worn boulders, the architects have constructed a building which represents an agony, a cry of horror. They have drawn the features of an unavailing despair. Almost it is an abstract portrait of a crematorium as seen by a man who enters it to die. It is a strange and perturbing place, and perhaps it is the nearest men will ever get to building a memorial to that senseless crime.

Lake Huleh

A man in Haifa told me how a lake died. It was a slow death, and he helped it to die.

The lake is still shown on maps, though for many years now it has ceased to exist. Above the Sea of Galilee it appears as a blue tear-drop lying at the feet of Mount Hermon, the first and highest of the three lakes in the Jordan drift. Into this lake poured the melting snows of Lebanon and Hermon, which later spill into the Sea of Galilee, and later still into the Dead Sea nearly thirteen hundred feet below sea level. In ancient times it was known as the Waters of Merom. On the shores of this lake Joshua pitched his tents and heard the voice of the Lord saying, "Be not afraid of them, for tomorrow about this time will I deliver them up all slain before Israel," and so it happened. Here, too, many centuries later Jonathan Maccabeus, the High Priest, defeated an army sent by Demetrius I, who called himself "Nicator," the bringer of victories. Here Herod the Great came in his young manhood to hunt the game swarming in the papyrus thickets, distinguishing himself with his javelin-throwing. So much history, so many legends, are associated with the lake that one can scarcely think of it vanishing out of sight; yet the lake has gone.

He was a tall man with a heavy, brooding face, and he did not look like an engineer; he looked more like a Roman emperor with his thin nose, his jowls, his enormous blue eyes. He had come to Haifa

77

from Germany in 1933. He was then a young man with a degree in engineering from Berlin University. He became a professor, then a consulting engineer, and then for a while he worked with one of the international oil companies while teaching at the Technion, which is Haifa's equivalent to Massachusetts Institute of Technology. During the war he joined the British Army; he had the rank of colonel in the Corps of Engineers and spent a good deal of time building bridges. He had once possessed a small farm on the hills overlooking the lake, and while he was building the canals which tore the lake to pieces, he would spend his weekends on the farm and look down on what remained of the lake as, day by day, it grew smaller and smaller until there was nothing left.

"It began a long time ago," he said, tapping the table with a gold-plated pencil. "The first surveys were made about 1905, under the Turks, and it might have been taken in hand even then if the Turks had somehow been able to collect the money for it. I've seen the surveys. They knew what they wanted to do, and the plan was substantially the same as the one we followed nearly fifty years later.

"Lake Huleh in those days was an extraordinarily beautiful place, full of wildfowl and wild flowers. Some people said it was just a malarial marsh, but that's nonsense. It had birds and flowers and wildlife which could be seen nowhere else, and it had something even more important—it had a soul. The Sea of Galilee is beautiful, but this lake was beautiful in another way. It was rather ghostly with its mists and the high mountains throwing their shadows on the lake, and the great stretches of papyrus thicket. It was hot and humid and intensely tropical, and you might have been on the shores of the Nile. The strangest birds came here. They nested here, and sometimes we were able to ring them, and the next we heard of them they had been found in Russia, or India, or South Africa. It was a little paradise.

"I first saw the lake the year I arrived from Germany. A few months later the old plans for draining the lake were revived, and I had something to do with the concession which was obtained for reclaiming the whole area. It was the time of the British Mandate. But things did not work well, and in fact very little was done. I had the feeling that no one really would get down to draining the lake. It was immortal and very beautiful, and it was unthinkable that it would ever vanish.

"Then in 1948 Israel came into existence, a small country which needed to put every drop of water to use. We could no longer afford to be romantic. One of the very first decisions of the new government was to put in hand the Huleh reclamation project. The actual work started in 1950. We thought we would drain the lake in four years, but it was seven years before we had finished with it. Then instead of the lake we had fifteen thousand acres of fertile soil and control of the waters flowing into the Jordan. It was the first necessary step before we could begin to feed water into the Negev.

"Most water engineers come to their profession because they have a passion for water. They love the colors and shapes of water, as the steel engineer loves the shapes and colors of structural steel. So most of us, I think, felt a pang of guilt about destroying the lake, and we had long discussions about the balance of nature and what would happen to these valleys when the lake had gone. We were very aware we were doing something dangerous, with unpredictable consequences, but there was one thing that was uppermost in our minds. We are a small land, but even if we use every last available drop of water we won't be able to irrigate more than half the irrigable land.

"I remember when we were destroying the lake, I spent more and more time on my small boat. I would tell myself I was going out fishing, but that wasn't the real reason. I was out on the lake because I was in love with it, because I wanted to be with it as long as possible. I didn't do much fishing. I anchored the boat among the water lilies, and just watched. The dragonflies hummed over the lake, and the kingfishers swooped down for fish. There must have been a million birds on the lake, and ten million frogs croaked and coughed every night. I used to be a good fisherman, but I had no heart for it any more. I watched the mists rising, the sun climbing up the mountains, the threads of light moving over the waters, the blinding mirror of the lake at high noon. There was a special anchorage where I would row on moonlight nights. I kept a journal in which I recorded every mortal thing that happened on the lake: the temperature of the lake three times a day, the birds I saw, the water snakes, the spiders, the praying mantis, and whatever the fishermen had found in their nets beside catfish, and I would count the pelicans and spoon-bills, and take motion pictures. I was the historian of the dying lake.

"I remember I would always go somewhere where I couldn't see the machinery which was being brought along to devour the lake, and when the dredgers came, I always took my boat to a part of the lake where they couldn't be seen. Then, when I had to superintend the machinery or discuss the drainage operations, I was someone else altogether. I was the practical engineer, and the lake was just an inhuman body of water which had to be carved up to serve the interests of the land. As always, the lake birds and the shore birds were fighting for their share of the lake. They did not know it was doomed.

"There were days when the lake was so quiet that there was not a ripple on the entire surface, but when the storms came, driving down from the mountains to the east, first with a muffled rumble and then with the sound of a thunderclap, it was as though a great hand had suddenly slapped the water, and then the water would boil and thrash about. There was a tremendous power in the lake. The storms were terrible. All creation seemed to be screaming, caught up in the storm.

"The dredgers came and nibbled their way across the lake. Weeks, months passed, and nothing had changed; only the huge dredgers gleaming in the sunlight. Meanwhile we had widened and deepened the river channel south of the lake, and we had cut an outlet through the basalt rocks which formed a sill across the valley, but we were not yet ready to let the water go. The dredgers carved two enormous tracks in the lake bottom; they dug up vast quantities of earth on which the sun had never shone and which no one had ever seen, and some of it was peat. We mapped the peat areas; we would need peat for fuel later. And gradually the birds began to go. They seemed to know what was in store for them.

"The dredgers tore and scooped into the lake, and turned it muddy. There was the horrible screaming, hammering sound of machinery, drowning out the bird song. And already the lake was shrinking a little, and the anchorage where I took my boat on moonlight nights became a mud flat, and here and there the fish were marooned on the muddy shores by the receding waters; and the mud dried in the pitiless sun, and the fish and the lake creatures died. Fires broke out, and for days and even weeks there were heavy black clouds hanging over the lake, as the papyrus thickets smoked and burned, and I think this frightened the birds more than anything else. They would stand along the shore watching the fires and shaking their heads. Something incomprehensible was happening and they chattered to one another, demanding answers.

"I thought of making a museum of the lake. I would collect the dead animals and the strange things found in the lake, but I gave it up. One day we opened the breach in the basalt rock and watched the lake go. One day there was a small shimmering expanse of silver, the next day there was nothing at all—only the black mud and the burned papyrus and a tangle of dead lilies. We had done what we set out to do.

"Now there are rich farmlands and a few fishponds and there's even a small patch which we call 'the wildlife reserve' where the birds and animals that haunted the shores of the lake can be seen, but I don't go there very much. I saw the lake die, and I don't see any point in keeping a little piece of it alive by artificial respiration. A whole new generation is growing up which never knew there was a lake at all!"

He sat there, staring into space, drumming his gold-plated pencil on the table.

"Do you still have your farm there?" I asked.

"Oh, no, that went a long time ago. I'm too old for farming. Nowadays I only go up there when I have to. These days I have my office in Haifa, and I stay here most of the time. Well, the truth is I haven't been in the Huleh development area since we finished off the lake."

I asked him about the Sea of Galilee. Would that be drained, too? He shook his head.

"I've seen some plans for it," he said. "But they won't do it in my lifetime. It's too difficult, too dangerous altogether. The problem now is to preserve the water in the lake from evaporation, and they are tinkering with various films which can be spread over the surface. They talk of spraying the lake from airplanes, but only God knows what that would do to the ecology of the lake.

"You see, we need water more than anything else. Moses struck the rock and found water, and we are beginning to do the same. We are tapping the water in the earth's crust. We are still experimenting with desalination processes, and not getting very far—it's too expensive. We are learning how to clean water which has been used in industry, and setting it in motion again. We are planting millions of trees, and that will help, too, to keep the water flowing where we want it to flow. We are learning to intercept storm-water runoffs. There are a thousand tricks, but some of the best of them like seeding clouds and desalinating sea water are proving to be less successful than we had hoped. We have a population explosion on our hands. Sometimes we wonder whether we shall have enough water to keep pace with the population."

He stopped drumming with the gold-plated pencil, and for the first time during a long conversation a smile lit the heavy Roman face.

"Do you know what the answer is? It's simple. We'll get it wherever we can find it. No easy solutions—a fight on all fronts."

A few days later I took the long road in northern Galilee which skirts the Lebanese frontier. There had been no rain for months, but the air was as clean and sparkling as though it had been washed in the rain only a few minutes ago. The hills of Zebulun and Naphtali shone with a fierce limestone glitter, ice-blue in the shadows, and here and there we came upon the patches of emerald green which indicate the presence of a *kibbuts*. We had the road to ourselves; there were almost no trucks or cars on the road, and this was disturbing, for the absence of traffic pointed to the poverty of those barren uplands. And then, coming down the winding mountain road, we suddenly saw a view which Moses dreamed of. There was Mount Hermon before us, bluish-gray in the morning light, shining like steel against the blue of the heavens, with no trace of snow among the jagged peaks, with a vast valley stretching at its feet. The valley was Lake Huleh transformed into rainbow-colored fields. There were yellow and purple fields, and some were silvery blue, but these turned out not to be fields at all; they were the famous fishponds. There were patches of red and magenta and emerald green. They were all luxuriant colors unrolling like a royal carpet along the whole length of the flowering valley. There were the wide channels where the river flowed, and the neat white houses, and the small roads winding among the fields. Here at last was the land flowing with milk and honey, so rich, so succulent, that it took the breath away.

They killed the lake, but they made a small paradise instead.

IN THE KIBBUTS

We had stopped for a while in a *kibbuts* where the workers were packing peaches on a conveyor belt. Most of the workers were women, long-legged, wearing shirts and shorts, their faces browned by the sun. There were perhaps twenty women there, and they were all young. There was a pleasant smell of fresh peaches and fresh wood.

It looked as though only women lived on the *kibbuts*, and when I asked whether there were any men, they burst out laughing, and one of them said, "There would be no life without men." It was dark inside the shed. The conveyor belt moved slowly down the middle of the shed, laden with its small white glittering boxes. Outside, some chickens pecked in the dust. Far away, beyond the orchards, were the red-roofed houses where the women lived.

I had been in the shed about twenty minutes when I was aware that a change had come over them. They still laughed and talked, their hands still moved dexterously over the conveyor belt, they still flashed their smiles, but their heads were bent a little lower and they were a little more attentive to their work.

Someone whispered, "Gideon has just come in."

"Who is Gideon?" I asked.

No one answered, but a ripple of laughter went the whole length of the conveyor. It was absurd, it was astonishing that anyone could come on the *kibbuts* without knowing Gideon.

Later, when I met Gideon, I realized why there had been that ripple of laughter, that sudden quiet explosion of energy. Gideon was a short, heavily built man with blue eyes, red hair, a heavy jaw, thick eyebrows, a square rather arrogant face. He smiled easily, but he was conscious of his power. He was leaning against the wall of the shed with the sun in his eyes, his body taut like a coiled spring. He was the

manager of the *kibbuts*, the elected leader, the man who superin-
tended the ten or twelve different activities which were carried on
simultaneously. It was not difficult to understand why he had been
chosen for the job.

He talked casually about life on the *kibbuts*, where everyone shared
and shared alike. It was a good life lived in community, with no
money problems, for everything necessary was supplied to the workers.

"Here," he said, "we are all equal, and therefore we can live our
lives fully. There are no quarrels, no jealousies. All the problems that
affect capitalist society are done away with. We envy no one, and
least of all do we envy the fat cats in Tel Aviv. We have found a way
of life which is completely rewarding."

Faintly disapproving, I said, "The trouble about equalitarian
societies is that they usually lead to dictatorships. Everyone is equal,
but the dictator is more equal than the others."

He took this well, but his cheeks flushed and his blue eyes had an
angry fire in them.

"I'm not the dictator," he said. "I've managed the *kibbuts* for three
years. I've been elected every year. I don't order people around. There
are some *kibbutsim* which are little dictatorships, but not this one.
We serve the common interest—everyone is encouraged to speak,
and that's why, in the last analysis, we waste such an appalling amount
of time. Everything has to be discussed, everyone must take part in the
discussion, even the children are encouraged to give their views, and
in the end we are haggard with talk."

"Then why do you do it—why have so much talk?"

"Because there is no other way," he replied, and then smiling: "No
other way to avoid dictatorship or a purely managerial system. In the
kibbutsim we are dedicated to one another. There is no question of
anyone exploiting another. At least that problem has been solved.
There is no resentment or envy under this system, because we are all
in it together."

I suppose Gideon was about thirty-five, but he looked younger.
There were small crow's-feet under his eyes, for he worked harder
than anyone else and took his responsibilities more seriously. Yet it
was easy to distrust him, for there was so much vital energy in him, so

much deliberate charm, such an easy assumption of power, that one felt on one's guard. I was not surprised to hear later that he had been one of the military leaders during the war with the Arabs; he was a man who commanded obedience.

So we talked at length about the communal *kibbutsim* and the rather less communal *moshavim*, where the workers are paid in cash. In his view the *kibbuts* represented the final flowering of the socialist theories of the nineteenth century; here was a social community which lived within the purest form of social contract. They had abolished fear, because all the members of the community served one another. The children were cared for in communal kindergartens, but the parents saw them every day. I saw the children, and they were well fed and quite obviously happy, and there was no doubt that the workers on the *kibbuts* had an an air of well-being.

"What do you think of it?" he said at last.

I said I would hate it if the whole state was given over to communal farms. It seemed to work in Israel because there were so many other kinds of economy in existence. Here was a small state of only two million people, and there were four or five entirely separate kinds of economy being practiced simultaneously, with no interference, and the miracle was that it could happen at all.

"No, it's not a miracle," Gideon said. "It could happen in any country. People should be allowed to work out their social and economic salvations in their own way. Sometimes I think that is why the Soviet Union is so bitterly determined to crush us. They want to turn the whole state into a *kibbuts* where no one except the government does the talking. Well, we don't want it. We want freedom to experiment. Let the most dedicated come to the *kibbutsim*, and let the others practice whatever form of economic life they like!"

We were walking near a barbed-wire fence on the other side of the peach orchard when he said, "There will be war in 1964. I don't know how it will come, but I know it will come. We are two million surrounded by forty million Arabs determined to annihilate us."

"Who will win the war?"

He said nothing. He was staring into space, towards the bleak hills of Syria in the distance.

Suddenly he turned and said, "Do you know how far we are from the frontier? About fifty yards. So you see it won't be easy to defend this *kibbuts*. It might even be impossible. We'll withdraw—if there is time to withdraw."

"And if there's no time?"

"Then we'll be massacred."

He said these last words very quietly.

We returned to the shed where the women were packing peaches. They were laughing, and once again there was the smell of peaches and fresh wood, and the slow conveyor belts were carrying the boxes to the waiting trucks. This *kibbuts* did not look like a frontier post, but it was.

From the hills the enemy was watching them every day of their lives.

Hazor

Mount Hermon shone misty blue and the fields were yellow and gold as we drove beyond the vanished Waters of Merom into the low-lying hills. The wind sang, and all the ripe pastures were gleaming. Hawks hung in the sky, the workers were out in the fields, and there was nothing in the least to suggest that we were coming to one of those star-bright, legendary places where history was made for twenty centuries.

We came through a village where an Arab girl stood alone in the market place, her dark face shining among the coils of her white head-dress, and heaven knows what she was doing there, for there was not another Arab for miles around. She stood there very quietly in the shade of the cypress trees, immobile and proud, lost in her own dreams, looking as though she were made of hammered bronze, the wind stirring in the folds of her gown, and I remember being haunted by the heavy eyelids and the darkness of her sculptured face as we drove towards Hazor in the bright afternoon, while the birds sang and the winds turned the fields to silver.

It was one of those heady days when the world seems to possess an excessive brightness. The sky was a richer blue, the grass was a richer green, the air more transparent, than they have a right to be. All the time I was in Upper Galilee, I had the curious impression that I was hovering in a low-flying airplane over an unearthly land parceled out in neat squares of orange and ocher and emerald green and the blue of an eagle's wing. There was something absurdly extravagant in the beauty of those landscapes.

"Well, there's Hazor over there," someone shouted, but it was only another hill like all the others.

We had seen excavations before: a few trenches dug in the soil, a rubble of ancient walls, and perhaps the stone base of a statue removed centuries ago. There is usually little left after the archaeologists have removed the clay tablets and the small pottery ornaments to the safety of the museums. So we showed no very great interest in this hill as we drove down the long road white with eucalyptus trees. There was a *kibbuts* called Ayelet Hashahar, and we thought we would have a late lunch there and ponder whether we would climb among the ruins later.

I went to many *kibbutsim*, but this was the cleanest, the neatest, the handsomest of all. It looked like the newest, but it was in fact one of the earliest, having been founded in 1916. Ayelet Hashahar means "the morning star," and perhaps this was why they were determined to keep it fresh and sparkling. There was a new swimming pool and new guest houses, and the restaurant was decorated with so many vivid mosaics and paintings and sculptures that it looked like an artists' colony. Girls in bikinis were wandering about in the sunlight, and you could hear the laughter from the swimming pool. Young Yemenite women waited at table, and like the Arab girl in the market place they were almost too beautiful to be true. So we talked about the Yemenite women and forgot the legendary kingdom of Hazor; and when, weary of talking, we went down the long drive to the main highway, the hill looked no more inviting than before. The archaeologists had abandoned it in despair. Then why should we clamber among the ruined walls?

There was a small museum at the foot of the hill. We thought we might salve our consciences if we had a look at it. The museum keeper was in the swimming pool. It was half an hour before we found him, and then we wondered why we had gone to the trouble, for there was little enough in the museum—a few pieces of pottery, a few blown-up photographs, no inscriptions, no statues, nothing that could give you the least suggestion of a formidable imperial capital with a history going back five thousand years.

I think it was the emptiness of the museum which made us determined to go up the hill; that, and the strange reddish heap of potsherds near the museum gates. The heap was waist-high, and we wondered what it was doing there until we realized that it was nothing more than the discarded fragments from the excavations, the cups and plates that no one had been able to put together. There were thousands upon thousands of these fragments. Some had numbers painted on them, to guide the archaeologists who had once hoped to see a wine jar emerge from fifty fragments before they abandoned the jigsaw puzzle forever. They told us to take as many as we liked, and we filled our pockets with them. Then, heavily burdened, we walked towards the hill.

THE DRAGONS' TEETH

In King Solomon Street in Jerusalem there is a brown ugly building which might be taken for a small warehouse. It has a tired look about it, as though weary of its ugliness, and it is no more attractive when you have climbed up four or five steep steps and find yourself in a narrow hallway with a guardroom off to one side. There are some dust-covered pamphlets on the wall. There are some uniformed men, heavily mustached, with the embittered looks of policemen who are kept continually at desk duty, and therefore have every reason to be abrupt and uncooperative. The entrance suggests an obscure provincial police station. Decidedly an unimpressive place.

But once you have passed those frowning and suspicious guards, you discover that you are in one of the most romantic places in Jerusalem, for the drab building is the headquarters of the Department of Antiquities in Jerusalem. Here, in small crowded rooms, are the treasures unearthed in Israel since 1948, and some discovered long previously. Glittering mosaics, Roman statues, horned altars, ancient tombs, Canaanite statuettes, inscriptions in Aramaic and Hebrew, gold rings, all the shapes of the vanished past, are gathered here in profusion. Here is the dedicatory stele erected by Pontius Pilate in the theater at Caesarea, found only a few months ago by an Italian expedition: it is the only inscription known which bears the name of Pilate. Here are the wonderful mosaics from Nirim, including the one with the hen laying an egg, and the egg seems to be laughing aloud with joy at being born. All these treasures, and many more which lie crated in the cellars, will one day occupy the new archaeological museum which is being built near the university.

The museum is overcrowded, but upstairs there is an air of spaciousness. Here a small group of experts work quietly, piecing together the fragments turned up by the archaeologists' spades, and collating the reports sent in by the seven or eight expeditions which are always in the field. Dr. Biran, the Director of Antiquities, has an office there. A wiry, broad-shouldered man with a deeply tanned face, deep-set eyes and shaggy eyebrows, he gives an impression of perpetual motion, a spring continually coiling and uncoiling, darting out in all directions. I never saw him walking. Even to cross the room to consult a book, he would move at the speed of a long-distance runner. He had the serenity which often, but not always, goes with the dedicated archaeologist, and at the same time he was at the mercy of a mind that moved like greased lightning, so that sometimes he seemed to be pursuing four or five different lines of thought at once.

That afternoon he was in high good humor, debating with himself whether he should write a book about archaeology in Israel. He had little enough time; he was continually moving about the country to inspect archaeological sites; there were a hundred administrative details to attend to; there were papers to be written on individual finds, and the new museum to be attended to, and far too much correspondence.

"Where the devil does one find the time to write a book?" he asked. "I don't know what it is like in other countries, but in this country there are two million archaeologists—everyone is playing at the game. It makes things easier, but it also makes things harder. It is like being near the top of a volcano; the past is continually pouring out and threatening to drown us. So much of it, and so little time to put it in order, to think quietly and make the proper conclusions."

Recently an expedition from the University of Rome had been working in Caesarea. They had dug up the famous dedicatory stele of Pontius Pilate and a headless statue of Diana of the Ephesians, the lady of the myriad breasts. There was a regulation that unique objects were to remain in Israel, while all other objects were divided equally between Israel and the foreign archaeologists.

"So we had to discuss what should happen to these two objects, both of them unique. The Italians desperately wanted to keep the Pilate stele. They claimed that Pilate was an Italian and would do more honor to Italy than to Israel. They brought up powerful arguments to prove that the stele was not particularly important, hundreds of dedicatory inscriptions had been found, why should we concern ourselves with a man of an admittedly bad character, who was a nuisance to the Jews? They brought up more arguments to prove that the headless Diana was equally unimportant. I admit I was sometimes shaken by the arguments, but in the end we had to keep them.

"Then there are the Japanese. They sent an expedition here a little while ago and discovered fragments of a human skull near the Sea of Galilee. It was a Paleolithic skull, perhaps older than the famous *homo galilensis* discovered in 1925. They were perfectly aware that it was unique, but they asked permission to take it to Japan for study. We asked them how long they wanted to study it, and they answered it would take eight years and two weeks before they could bring in a final report. Now why do you think they wanted eight years and two weeks?"

I made a rapid and inaccurate calculation.

"That makes a hundred months—a nice round number."

"Nonsense! They had worked everything out to the last detail. So many weeks for this, so many weeks for that—spectroscopy, carbon tests, heaven knows what else! They produced a time-chart. It was a glorious time-chart and covered a good many pages, and there was no fault with it. So they will have it for eight years and two weeks, and there will be a report in four- or five-octavo volumes on three or four little pieces of bone!"

Soon he was talking about the recent archaeological discoveries, rolling off a long list of sites—Hazor, Tel Nargila, Avad, Shavei Zion, Ramat Rahel and many more. In time I was to see nearly all the places he mentioned, but they were still fresh to me, and so he discussed them at length. He had a special fondness for Tel Nargila, which might perhaps turn out to be the long-lost city of Gath. Of Hazor he spoke with something approaching awe.

"It's such a huge city that we may never get to the bottom of it," he said. "When Yigael Yadin was excavating there a few years ago, he calculated that with our present resources it would take eight hundred years to uncover the whole city. There is a tremendous grandeur in the place. You won't see it at first, but it will grow on you."

I remembered these words when we climbed the low hill and saw only a few white walls rising like splintered bones from the blood-red earth. There was another hill, not far away, with more bones rising. They were not the closely fitted walls which you find in Mycenae; these were rough-hewn, stark, elemental, not intended to please the eye but to keep out invaders, the walls of a fortress built by giants. There were rows of columns, which probably supported the roof of a small palace, and they too were rough-hewn, without any pretensions to art. There was power in them, and they looked like dragons' teeth.

Only scrub grew on this low hill, and the winds came beating across the wide valley as the afternoon wore on. We wandered along streets where the Canaanites had ridden in their chariots, and through sanctuaries where the snake goddess was worshiped. Here and there, where the archaeologists' spades had dug deep, you could see the telltale layer-cake effect which comes when one city has been built on the ashes of another. In one place there were eight layers, in another twelve. The excavators found altogether twenty-one layers representing a period of about twenty centuries. Time had sometimes frozen a whole century into an inch or two of compressed stone. The archaeologists are still puzzling over which layers represent the Canaanite cities and which was the city rebuilt by Solomon. Many more cities came after Solomon.

Hazor was first discovered by Dr. John Garstang of Liverpool University in 1928. He found the rows of monolithic pillars, which are still the most impressive objects on the hill, and he dug a number of trial trenches, which were oddly unproductive of Mycenaean pottery, and this led him to believe that in the fourteenth century B.C., when the influence of Mycenae and Crete were most extensive in Palestine, the city's importance had already come to an end. Lack of funds prevented him from continuing his excavations, while his conclusions puzzled the scholars, who were perfectly prepared to believe that he had found Hazor, while disputing his claim that the city was no longer of importance when, at some time in the thirteenth century B.C., Joshua took it by storm. The Book of Joshua describes the fate of Hazor:

And Joshua at that time turned back, and took Hazor; and smote the king thereof with the sword: for Hazor beforetime was the head of all those kingdoms.

And they smote all the souls that were therein with the edge of the sword, utterly destroying them: there was not any left to breathe: and he burnt Hazor with fire.

Now this reads like authentic history, and if it were true, then one might expect to find the trace of the burning and of the final overthrow of the Canaanite capital. And when in 1955 a new archaeological expedition set out to excavate Hazor, it was with the deliberate intention of discovering whether the conquest of Hazor by the Israelites had actually taken place. It was a large and well-organized expedition led by Professor Yigael Yadin of Hebrew University, the former Chief of Staff of the Israel Army, and it continued to work for four seasons. They soon discovered the missing Mycenaean pottery. They uncovered two Canaanite temples, one on top of the other, with the ritual vessels still in place. Up to this time very little was known about Canaanite art, but a potter's workshop, apparently abandoned in the midst of war, provided a number of ritual masks with faces of astonishing calm; and in the "Holy of Holies" there were lion reliefs and seated figures, all possessing that same untroubled and assured expression. One stele in particular, showing two hands raised towards a crescent moon, was particularly enlightening, for its very simplicity seemed to provide a clue to the nature of the Canaanite mind. They found a goddess holding a snake in her hands. In one rock-cut tomb chamber alone they discovered about five hundred small vessels, including many delicately fashioned pots from Mycenae. Always there was the sense of calm and order, the quiet assurance, the knowledge that they were unassailable. The ritual figures sit calmly on their thrones and gaze straight before them, undisturbed and unafraid. Then Joshua came, and over the layers of many Canaanite cities, there was the black layer of the burning.

For two or three centuries Hazor seems to have been uninhabited. Then gradually the city flickered into life again. Under Solomon it was rebuilt and fortified with a massive casemate wall. Then in the time of Ahab the city stretched out until it included the entire summit of the hill, and had regained its importance as a powerful strategic center dominating the Via Maris leading from Egypt to Mesopotamia, Syria and Anatolia. Later, in the time of Pekah, about 730 B.C., it was destroyed again. Yet for centuries the citadel remained. Assyrians, Persians, Greeks and Maccabeans fortified this solitary outpost commanding the road to Damascus. After the Maccabeans the history of Hazor seems to come finally to an end.

It had been a long history—how long we may never know. About 1700 B.C. it was already sufficiently important to be mentioned in the cuneiform archives of the Syrian city of Mari, but long before that it appears in the Execration texts published by the Pharaohs as spells intended to lead to the destruction of the city. Thutmose III, Amenhotep II and Seti I all claimed to have conquered it—the excavators found evidence of these conquests with Egyptian scarab stones of the appropriate date and dynasty lying among the ruins. Tiglath-Pileser III, King of Assyria, reduced it to rubble, and he too was represented in the debris found by the archaeologists. They found much that puzzled them. They found, for example, a fantastic number of infants buried in jars. But for the most part the layer cake with the twenty-one telltale signs corresponded to historical records. The pieces in the historical jigsaw fitted together almost too neatly.

After four seasons the work was temporarily abandoned; there were other and more glamorous archaeological prospects in store. Also, it was felt that future generations should have the opportunity of working there. Somewhere beneath these low hills the treasuries and the archives still remain hidden. Hazor has been mapped, but it has not yet been explored.

This ancient acropolis dominates the Valley of Huleh, as Mycenae dominates the Plain of Argos. Just to stand there is to know power, the sensation of commanding immense acres of earth. Blue shadows fell across the land, Mount Hermon faded into misty purple, but the sensation of power remained. Eagles hovered high overhead, wheeling so effortlessly in the cloudless sky that they might have been made of paper; there was no strength in them; they too would fade. While from the earth came the gleam of the dragons' teeth, still bright and dangerous after so many centuries.

Beth Shean

We had come a long way that day over the burning hills on the west of the Jordan, and sometimes there would be a splash of emerald green on the farms cultivated by the *kibbutsim,* but afterwards there were only the endless tawny rocks, the hills rubbed smooth by the winds, the sense of interminable desolation; and sometimes from the heights one could look down on the Jordan Valley, seeing the thin white thread of the river below, the hills on the other side burned white by the sun. I had thought the Jordan was luxuriantly tropical with myrtles and ilexes growing on its banks, and so it was near the Sea of Galilee, where I slipped down a bank and bathed in its waters, but from the hills the river looked bare and featureless, no more than a white scrawl on a dusty map. My companion, an expert on hydraulics, was amusing himself with visions of what might happen if Jordan and Israel came to some sensible agreement on the use of the river, each apportioning to himself what was properly his own, and then I would look down and see the river in the distance and wonder what all the fuss was about.

All the days I spent in Israel were hot, but this was the hottest of them all. The sun came down like burning rain, and the rocks seemed to melt in the glow. I could not understand how anything green could survive in that relentless heat, and there were not many green patches in those uplands. Sometimes the air above the rocks was shimmering,

Mount Zion, Jerusalem

Herzl's tomb on Mount Herzl

Menorah on King George V Avenue, Jerusalem

Mount Zion. Entrance to David's tomb

Montefiore windmill overlooking Mount Zion

Beth Alpha. Central medallion of mosaic

Kefar Bir'am. Synagogue

Judean wilderness near Jerusalem

as it shimmers above a caldron of boiling lead. Yet there was nothing in the least debilitating in the sun's heat. It was ferocious, and demanded a ferocious response; its very ferocity was invigorating. Somehow by cursing and fighting against it, you were able to absorb some of its strength. The Jews call the sun "Shemesh," the Persians call it "Shams," and in all the languages of the Middle East it has roughly this same sound. I used to think that "Shemesh" was a very soft and sweet sound; now I am reasonably certain that it was originally intended to reproduce the power of the sun's smashing blows.

I remember coming to Beth Shean with a feeling of weariness and intoxication, almost delirious with the heat. The sky was no longer the lovely trembling blue of Galilee, but a brilliant opaque purple. There were no clouds, and it was unthinkable that any clouds had ever traveled in that dark sky. Mercifully there was some shade in a little café run by some Moroccan Jews. They were playing a game like mah-jongg, and the rattling of the ivory tiles came as a pleasant accompaniment to their high-pitched voices. Dark-skinned, friendly and excitable, they wore the bright kaftans they had worn in Africa. They had arrived only a few months before, and my companion, the expert on hydraulics, said they were lazy and would take some breaking-in. And seeing them there, quarreling and laughing like schoolboys or moving about the place with an easy grace, I hoped they would remain lazy for a little while longer. By some odd chance these Moroccans were settled in a town which is among the most ancient in history. They were the last, the most improbable inheritors of a great citadel which had seen the coming of Philistines, Assyrians, Canaanites, Egyptians, Greeks, Romans and Scythians.

Today Beth Shean wears its load of history lightly. Most of the houses are new, few of them more than fifteen years old, and there are only a few streets arranged in orderly rows. The paint has not had time to flake from the brightly colored doors. There is a small cluster of shops. You would think you were in one of the mushrooming suburbs of Los Angeles, for all the brightness and neatness of the houses. But wherever you go in Beth Shean you are confronted with a yellow sulphurous mountain which rises clean from the valley, heavy and powerful still, though all the evidence of power has long ago been removed. You step through the doors of the Moroccan café, and it is there. You walk down the side street, and it glares at you from the end of the street. You go to the small museum, where some of the relics from the mountain have been collected, and it is still there, glaring at you through the windows. Imagine a lion with its tawny head buried in its forepaws close to the earth, and you have the shape of the mountain; but this sleeping lion is two hundred feet high and nine hundred feet long.

"Beth Shean" means "the house of rest," but there has been very little rest in its history, for the good reason that it lies on the great caravan route from Damascus to Egypt and is watered by four streams, and being an oasis on a main highway it was worth fighting over. Endless wars were fought for the possession of the yellow mountain, and with every new conquest new buildings and new fortifications arose, with the result that the mountain swelled with every successive invasion like a strange fruit watered by the blood of the defenders. We know almost to an inch how much it grew every century because an expedition organized by the University of Pennsylvania cut a deep trench through it.

What they discovered was rather more than they had hoped for. Every empire which had ever risen in the Near East had left its mark there. There were Turkish buildings on top, but these were easily cleared away. Then they found the ruins of an unfinished Crusader castle which had been begun by Adam, Lord of Béthune, who called himself Lord of Beth Shean. Beneath these ruins they came upon the tumbled debris of the Arab town, with fortress and mosque, which must have been built shortly after the Arab invasion of Palestine. There followed the Byzantine town with delicate columns, mosaics and bronzes, and there was a layer indicating precisely when the Byzantine churches were overthrown during the persecution of the Christians under Julian the Apostate; afterwards the churches were built again, to survive a little while longer until the coming of the Persians. They dug to a depth of seventy feet below the pavement of the Byzantine town and found layers of civilization almost beyond counting.

They found the ruins of a Greco-Roman temple erected in honor of Bacchus, with Corinthian pillars six feet in diameter, and below the debris of the Roman and Greek epochs they came upon the surprising relics of the Scythians, who swept into Palestine about the year 630 B.C. Under the Greeks, and for a thousand years later, Beth Shean had borne the name of Scythopolis. The modern historians were a little puzzled, and they wondered what the wild Scythian tribesmen were doing there. Herodotus had spoken of them, Jeremiah and Zephaniah had thundered against them, but no one had imagined that they had seized the yellow mountain and straddled the trade route between Syria and Egypt. But the evidence was unmistakable that the Scythians had poured out of southern Russia and penetrated deep into Palestine, leaving their relics for American archaeologists to ponder over. Below the relics of the Scythians were Jewish ceramics and some Cypriote pottery which could be dated about 1600-1400 B.C., but the best was still to come.

For hundreds of years Beth Shean had been one of the great frontier posts of the Egyptian empire. The archaeologists found five strata, indicating five separate occupations by the Egyptians. They found the superimposed ruins of Egyptian altars erected to Ramses II and Seti I lying on top of one another, and the charred walls of the Egyptian fortress still stood six feet high. They found Canaanite tombs and ramparts of unbaked brick which had been standing there long before the Hebrews entered Palestine.

The archaeologists from the University of Pennsylvania were puzzled, however, by one small gap in the stratification. Between about 1000 B.C. and 300 B.C. there was an inexplicable blank. For nearly seven hundred years the powerful fortress had remained untenanted. There were no blanks before, and none afterwards; then why during this particular period should the mountain remain silent? There seems to be only one possible answer. At the disastrous battle of Mount Gilboa, which took place about 1000 B.C., the Israelite army was destroyed by the Philistines. King Saul stabbed himself to death, for his three sons had died in the battle, and he had nothing to live for. The following day the Philistines found his body and hung it on the walls of the fortress of Beth Shean, only a few miles away from Mount Gilboa, and they hung his armor in the temple of the goddess Ashtaroth as a sign of their victory. The armor remained in the temple, but the king's body was later removed from the walls by some daring Israelites from the east bank of the Jordan, who carried it to their own town of Jabesh Gilead and buried it beneath an oak tree. From about the time the Philistines won their battle over the Israelites no more trace of them is found upon the mountain. The archaeologists have concluded that David must have attacked the fortress and destroyed the Philistine army. But if so, why is there no record of this victory in the comprehensive account of David's life in the Old Testament?

It is all mystery, with scarcely a hint of a clue. We may know more when the Philistine city of Gath is uncovered, or when ancient Ashkelon emerges from under the sand dunes, for there are gaps in our knowledge of Philistine history. Did they abandon the fortress because their lines were overextended? Were they destroyed by a pestilence? There is perhaps a small ghostly clue in the song of lamentation which David sang for Saul and Jonathan:

> The beauty of Israel is slain upon thy high places:
>> How are the mighty fallen!
>> Tell it not in Gath,
> Publish it not in the streets of Ashkelon;
> Lest the daughters of the Philistines rejoice,
> Lest the daughters of the uncircumcised triumph.
>
> Ye mountains of Gilboa,
> Let there be no dew,
> Neither let there be rain, upon you,
> Nor fields of offerings:
> For there the shield of the mighty is vilely cast away,
> The shield of Saul, as though he had not been annointed with oil.
>
> From the blood of the slain,
> From the fat of the mighty,
> The bow of Jonathan turned not back,
> And the sword of Saul returned not empty.

According to the Biblical account, the sword of Saul did return empty, and his army was defeated as no other Israelite army had ever been defeated. Something has gone wrong. Some words are missing, or a verse has been misplaced. It is just possible that David's song of lamentation conceals a song of triumph. But all we know for certain is that from the walls of the fortress on the yellow mountain there once hung the naked and headless body of Saul, the first to be called King of Israel.

THE COOL WINDS

It was one of those hot breathless days when there is no wind and the temperature is 110° in the shade. Yet, as often happens, the burning air was invigorating. In this well-watered valley Beth Shean remained green under the copper-colored sun, so green indeed that it was almost possible to believe the ancient saying, "If Paradise is to be found in Israel, then the gate of Paradise is in Beth Shean."

So we remained in the shade, and sometimes we would make short sallies into the open until we were driven back into shelter again. There is a pleasant and spacious museum, with flowering trees and ancient columns in the garden, the columns flashing milky white, the green so rich and dark that we might have been in Ireland. An old Arab was in charge of the museum. He had the good sense to have an electric fan, which he set up on a table near the door, and in the intervals between gazing at mosaics and swords encrusted with the patina of fifty centuries, we would hurry back to the fan and bathe in its coolness. In the garden not a leaf stirred; the air was still on fire.

My companion, the expert on hydraulics, was also an expert on Roman history, and he knew every village and hamlet which the Romans had passed through in their travels backwards and forwards across Palestine.

"If you come with me down the valley," he said, "I'll show you the best-preserved and most impressive Roman theater in Israel. It beats the one in Caesarea hollow."

No doubt it did, but I was in no mood for walking into the boiling valley. It was even pleasant to stand for a few minutes in the sunlight, defying the sun's majesty and power. I had another reason for not walking. I had bought leather sandals at Haifa, and the thongs were biting deep into the flesh and drawing blood.

"How far is it to the theater?" I asked.

"Not very far. We could do it probably in five minutes. Five minutes to get there, five minutes to get back, say twenty minutes altogether."

"Then we can go and have a drink?"

"Yes, you can go and have a drink."

He had the pitying look of a professor. He described the long history of the Roman theater from its origins in Greece to its final apotheosis in the superb theater at Scythopolis, where for the first and last time a theater had been built worthy of the Roman genius. It was a theater to end all theaters, and only a fool would miss it. Recently some archaeologists had uncovered large areas of it, and only a few people had set eyes on the entire expanse, and this was all the more reason for going down into the valley.

"It's not something you can see from outside," he went on. "You have to be down there. It's an amazing place. Of course, if you are not interested in Roman history—"

Limping, I followed him down the valley. There were no trees, no shade at all. Rising from the other side of the valley was the huge yellow mountain which acted as a mirror, concentrating the sun's rays on us. It grew hotter and hotter as we descended, but the heat of the sun was less bothersome than the thin gray dust on the slopes of the hill. The dust was ankle-deep, and it was like wading through a lake of fire. I was in agony. The dust bit deep into my sandaled feet, searching out every scar and wound. I have never known dust like this: so hot, so soft, so fine and so piercing. The dust was hotter than the sun.

"We could never get down this slope in winter when it rains," he went on. "In winter it's nothing but a sea of mud."

I wished devoutly it would start raining. He bent down and gathered some of the bright red-hot dust in his hands.

"There's another curious thing about this dust," he said. "There's nothing like it anywhere else so far as I know, not even in Egypt. Have you noticed how fine it is?"

"Yes, I've noticed it."

"It's like silk, isn't it? Soft as silk. It's probably the oldest inhabited dust in the world. It's not the dust of centuries. It's the dust of millennia." Then he said, "In another five or six minutes we ought to be at the theater. We'll see it soon. Are you having any trouble?"

"No."

"Well, you can have a rest when you get to the theater."

He went trotting downhill, and sometimes through the sun's glare I would see him waving his arms. The surprising thing was that he had been ill until the previous day. He had been lying in bed for a week, suffering from some intestinal trouble, and he had eaten nothing at all. He looked a little like Disraeli, with a heavy upper lip and very bright eyes, and moved like a dancer.

Down, down into the valley we went, through the burning lake of dust, which rose high in the air, blinding us and scorching our faces. It was hotter than ever in the valley, where the theater lay, a dark and austere half-circle of carved stone at the foot of the yellow mountain, trembling in the heat haze. We dared not sit on the stone seats: they were scalding hot. Broken Corinthian columns lay scattered in the grass nearby, and there cannot have been one less than six feet in diameter. Giants had inhabited the place, and giants had built this small and perfect theater under the yellow mountain.

The expert in Roman history was quite pitiless. Standing bare-headed in the sun, he pointed to the marble chairs where the priests of Dionysus once sat, and the traces of the conduit which brought water from the river into the theater so that sea fights could be staged by gladiators. There were granite pillars which came from distant Assuan in Egypt. There were panels carved with delicate Hellenistic designs. The stage area was a ruin, but it could easily be restored. What did I think of it?

I said it was very small compared with Epidaurus, but comparable with the theater of Herodes Atticus in Athens; at which he grunted, and pointed out that the theater in Beth Shean had better acoustics than either. He went on to discover more and more virtues in this theater, which looked in spite of the ruined stage as though it had been abandoned only yesterday. He knew his architectural history, and his judgment was sound. Here at Beth Shean, at the bottom of a valley in Galilee, four hundred feet below sea level, was the best, the most perfectly designed of all the Roman theaters in Israel.

He had been discussing the fine points of the theater for what seemed half an hour, though it was probably no more than ten minutes, and suddenly he said, "I suppose you would like to get out of the sun?"

"Yes."

"Then we'll shelter under the arches. There's something there I want to show you, and I think you'll enjoy it."

He danced lightly up the stone steps, while I clambered slowly after him. There were fifteen tiers of weathered limestone, and more tiers of black basalt. From the curving uppermost tier nine archways led over crumbling pathways to the world outside. It was through these arches that the poor, who occupied the upper seats, entered the theater; the rich and influential went to their seats through ornamental tunnels below.

"Notice anything?" he asked, his eyes glinting with pride.

"No."

"Nothing at all? Surely you notice something? It's cooler here, isn't it?"

I was going to say, "Of course it's cooler. We're in the shade." But I said nothing, for as always he was absolutely right. No leaf stirred outside. The gray dust was smoldering lethargically, and the sun was still blazing off the yellow mountain. Beyond the mountain lay the eternally boiling blue sky and the pitiless sun.

Under the archway cool winds were stirring. Mysteriously they seemed to exist only within the archway, dying once they were outside. I opened my shirt, and the cool winds poured round me, coming from nowhere, belonging to the shade, dying on the sunlit air. It was like bathing in a spring to be under those great basalt vaults, in those fresh and lovely winds.

There was no wind outside, but there was wind in the shade. Even today I do not know where it came from, why it was so sweet and cool.

"It's simple," he said. "The Romans knew a terrific amount about engineering. Air ducts, ventilation shafts, the proper angling of the arches. Wonderful people the Romans!"

THE MONASTERY OF THE LADY MARY

In fear of death and in love with heaven, the Lady Mary built a monastery on a hill overlooking the yellow mountain, on the other side from Beth Shean. It was not a very large monastery, being about a hundred feet by a hundred feet, but it must have been a thing of splendor when it was new, standing there on the crest of the hill with its marble columns and red roof tiles and sumptuous array of mosaics covering the floors. Nothing remained of the monastery except the mosaics and a few stones inscribed in Greek. Of the Lady Mary we know very little. She may have been the wife of the provincial governor; she certainly had a son called Maximus; and she founded the monastery about A.D. 567, and was so pleased with it that she ordered her name to be written in three or four places on those jeweled floors. One inscription near the entrance of the church reads: "O Christ, God, Savior of the world, have mercy upon the Christ-loving Lady Mary and her son Maximus, and grant rest to their forefathers, through the prayers of all the Saints. Amen." She does not mention her husband's name, and we are therefore permitted to imagine an elderly widow, very devout, full of good works, intensely aristocratic, proud of the accomplishments of her son, and rich enough to import mosaic artists from Constantinople. She had a right to be pleased with herself, for there are no more brilliant mosaics in Galilee.

Only a dirt road leads to the mosaics, which are sheltered from the elements by a low wall and a corrugated-iron roof. Between the wall and the roof there is wire netting. Through the netting a small blue pigeon had flown a few days before we arrived, and being unable to fly out again it had died of exhaustion and lack of food. Now the pigeon lay on the broken floor, very small, very quiet, and sometimes the feathers stirred in the wind. In the half-light under the corrugated-iron roof the pigeon was brighter than the mosaics.

At first you can hardly see the mosaics at all. Everything inside that rambling low-roofed barn is gray with cobwebs and yellow with dust. In the dim light there is only the queer purplish rubble of small stones embedded in the floor and stretching across the whole length of the barn, with some depressions here and there where the stones have crumbled away. Blow the dust away, throw water on them, and the purplish rubble becomes a sheet of mosaics glittering with scarlet and yellow and cobalt blue!

There had been chapels and dormitories and private rooms, each with its separate mosaics, but now there is only one undulating floor with five or six strange and intricate designs. In one we see the months wheeling round the blazing sun and moon; they have the shape of twelve farmers. February carries a spade on his shoulder and a sapling in his hand. June carries baskets of fruit, July carries sheaves of wheat, December sows seed in the ground. They are not ordinary farmers. They are saints with uplifted eyes, rapt in adoration. The sun wears his flaming crown and the moon wears a crescent, and both wave their fiery torches. No one knows why the sun and moon should be represented in such pagan terms, while the months are so evidently Christian. The immense wheel seems to revolve, the colors flame up—purple, blue, ocher, gold—and all creation is set in motion.

There is nothing playful in these mosaics. They are grave, austere, and so they must be, since they belong to the time of Justinian, when a graceful severity was the rule. But sometimes humor creeps through. There is a panel showing the gathering of the vintage and the pressing of the grapes, and all the small scenes are depicted as they might be in a medieval *Book of Hours* in leafy circles of vine branches, and already there is the beginning of a dance. There are birds wading in white streams, not unlike those on the sandy hill in Caesarea. There is a Negro leading a camel down a dusty road, while a peasant plays on a flute to a dancing bear. You have the impression that the artist looked up, saw the Negro, the camel, the peasant and the dancing bear, and decided that the scene must be recorded forever. They, too, were a part—a very important part—of the scheme of things, the divine economy of the universe.

The bear dances and its tongue lolls, as it stands on its hind legs and prepares to perform a graceful pirouette, while the peasant watches with a bemused expression, wondering whether the bear will succeed in keeping its balance; and the Negro boy, walking like a prince, wears the same bemused expression as he half-turns towards his diminutive camel, wondering whether it is really there. The wonder, the eagerness, the calm joy is everywhere on those miraculous mosaics under the corrugated-iron roof, lost among the hills of Beth Shean.

Poor Lady Mary! She built for eternity, but her monastery had a very short life. From inscriptions we know it was built about A.D. 567, while the last coins found among the ruins bear the portrait of the Emperor Heraclius and date from about A.D. 610. So we may assume it was sacked by the Persians when they invaded the territory a few years after she had built the beautiful church to the glory of God and of herself and her son Maximus.

THE CHARIOTS OF THE SUN

One should look for mosaics wherever they can be found. Statues lose their heads, paintings are eaten away by the acids in the air, but mosaics remain, defying fires, earthquakes and wars. Those chips of stone are as nearly immortal as anything on this earth.

In Israel, where everyone is an amateur archaeologist, the search for mosaics has been going on relentlessly, ever since a British shell in World War I turned up the first of them. Roman mosaic pavements, of course, are turning up all the time. Byzantine pavements are rare. Rarest of all are Jewish pavements, though they are beginning to appear more frequently now that the Israelis are beginning to know where to look for them.

One of the first Jewish pavements to be discovered was so startling that some people claimed it must be a fake. It is odd that they should have pursued their claim in the face of the extraordinary artistry of the mosaic, which depicted in three registers the Torah shrine flanked by seven-branched candlesticks, the chariot of the sun surrounded by the signs of the zodiac, and the sacrifice of Isaac. But no one had ever seen a mosaic composed quite in this way, rough, provincial, with bold and wiry outlines, by artists evidently in a state of wild exuberance. The making of mosaics is largely an aristocratic art, careful and ponderous. These village artists threw care to the winds, and far from being ponderous they designed the three panels with an insistence on

a kind of primitive joy. They were serious and at the same time determined to amuse themselves.

The mosaic was discovered in December, 1928 by workmen digging
an irrigation channel at Hephzibah, a few miles from Beth Shean.
They cleared a small part of the mosaic and then sent for Professor
Sukenik, the leading archaeologist in the Hebrew University at Jerusalem. Professor Sukenik came at once, and by the end of January,
1929, most of the mosaic, forming a square about thirty feet wide and
thirty feet broad, was uncovered. In the following years a simple corrugated-iron roof was put over it. Today it is housed in a solid wooden
building of admirable proportions, well lit and provided with a terrace which enables you to look down in comfort at the entire expanse.

Most mosaics are unsigned, and art historians are put to a good deal
of trouble by the anonymity of the mosaic artists. We do not know the
names of the great mosaic artists of Constantinople, Ravenna and
Palermo. As it happens, we do know the names of the artists who designed the three panels at Hephzibah, for one of the panels bears an
inscription in Greek reading: "May the craftsmen who carried out
this work, Marianos and his son Hanina, be held in remembrance."
Marianos is a Greek name, Hanina is Aramaic. So the inhabitants of
this obscure provincial town on the slopes of Mount Gilboa—the
town is believed to have been Beth Alpha—may have been of mixed
Jewish and Greek descent. A fragmentary Aramaic inscription adds the
information that the floor was laid down in the reign of the Emperor
Justinian.

Marianos and Hanina had no formal training, but they had evidently studied the mosaics at Beth Shean and were determined to em-
bellish their own small synagogue with equally rich mosaics. They
aimed high. Profoundly complex relationships, vast ideas, mysterious
beliefs seethed in their brains. They had only a rudimentary conception of the human figure, but they possessed a glorious sense of
color and a vivid gift for dramatic expression. A child could have
drawn the Abraham who sacrifices Isaac, but only a child of genius
could have depicted the entire scene, beginning with the arrival at
Mount Moriah on donkeyback and ending with the smoke and flames
of the sacrificial altar. Abraham wears a sun helmet, Isaac a green cap,

God is a small dark cloud out of which a crimson hand emerges. The servants watch eagerly, while the ram, tied to a tree by a scarlet cord, reaches up to the succulent leaves on the topmost branches. Abraham, Isaac and the servants all have fair hair. Why this should be so no one knows. The artist has printed the names of his characters over their heads, so that there shall be no mistake. Beside the crimson hand of God are the Hebrew letters meaning "Lay not . . ." Isaac is not to be offered up as a burnt offering. Abraham's head is bent in assent. He has heard, and he has not heard, for Isaac is still flying in mid-air and the knife is still being brandished. The artists have caught the exact moment when the crisis is at its height. All this is accomplished with precision, with gaiety, and with a deep religious feeling by artists who were so incapable of drawing human figures that Isaac's body resembles a child's doodle and the angel is little more than a beanpole, a triangle and a pair of legs.

The artists' happy inadequacy is seen to its best advantage in the medallion depicting the Chariot of the Sun. Helios is reduced to a head and a tubular neck, while the horses' heads resemble lumps of colored putty in which red mouths and black eyes have been inserted. There is a shieldlike object which may be the front of the chariot, there are weird curving shapes which seem to be parts of wheels and legs spread out before us. The reins fly in the air. Helios wears the diadem of the sun, while the crescent moon rises beside him and the morning stars explode at his feet. Everything is wrong, and everything is prodigiously right. The Greeks carved the Sun with every hair in its proper place and every human muscle carefully outlined. Marianos and Hanina painted him with the inner eye, seeing only the heavy, luminous face, the abstract forms of power. Ultimately this sun god derives more from ancient Canaanite sources than from Greece. He is not so much Helios as an expression of the creative power informing and governing the universe.

The third panel shows the Torah shrine lit by the light of the seven-branched candlesticks. The shrine is guarded by the birds of paradise and by two lions which look no more formidable than kittens. That the *ner tamid*, the "eternal light," should be guarded by kittens and birds of brilliant plumage is in keeping with what we already know about the imaginations of the artists, who submitted to no laws but the laws of their own gay improvisations.

When you enter the building which shelters the mosaics, everything is dark. Your first impression is that this might be a small swimming pool, for the eye is immediately attracted to a square sunken space where mysterious shadows swirl. Then the lights come on, and the floor is instantly transformed into a sheet of flaming colors, so bright and dazzling that they hurt the eyes. They were found in a wonderful state of preservation, and only a small amount of restoration was needed; and like the mosaics in the nearby monastery of the Lady Mary, they seem to have been preserved because the building over them was fired during the Persian invasion.

Today whenever a new mosaic is found in Israel, it is judged by the mosaic found at Hephzibah. It is the earliest example of Jewish mosaic, the richest and most poetical. These obscure craftsmen worked better than they knew; fourteen hundred years after their deaths their mosaic has become one of the supreme treasures of the state of Israel.

For this work is like a battle flag, a thing men can live by. This artless refinement, this passionate visionary quality, speaks to the present age more clearly than the prophets and the sages. The shrine, the wheeling sun and the Covenant of Abraham are brought together in simple confrontation, and shine on one another. Here the voice of Israel is heard with perfect clarity.

Beth Shearím

That day the sky was very high, and there were long clouds like feathers streaming in from the sea. We had come from Beth Alpha and the highlands had been left far behind. Now, returning to Haifa along the Plain of Esdraelon, we saw the new settlements glinting in the sun, and the earth was green again. Everywhere there were ripening fields of cotton and wheat, and the portable sprinklers were twirling, shooting off little tents of sparkling spray. There were cypresses near the road, of a lighter green than I have ever seen them. There were bathing pools and shouts of laughter, and young bodies could be seen dimly through the cypresses. It was the late afternoon of a hot summer day, but there was the freshness of the dawn in the shining sky and the ripening fields.

Not long ago the Plain of Esdraelon was a malarial swamp, and the Arabs called it "the gateway to hell." It was the habit of the Turks to send Arab tribesmen there whenever they were recalcitrant. They would be told of a green valley sheltered from the winds where they could raise horses to their hearts' content, and it was true that the valley was green; but they died like flies. The Jewish National Fund acquired the land in 1921 during the early years of the British Mandate. Forty years of draining, tilling and plowing have gone to make the flowering of the plain.

There are few pleasures greater than driving at a fierce speed through a land colored in every shade of green. Everything looked sleek, glossy, youthful, brimming with vitality. We passed a girl riding on a gray and white donkey; the donkey was fat, and the girl had red cheeks and looked vibrantly healthy. So it was along the whole length of the road, until we came to a turning and entered the city of the dead.

And what a city! There were vast, silent streets of stone carved out of a mountain, dark and clammy, with houses lying in row after silent row. One street opened into another, and some of the streets were separated by stone doors, which opened quietly on stone hinges and were carved to represent wooden panels. The houses too had carvings on them: of lions and crowns and seven-branched candlesticks, of fruit trees and strange shell-like objects, and the head of Hercules. There were many inscriptions, most of them in Greek. Nothing lived here, only some strange green moss, soft as thistledown, which came to birth wherever a lamp shone on the stone. You blew on it, and the moss vanished. Then there was only the lifeless street, the glint of limestone, the endless roads and corridors of the dead.

One could drive an automobile through some of these streets, and still have room to maneuver in. There is a sense of ordered spaciousness, of generous town-planning. The roof is high, the paving smooth. Here and there you come upon the litter left by tomb robbers, heavy slabs prized off the tombs. There are even ruts occasionally in the rock floor, suggesting a large carriage trade. Here and there you come across slabs of marble, but the marble tombs vanished in the medieval lime kilns. Those that remain are of limestone.

You wander through the city of the dead with a sense of bafflement at the orderly array of ghostly white houses. The city seems to have been abandoned only a few hours ago; it is hushed and absorbed in its own stillness. The dead have fled. There are no bones, not even the dust of bones. Everything has been rifled, desecrated, invaded by generations of tomb robbers. Everything that was valuable or movable has been taken away. The dead have vanished, and left us their city.

Until the spring of 1936 no one ever guessed that such a city existed. All that was known was that somewhere in the neighborhood the priestly court of the Sanhedrin had settled in the second century under the presidency of the great Rabbi Judah ha-Nasi, a wealthy and learned patriarch whose spiritual authority was acknowledged by all the Jews of his time. "Ha-Nasi" means "the prince," and Judah combined the roles of earthly ruler and patriarch. The Romans were still oppressing the Jews, and he therefore chose as the site of the Sanhedrin the little town of Besara, a quiet place, far from the military roads and not under direct Roman occupation, for it formed a small domain belonging to Berenice, sister of Agrippa II and Queen of Chalkis. Here he ruled his flock, while pursuing his studies and completing his compilation of the Mishna. He died about A.D. 217 at the age of eighty-five, his eldest son inheriting his high position. There was a saying current during his reign: "Justice, justice shalt thou follow? Then follow Rabbi Judah to Beth Shearim." Beth Shearim was the name he had given to the small town of Besara, and it meant "The House of the Gates."

A good deal is known about the princely Judah ha-Nasi, but until recently Beth Shearim was no more than a name which kept continually recurring in accounts of the rabbis and sages who had lived there. It was assumed that the gates were spiritual gates, not to be seen with mortal eyes. Then one day in the spring of 1936 a forester called Alexander Zaid, a Siberian Jew who had settled in the area when it was bought by the Jewish National Fund, clambered down the side of a small hill thickly covered with timber and underbrush and found a carved stone gateway hidden among rubble. The first of many gates had been found.

The forester forced a passage through the gate and what he saw convinced him that he would have to summon the archaeologists, who were startled by the immense size of the catacomb winding into the rock and still more startled to find representations of human figures on the carved tombs, as though the commandment against the making of graven images was being deliberately disobeyed. At that time the influence of Greek designs on Jewish art in the third and fourth centuries A.D. was still unknown. But what puzzled the archaeologists even more was the prevalence of Greek inscriptions. Since then many more catacombs have been opened and many more inscriptions have been read, and they are still puzzled by it. Of nearly a hundred and twenty inscriptions found in the catacombs, only about twenty are in Hebrew. There are half a dozen in Palmyrene, the rest are in Greek.

The scholars went to work, hoping to discover more about the mysterious town of Besara, which Josephus had described as "in the Great Valley, in the southernmost part of Galilee, twenty stadia east of Gaba Hippeum." Now Gaba Hippeum was known—it was the town where Herod the Great settled his retired cavalrymen and adjoins Carmel—and the description fitted the site of Beth Shearim exactly. Then they went to Talmudic sources, and gathered together all the references they could find about the town. They learned that when the ancient Jewish cemetery on the Mount of Olives in Jerusalem became closed to the Jews after the Bar Kokba revolt in A.D. 162, and after the burial of Rabbi Judah ha-Nasi in Beth Shearim, these catacombs became the new burial center for pious Jews. But in all the Talmudic sources the archaeologists consulted they found no references to a great city of tombs beneath a mountain, with pillared vaults of living rock opening into funeral cells, with reliefs of animals and plants and candelabra and human faces, with rich mosaics and ceremonial halls, all carved in designs which were essentially Greek. It was known that Greek architecture had influenced the design of synagogues in the second and third centuries A.D., for the façades of the synagogues at Bar'am and Capernaum, long known, possessed a purely Greek elegance. It was known, too, that Greek words and ideas had invaded Jewish theology, but in the process they had been subtly altered so that their Greek origins were often forgotten. No one doubted that there had been a persistent Greek influence among the Jews ever since Alexander the Great led his armies through Palestine. But why should the inscription on the tomb of a rabbi be in Greek? Why should the Jews build a Greek city for their dead?

Even now the scholars are not certain of the answers to these questions. They are acutely aware that great and unexpected changes occurred in the minds of the sages of Beth Shearim during the years when the Sanhedrin held its meetings there. There was a new hope, a sense of liberation, a refusal to be bound by laws which had lost all contemporary meaning. The inscriptions showed a particularly strong belief in the resurrection of the dead, previously very rare. There were no Aramaic inscriptions, and this was puzzling because Aramaic continued to be the language of the common people. Judah ha-Nasi is reported to have said, "Why speak Aramaic in Palestine? It is better to speak Hebrew or Greek." Perhaps this was the clue. Perhaps the tide of Hellenization reached its peak during the years at Beth Shearim. They were the years when Rome was saturated with Greek feeling, and the Antonine emperors customarily spoke and wrote in Greek. Judah ha-Nasi enjoyed the goodwill of the Romans, and was said to have been on intimate terms with Marcus Aurelius. So it is possible that this Greek influence came by way of Rome.

But if the scholars were puzzled by the inscriptions in a language which was not thought to have had deep roots in the country, they were even more troubled by the large numbers of representations of human figures. Had the second commandment been abandoned? Or had there been as the result of a long process of Hellenization a gradual acceptance of these painted and carved figures as being purely decorative, without idolatrous significance? Scholars are still disputing the question. For the more rigid Jews Beth Shearim came as a shocking surprise, and the open wounds have not yet healed.

The first excavations took place under Dr. Benjamin Mazar between 1936 and 1940, and led to the uncovering of eleven catacombs. The excavations were interrupted by the war and the long aftermath of fighting in Palestine, and were only resumed in 1953. Since then many more catacombs have come to light, including one bearing inscriptions in Greek and Hebrew saying that the Rabbis Shimon, Gamaliel and Hanina are buried there. The archaeologists were heartened by the discovery, because it seemed to indicate that they had come upon the tomb of the family of Judah ha-Nasi himself. Shimon, Gamaliel and Hanina were the names of his sons. It was recorded in the Talmud that he desired to be buried in Beth Shearim, and what more likely than that he should be buried with his sons? But no trace of the tomb of Judah ha-Nasi has yet been found.

Only a few tombs seem to have belonged to rabbis. Most of them belonged to rich officials and businessmen and their families. So we find bankers, perfumers, silk merchants, all people of substance, together with lawyers and town councilors. The catacombs belonged to the rich and powerful. If the poor were buried there, their graves are still unknown.

Very early in its history this cemetery honeycombed out of the rock came to be regarded as holy ground, sanctified by the presence of Judah ha-Nasi. Accordingly Jews from far afield asked to be buried there, and the towns and provinces they came from are sometimes included in the inscriptions—Antioch, Byblos, Sidon, Beirut, Palmyra, Pamphilia, Mesopotamia, even Yemen. From Egypt, Parthia and the Euphrates came the long camel trains, bearing the lead coffins and the wooden boxes of bones. For about two hundred years this small hill lying between Carmel and the highlands of Lower Galilee became another Jerusalem.

No one knows for certain when the cemetery was abandoned, but the last coins found in Beth Shearim can be dated about A.D. 350, and this accords well enough with the possibility that the small town was sacked in A.D. 352, when a Jewish revolt in Galilee was suppressed with fearful severity by Gallus, the brother-in-law of Constantius II. Thereafter there were no more burials and nothing was ever heard of the catacombs. The city of the dead died and was forgotten, to be reborn in our own day.

Green lawns have been planted on the approaches of the hill, cypresses crown the summit, and there is an air of quiet holiday-making around the catacombs, as visitors come and go. But once they have passed through the sculptured gates they walk silently, awed by the immensity of the spectacle which unfolds before them. The sheer size of those immense shafts driven into the hillside is frightening, and there is always the sense of strangeness at the sight of Judaism wearing the colors of Greece. Sometimes these shadowy tombs have a monumental delicacy. There is one in particular, known as the "shell sarcophagus," weighing five tons, which has three shells carved on its surface, together with an eagle and the head of a bull between two lions, and there is another lion further down. The lions, however, have no ferocity in them; they look like dolls made of cloth and stuffed with straw. The eagle, too, looks like a child's plaything. All these separate objects are joined together by intricate lacy designs in charming confusion, so that the massive tomb acquires an air of monumental gaiety. It is as though a child had toyed with a five-ton block of stone and carved whatever his fancy demanded. Yet somehow, out of shells, lions and eagles he has contrived a small masterpiece.

Huge seven-branched candlesticks are carved into the wall, Leda wrestles with her swan, and riders go off to war, brandishing swords. The head of Hercules—or is it Zeus?—stares down from the walls of a tomb. All these reliefs possess a happy, primitive quality. They are rough-edged, not smoothed over, all the more charming for their lack of finish. They proclaim, not the severity of death, but a kind of joyful innocence.

How innocent they were, and how joyful, can be seen from a Greek inscription carved near the entrance of one of those enormous catacombs. It is high up on the wall, and written in bold letters. *"Eutykhos ti humon anastasi,"* reads the happy inscription. "Good luck on your resurrection."

Nazareth

For century after century the pilgrims have been coming to Nazareth to see the Cave of the Annunciation and the grotto believed to be part of the house in which Jesus lived, and I suspect that most of them have been disappointed. The grotto does not differ from many other grottoes in these hills, and the cave is so small and cluttered a place, with its Victorian oleographs and creamy altars of Carrara marble and red granite columns, that it is almost impossible to detect any numinous quality. The Cave of the Annunciation is about the size of a small coal cellar. It is shapeless and ugly, and there are too many hanging lamps, too many oleographs, too many collection boxes. Below the altar, on a kind of marble table, there is the inscription in gold letters, VERBUM CARO HIC FACTUM EST, but only the most credulous could believe with certainty that this is the precise spot where the Word was made Flesh. An Arab Christian leads the pilgrims down the stairway to this cellar, intoning a litany which has lost all meaning by repetition. "Please, ladies and gentlemen, observe the columns dating from the fourth century. On the left is the column representing the place where the angel appeared, on the right is the column representing the place where Mary was standing." The columns are very close together; it is only just possible to squeeze between them. The Italian painters did it better. They gave a sense of spaciousness to the scene. They painted Mary quietly kneeling in a spacious house while an

118

angel alighted in the garden outside, his brilliant wings echoing the vivid colors of the flowers. Peacocks wandered on the lawns, and the doves looked down from the roof beams. There was no clammy cellar, no walled-in horror of bare rock encrusted with marble monuments dating from late Victorian times. The medieval French pilgrim Bertrandon de la Brocquière said of the Cave of the Annunciation that it was "pitiful to see," and in his day there were no lurid oleographs on the walls.

But if the guided tours through the sacred places are disappointing, there is still much to see in Nazareth. Above all there is the town itself, clinging to the slopes of an abrupt limestone hill, dotted with white roofs, strangely unchanged through the centuries, so that you can wander through the narrow streets and feel yourself back in the time when Jesus walked those same streets where the gray donkeys climb. The women still walk splendidly, though they no longer come to Mary's well for water and balance pitchers on their heads—the Israelis have run pipelines to the houses, and left the well desolate. Some things have changed. There is an entire new Jewish town on a great shoulder overlooking the old town. The buses roar along the main street, on their way to Tiberias. The black-cloaked Franciscans are everywhere, and the Vatican is busy building more and more convents and churches along the sides of the hill, so that you have the impression that it will eventually capsize under their weight. Still, for a little while longer, the unhurried side-streets in the shade of the cypresses will continue to speak of the ancient days. Especially at night, in moonlight, when the donkeys come treading delicately along the slopes, and the faces of the Arabs are hidden in the shadows of their keffiyehs, and the silence settles, then the illusion of being hurled back into the remote past is inescapable. The churches vanish; there are only the winding roads.

Yet the glory of Nazareth is not so much in the white town as in the soaring hills. Jesus of Nazareth has fled from the holes in the rock, and if we would encounter Him anywhere, it is on those broad and sinewy hills, where the air is sweet and pure, and the sounds of the market place are no longer heard. From those hills you have the impression that the whole earth is laid out before you. On a clear day you can see the great cliff of Carmel and the sea to the west, and Mount Hermon, silvery even in summer, to the north, and the rich plains of Esdraelon lie at your feet with the rolling blue hills of Samaria slumbering on the horizon. There is Mount Tabor with its oaken groves, grayish-blue, shaped like an inverted cup, so perfectly proportioned that one imagines it has been made on a potter's wheel, and beyond Tabor are the long ridges of the Galilean hills running up towards the mysterious city of Safed. I used to wonder why the Psalmist spoke of the hills leaping with joy, but I wondered no longer after Nazareth. There are so many hills, of so many different shapes, and all of them seem to be arranged artfully like the carefully contrived landscapes of gnarled rocks in Japanese temples, to produce the greatest pleasure in the beholder. Nazareth is like an eagle's eyrie, and any shepherd boy on those hills would rejoice in visions of the earth lying quiet at his feet, all gold at sunset.

The astonishing thing about Nazareth is that it tells us so much about the hidden years of Jesus, even without benefit of caves and grottoes. The Arab Christian guide will lead you to a cave which may have been a granary, and he will say that Joseph and Mary lived there, and took food from that ledge of rock, and built a fire in this chimney corner, and he claims that a little hollow in the rock is a manger in which the Christ Child lay. But all this is unnecessary. We learn more about Jesus from the sweep of the hills, which are broad-shouldered and muscular, not for weaklings. Living on the slopes of those hills, a boy would grow strong without effort, and to the end of his days he would have the sense of living at the hub of the earth, for all Lower Galilee seems to revolve like a wheel around Nazareth. Oddly, the town had no history of its own. No battles had been fought there, no great scholars had settled there, and it was not mentioned in the Old Testament. But from the hills the boy could look out on places which had grown dear and familiar to him from the Old Testament texts. He could see Mount Tabor, where Deborah and Barak assembled the children of Zebulun and Naphtali to fight against Sisera, and Gilboa where King Saul fell in battle with the Philistines, and the valleys and plains where the armies had marched to battle for centuries. To the north lay the white houses and temples of Sepphoris-Diocaesarea, the capital of Lower Galilee, where there was a Roman theater, schools, baths, race courses, eighteen synagogues and many scribes; it was no more than two hours away by road, on the other side of the hill of Nazareth, in the midst of a vast plain. As a shepherd boy on the hills Jesus may have seen the city in flames when the Romans under Varus attacked it in the days when Judah, the son of Hezekiah, raised the flag of revolt. Then for a few years Sepphoris-Diocaesarea was no more than a tumble of ruins.

But all the time Nazareth lay outside history, secluded among the quiet hills, the main road lying beyond the town, the people at peace with themselves, going about their daily affairs as though they were spectators, remote from the world. It was a town where nothing had ever happened, and nothing was likely to happen. It was not rich or poor, and there was only one fountain to serve the whole community. When people in Jerusalem remembered the town they would say, "Can any good thing come out of Nazareth?" and shake their heads, meaning perhaps that it was a small thing and hardly worth wondering about. In this silence, in the eagle's eyrie, Jesus spent nearly all the years of his life.

THE TREMORE

He was a tall man, well built, with a fine sunburned face and an expression of nervous serenity. I remember how his face would light up at the sight of a beautiful child, and how, when there was nothing better to do, he would lie down on the grass and lose himself in a book, becoming so completely absorbed in it that he lost track of the passing of time. There was a strange gentleness in him, but this gentleness was illusory. He had been a member of the Haganah, the Jewish secret army, in charge of gun-running, and he had fought in many skirmishes with the British and the Arabs. "We captured arms and hid them and we had to bring them out of their hiding places when they were needed," he said. "It went on for years and years, and I thought it would never end." Now it was all over, and he was an old soldier trying to forget the times when he killed to obtain arms, and lived in a house with dynamite behind the wallpaper.

As a young man in the early thirties he came to Palestine from Hungary, and the first sight of Haifa made him decide to stay there for the rest of his life. But though he loved Haifa and Mount Carmel with a passionate devotion, he liked to wander through Israel. He knew every hill and valley, and he had read all the books about his country he could lay his hands on. He was my companion during many days of wandering around Galilee.

We were standing in the dusty market place watching the bus-loads of pilgrims making their way up to the Church of the Annunciation when he said, "Have you seen the Tremore?"

"No."

"Then you should. It's the loveliest thing in Nazareth. It's a very small church, and they say that when Jesus preached in the synagogue and was driven out and the people wanted to cast him headlong from the Mount of Precipitation, then Mary followed them, hoping to save her son. She was running along the hill, but suddenly her strength gave way and she could run no more. She fell to her knees, giving herself up to despair. At the place where she fell, they erected a church which they called Our Lady of the Trembling—the Tremore. I don't know anything about the church, but it is very human and beautiful that they should have built the church there."

"Who built it?"

He shook his head.

"I don't know. It may have been the Crusaders, but the Catholics are silent about it. It's all a mystery to me. I've never visited it. I've only seen it from a distance, and always marveled at it. Shall we go there?"

So we went in search of the Tremore, which had been invisible earlier in the morning when we stood on the great bluff overlooking the craggy cliffs of the Mount of Precipitation, with their sheer drop of a thousand feet, the great Plain of Esdraelon lying below. The Mount of Precipitation is like a heavy shoulder flanking the town of Nazareth, all bare and yellow in the sun, with only a few cactuses and carob trees, and no sign of habitation. There was a dead, heavy strength about the mountain, rising slowly towards those imponderable cliffs, very sure of itself, unable to take part in the life of the town though so very close to it.

By this time it was midday, and the streets were gradually emptying. A few children were playing. A few Arabs with black headbands and white keffiyehs were still wandering aimlessly in the deserted streets. There were no more buses. The quietness of noon was settling on Nazareth.

According to the map there was a road leading to Tremore, or very close to it, but we never found it. Occasionally there would be a glimpse of a small white church lying on a saddle of the mountain, very far and remote, vanishing stealthily at the next turning of the road. In the end we found a road leading to a limestone quarry, a huge white gash carved into the side of the mountain, smoking with dust, derricks and bulldozers, and we walked through the soft, suffocating dust up to our ankles in search of a path up the mountain. We were sure that Tremore was somewhere near, but it had a habit of eluding us.

The workmen had gone home for lunch, and there was no one about except an Arab foreman with a clown's face white with dust, and he knew nothing about the church and cared less. Strangely, an enormous turkey with a brilliant scarlet neck suddenly emerged out of the shade of the rocks, and in the blinding summer light, against the white dust, the neck was the color of fresh blood. The turkey kept pecking at us, dogging our footsteps.

Many strange things had happened that morning, and perhaps the strangest of all had been the gray candlelit Cave of the Annunciation filled with the troubled faces of the pilgrims, the intolerable oleographs hanging on the walls. I remembered an old woman in a black dress whispering to a priest and giving him an envelope to lay on the marble table where the gold letters proclaimed that the Word was made Flesh; and very gravely the priest lit a candle and knelt beside the envelope, which in that light resembled a slice of bread waiting to be toasted by holy flames. They prayed together, and then the priest returned the envelope to the woman, who thanked him and dropped some coins in the collection box. I had not expected it, never thought that such a thing was possible in the present age. So now in the quarry it seemed incredible that a venomous-looking turkey would flutter round us like an emissary from hell, trying to prevent us from reaching an obscure church in Nazareth.

There was nothing to be done except to climb the mountain in the hope that the Tremore was somewhere near, for we had long ago lost sight of it. There was no pathway. It meant climbing the steep outcrops skirting the quarry, but at this point the mountain was still low, no more than forty or fifty feet high, gathering strength for the great thrust which would bring it eventually to a thousand-foot precipice. So we scrambled up to the ledge where the giant sea-green cactuses were sunning themselves, and found a pathway which led to some abandoned tombs, and beyond the tombs lay the Tremore.

It stood there framed by carob trees, and then as we climbed higher it broke free of them in proud isolation, alone in that immensity of barren sunburnt rock, so beautiful a thing with its slender columns and open vestibule and stairway curling over a crypt that it took the breath away. It was all delicacy and grace, perfectly appropriate to its lonely setting, with the mountain rising in a broad sweep beyond it, and in its proportions there was no severity.

I have never seen a church which gives such an overwhelming impression of calm elation. Every line of it spoke of certainty and faith. The ample archway supported on the slender columns was an arch of triumph, balanced by the semicircular opening of the crypt under the stairway. The purity of the proportions suggested early Romanesque, but there were moments when I thought I detected a Persian influence, and I was reminded, especially when seeing the church in profile, of the sumptuous palace of Ali Qapu in Ispahan. The door was closed, but through the keyhole it was easy to see that it had been abandoned; there was nothing inside. The crypt, however, was open, and filled with debris. There were some bullet holes, and a Pole who had visited the crypt twenty years ago had signed his name and the date. On the locked door of the church the Greek letter Φ was painted, indicating that it was in the possession of the Greek Orthodox community.

I never discovered who built the church, or when, or why it was left abandoned. I have searched through half a library of travelers' books on Palestine without discovering more than an occasional and uninformative reference to it. Writing in 1923 Father Barnabas Meistermann, the author of a learned *Guide to the Holy Land*, says: "The Greeks have built a little chapel with an open vestibule near the road that makes straight for the precipice. It is there that they show to their pilgrims the place of the Fright of Mary." He adds that the sight has "neither the appearance of reasonableness nor the excuse of good faith." But such a consummate work of art cannot have been built without reasonableness and good faith. On that broad, flinty mountain someone, at some unknown time, built a small palace for the Virgin.

Today few visitors to Nazareth pay much attention to the Mount of Precipitation. It was otherwise in the Middle Ages. At the time of the Crusades, and even long before, the mountain was regarded with almost as much reverence as the Cave of the Annunciation. "In Galilee, in the holy city of Nazareth," wrote the unknown author of the *Commemoratorium* about A.D. 808, "there were twelve monks. A mile from Nazareth, where the Jews wished to throw Christ our Saviour over the cliff, there has been built a monastery and a church in honor of St. Mary; it is occupied by eight monks." The church and monastery were built on the very edge of the precipice; the ruins are still visible with their broken cisterns and crumbled mosaic floors. The medieval travelers rejoiced in the drama of the precipice. They invented, or found in old fables, the story that Jesus escaped His pursuers by leaping off the edge of the mountain in royal anger, to reappear a moment later "a bowshot away." The leap of the Lord, the *saltus Domini*, belonged to the stuff of their dreams. To them it was inevitable, and proper, that Jesus should perform an act of heroic daring, for it was inconceivable that He would simply "pass through the midst of them and go on his way." And in their minds this deliberate leap from a pinnacle acquired a special significance when compared with His deliberate refusal to leap from the Cross. The *saltus Domini* became, in fact, a central article of belief, giving color and dimension to His divinity, His divine power, His heroic authority.

There was no sanction for this belief in the Gospels, but this scarcely troubled the medieval Christians. They had only to look at the mountain and gaze down in fear and trembling at the precipice to know that it had happened in this way. For the same reason they *knew* that Mary had not dared to go more than a little way along the mountain, and so they built the small palace for her, giving her a delicately arched vestibule in which to receive her guests.

The Mount of Precipitation is shaped like a crouching lion, guarding the approaches to Nazareth from the west. In time more quarries will eat into it, and sooner or later expanding Nazareth will climb upon the rocks and build a suburb there, and the lion will die, and the legends will be forgotten. For a little while longer we can see the place where Mary trembled and the Lord leaped, then it will be as though it had never been.

AT GABRIEL'S WELL

The afternoon sun was beating strongly on the savage rocks, shining like mirrors under the indigo sky. All day there had been that steady, relentless heat pouring out endlessly over the barren hills, where the scrub was drying up, brittle as glass. There was no shade on the broad shoulder of the Mount of Precipitation. Some gray lizards scuttled among the stones, and only the swallows darting madly over the crest of the mountain seemed to have any life left in them. There were moments when the whole mountain seemed to be melting in livid, white fire.

So we left the mountain and took shelter from the sun in the small church which lies a little way behind the arched well, where for generations women came to fill their pitchers and visitors have written happily about them, seeing this well as the focal point of the living legend of Nazareth. But that well, so often painted, was built by the Turks and still bears the marks of Turkish workmanship. The real well, the Virgin's Spring, comes bubbling up within the church, which is called after the angel Gabriel and belongs to the Greek

Orthodox community. It was here, according to the apocryphal Gospel of St. James the Less, known as the *Protoevangelion*, that Mary heard the voice of the angel while drawing water at the well:

And she took a pitcher, and went out to draw water, and heard a voice saying unto her: Hail, Mary, full of grace, the Lord is with thee: blessed art thou among women.

And she looked to the right and left to see whence the voice came, and then trembling went into her house, and when she had laid the pitcher down, she took the purple, and sat down in her seat to work it.

And behold the angel of the Lord stood by her, and said, Fear not, Mary, for thou hast found favour in the sight of God.

When she heard this, she reasoned with herself what sort of salutation was meant.

And the angel said unto her, The Lord is with thee, and thou shalt conceive.

To which she replied, What! shall I conceive by the living God, and bring forth as other women do?

But the angel returned answer, Not so Mary, but the Holy Ghost shall come upon thee, and the power of the Most High shall over-shadow thee, wherefore that which shall be born of thee shall be holy.

Such was the story told in the *Protoevangelion*, which was written down at some time in the second century, and many learned doctors of the Church, including Martin Luther, have firmly believed in it. In time legends grew around the well. It was not enough that the voice of the angel should be first heard beside the well, but it was said that many miracles took place there; and nearly all the pilgrims to Pales-tine visited it. Sir John Mandeville, who may never have visited the Orient at all, though he based his story of his adventures on the au-thentic travels of others, wrote most poetically on the well without summoning any miracles to his assistance. "Near there is Gabriel's well," he wrote, "where Our Lord was wont to bathe, when he was young; and from that well he carried water often to his mother; and in that well she often washed the clothes of her son Jesus Christ."

So we went to the well with some trepidation, scarcely expecting we would be able to drink from it, but at least it would be cooler in the church. One does not normally find drinking water in churches.

Yet it was evident from the beginning that this was a church unlike any others. I had a confused impression of flashing gold icons and wheeling lights, and then suddenly we were being led down some steps into a small green-tiled crypt, originally part of the grotto, for some of the bare rock could be seen above the tiles, which were painted with green trees. The crypt was scarcely larger than a small bathroom.

There was a kind of slot in one wall, just large enough for a polished steel bucket to descend. A chain ran down from the roof, and all you had to do was pull on the chain and bring up the bucket and drink to your heart's content. The water came up, flashing silver, very cool and sweet. There was a complete absence of formality. There were no tablets announcing that this was one of the sacred places of Christianity. There were no offertory boxes, no solemn declarations, no candles glowing before icons; only the wellspring.

Here at last there was no need to put faith in legends, for there is no doubt that the Virgin came to this spring, and her son too, for there is no other spring in Nazareth.

We lingered long in this place, delighted to escape from the sun, delighted to be at the Virgin's Spring, delighted by the informality. Children came and slaked their thirst, and went running out again. There were strings of electric light overhead, and more light came down through an air shaft, which provided a fresh and pleasant breeze, so that the lamps kept swinging. Clearly the place has not changed very much since Saewulf saw it in the year A.D. 1103, reporting that "the Spring of the Virgin is adorned with columns and tablets of marble." Here and there among the tiles were medallions bearing the portraits of women, but the colors had faded, and it was impossible to distinguish whether they were saints or ancient empresses.

"Very few Christians who are not of the Greek Orthodox faith come here," said my companion. "I can't think why they avoid it. It's so very human." He had used the same word when speaking of the Tremore.

Spilled water shone on the tiles, coolness came from the walls, there was a pleasant rattling sound as the chain ran down into the well. Outside the sun was beating down harshly, but here there was only

Porphyry statue at Caesarea

Herodian capital at Ashkelon

Winged Victory at Ashkelon

Hazor. The Dragons' Teeth

Beth Shearim. The Catacombs

Beth Shean. The Roman theater in foreground, and the fortified Tel in background

Capernaum. The synagogue

Massada

quietness and a sense of remoteness from the burning countryside. We splashed our faces and our hands, and drank like camels. Children were padding up and down the worn stairs, water was splashing everywhere, and there was the sound of laughter.

It was the same in the church above, which was unlike any church I have ever known, the walls covered with an incredible collection of garish icons haphazardly restored, the golden-haloed saints with monstrously large eyes seeming to be the work of one of those artists employed to paint merry-go-rounds at a fun fair. There was a cross outlined in naked electric lights. Innumerable hanging lamps hung from the ceiling. A coffeepot was boiling behind the altar screen. Perhaps a hundred lamps were burning, while the sun poured in through the wide-open doors. But what was still more astonishing was that children were playing tag between the pews, while the priest paid not the slightest attention to them. He was a dark, heavy-set Arab with a beautiful beard, who laughed easily. At that moment he was preparing to baptize an Arab baby with water from Mary's well.

Gradually the pieces of the jigsaw began to fit together: this was, after all, a Greek Orthodox church serving the large Arab community in Nazareth. Nearly all of them were Christians, and they had elected to remain when Israeli forces conquered the town. Like the Greeks, the Arabs have developed a fondness for strings of electric light, and this explained why so many were burning on the hottest and brightest day of the year. The garish icons also betrayed an Arab influence. Arab, too, was the informality, the indifference to order, the delight in noise. People kept coming in and out, to greet the priest and go on their way. A janitor with ballooning trousers and an enormous Turkish mustache dyed in henna came from behind the altar screen with a small cup of coffee which he presented to the priest. I could not imagine this happening in the middle of a service in an American church, but it seemed perfectly natural here. An old white-bearded Arab came out of the sunlight, removed the headband of his keffiyeh, and began to kiss the icons passionately, making a smacking sound with his lips, then staring at each icon gravely, as at a familiar friend, before passing on to the next. Meanwhile the baptism went on, the baby yelling, the parents fussing over it, and the priest reading at great speed from an Arab text. There was no gravity, no unction in his voice. He was hugely enjoying himself, and so, I suspect, was everyone else in the church. Even the baby grew quiet at last, and then the priest took it in his arms and kissed it. He made a good smacking noise.

The bright lights, the smell of coffee, the children shouting, the janitor sitting cross-legged beneath the altar screen, the dark, strong-faced, vigorous priest raising his hands in benediction, and the old bent Arab who seemed intent on kissing every one of the hundred icons in the church—all these produced an effect of shattering incongruity. At first I thought something had gone hopelessly wrong, until I realized it was all hopefully right. There was a feeling of life flowing through the open doors. There were no stern creeds to be obeyed, only the joy of life. In that church there was nothing that suggested an austere, impenitent faith. Instead, there was kindness, gentleness, an overwhelming tenderness. There was a priest who looked like the young Jesus, and there were children who splashed their faces with water from a well and went running about with shining cheeks.

I suspect there are lessons to be learned from the Church of the Holy Gabriel at Nazareth, among them the very serious and important lesson of bringing gaiety back into Christian life. Studied gestures and unctuous voices are the death of faith. We need more informality. We need bright, garish pictures on the walls of our churches. We need to have children playing among the pews. We need to throw open the doors and to let the light in. The Church of the Holy Gabriel speaks with some authority in these matters, for it possesses the wellspring.

I went back again to the well, for the heat was still blazing outside and there would be no more slaking of thirst until we reached Galilee. The children had gone at last. It was very quiet there, among the bright tiles. Then for the first time I heard the murmur of the spring water, like someone singing very far away.

The light shone on the tiles, those greenish-blue squares set into the wall centuries ago, the gift of the Kings of Armenia when that country was a vassal of Jerusalem and allied to the Crusaders; and though they have faded a little and acquired pastel shades, the glimmering of these tiles was perfectly in keeping with the murmuring waters.

In the green grotto, in the glimmering light of the wellspring, it was easy enough to believe in the presence of angels.

Mount Tabor

Wherever you go in Israel, you are confronted with the furious poetry of names. The road signs are not like road signs elsewhere: they do not point simply to towns: they point to legends, visions, dreams, the places where prophets spoke and angels descended to earth. The fingerpost in the Valley of Hinnom says: TO MOUNT ZION, and it is almost beyond belief that you can climb from the Valley of Hinnom to Zion in about seventy steps, but it is so. Around the Sea of Galilee there is hardly a signpost which is not charged with emotions. The trucks roar past, the garagemen are at work, the farmers are in the fields, smoke rises from the factory chimneys, and life goes on almost as though no prophets or sages had ever walked these roads, and suddenly you come to a road sign which has the effect of a beacon light, and you are transported immediately into a legendary country where everything is larger than life, and more luminous. In this legendary country the air is full of angels.

Nazareth, Cana, Tabor, Sepphoris, Nain, Magdala, Capernaum and Tiberias are all within a day's walk of one another. Today we can roar through these places in automobiles, visiting all of them, if need be, in a morning, but it is pure recklessness to travel in this way. The donkey's pace is best: a slow amble, which gives you time to observe how the landscape changes its character every five hundred yards.

For what is chiefly surprising in this small corner of Galilee is the

132

quickly changing landscape. Nazareth is a soaring sharp-edged mountain, robust and flinty, with the long protecting shoulder of the Mount of the Precipitation sweeping before it. The shape of Nazareth is intensely masculine, but Tabor, only a few miles away, is gentle and rounded in a purely feminine way, rising like a green breast over the plain. Then beside the Sea of Galilee lies the Plain of Gennesaret like a long flowerbed stretching from the lake to the mountains, but the nearby Wadi Hammam, honeycombed with caves, is as ferocious and austere as the Judean wilderness. Here the desert and the sown lie side by side.

This meeting of many landscapes gives Galilee a quality of its own; it is as though all the worlds were set out before you, and you had only to saddle a donkey and by nightfall you would have passed through all of them. And because all these worlds lie so closely together, there is the sense of being in a closed universe. "*Galil*" means "circle." A man in Galilee has no need to travel outside his magic circle, for he can see everything in his own land—the sea, the mountains, the plains, the deserts. He can see it all in a moment of time if he stands on Mount Tabor.

When Arculf climbed Mount Tabor in the seventh century, he found on the top a pleasant meadow surrounded by thick woods, with a great monastery standing in the middle of the meadow. The woods and the meadow and the monastery are still there, though they have been fought over many times since Arculf's day. The mountain has been set on fire and everything on it destroyed, when the Sultan Baybars led his army from Egypt and established his camp at the bottom. A pilgrim coming to the mountain in A.D. 1283, twenty years after it was sacked by Baybars, found nothing but ruined palaces, cloisters and towers, and the dens of lions and other wild beasts. He may not have been exaggerating when he spoke of lions. Until quite recently leopards and hyenas prowled in those woods, and there seem to have been lions in Palestine until the late Middle Ages.

Beside the Franciscan basilica are fragments of the rough fortress walls of the Crusaders. From the topmost wall there is a stupendous view of the entire circle of Galilee. Northward lies Mount Hermon, ice-blue in the depths of summer, icecapped in winter, with the rolling

Galilean hills below; to the northeast a blue thimbleful of the Sea of Galilee; to the east the savage and sun-parched mountains of the Hauran beyond Jordan; south and west the Plain of Esdraelon where the armies of Deborah defeated the scythed, iron-sided chariots of Sisera. Carmel can be seen on the west, and Mount Gilboa on the east. Nazareth—the new Nazareth built on a sprawling mountain-top—can be seen clearly, no more than five miles away. From that high perch of the ruined Crusader fortress, mountains and plains seem to be in perpetual revolution, swimming in soft pastel shades of green and russet and purple and blue, wheeling into the distance. The world seems to be spinning away.

Climbing down from the Crusader wall and entering the basilica, all marble and alabaster, there is a sudden sense of security. The world is no longer spinning away. Under this vault anchored to the earth by heavy columns, one seems to be enclosed in an enormous white shell. The basilica has the color of a Christmas cake; one expects the icing to melt in the summer heat. There are no aisles. There is no transept, nothing to suggest the normal form of a basilica. Designed by Antonio Barluzzi, who was responsible for many of the cream and gold churches in the Holy Land, and modeled on the ancient churches of Byzantine Syria, it suggests an opulence which seems to be altogether out of keeping with the Transfiguration it is intended to commemorate. One expects something stark, brooding, urgent, the flash of sudden fire, the disciples falling in pure terror at the feet of Jesus whose face "did shine like the sun, and his raiment was white as the light." But there is only the pale white marble shell. Towards sunset light pours through an alabaster screen above the doorway onto the mosaic figure of Jesus above the altar. There comes a moment when the face is illumined with the trembling colors of the dying sun. Then gradually the light vanishes, and the basilica becomes a vast cave haunted by shadows.

In the old days men climbed on their knees up four thousand steps to reach the top of Mount Tabor. Today there is a motor road with seventeen hairpin bends, and the climb is made in ten minutes. I prefer the modern way. To come freshly to that high Crusader wall and to see all Galilee stretching below is to know magnificence. The Transfiguration is beyond all human comprehension, but Galilee once seen is a possession which remains for the rest of one's life.

CANA

The Arab boys were running through the small, huddled streets of Kefar Kannah, shouting at the top of their voices. They were moving their arms and their dark faces were alight with happiness. Some slithered over the low walls between the hollyhocks and the pomegranate trees, while others emerged from houses which seemed to have been boarded up and shuttered centuries ago. Something of momentous importance had happened, and they were all hurrying breathlessly to see it. No one had sounded the alarm. In the mysterious way of children they knew they must hurry to the spot.

We thought there had been a fire, or perhaps one of their comrades had fallen and hurt himself, or perhaps a dog had gone ravening mad—there was so much excitement in the air, so much flaying of arms, so much eagerness in their faces, that anything less was unthinkable. But in fact, when we made our way through the crowd of wildly excited children, who had come from all parts of the town, and who were still coming, we discovered that the excitement was caused by a chameleon. It was very large, very old and very gaunt. One of the boys had found it, and was proudly showing it. It was swaying on top of a cardboard box, terrified out of its wits by the incessant shouting and the faces peering at it. The crowd was pressing close, and there was the danger that the chameleon would fall from the box and be squashed under their feet.

Evidently chameleons are not found every day in Kefar Kannah. This very large, ungainly, gray-mottled chameleon looked as though he had been hibernating for centuries and would gladly hibernate for a few more centuries. There were no insects in sight, and so the long tongue did not unroll. The chameleon only trembled and shifted about on the cardboard box, which was too small for it, so that the long tail overhung the box. Everyone was looking at it and studying it, as though it were some wild beast in captivity. So for about five minutes all the boys of the village feasted on the spectacle, and then they gradually lost interest in it. When the crowd melted away, the boy who had discovered the chameleon simply dropped it inside his shirt and went whistling on his way.

We saw the boy later when we were trying to enter the Greek Orthodox Church. He was about twelve, with a lean intelligent face and enormous dark eyes, but the most extraordinary thing about him was a kind of rippling gaiety. He was always laughing quietly, amused by everything. He was amused when we asked him how we could enter the church, and ran off gaily to return with a key almost as large as himself. And since there was not very much to see in the church except two old and worn stone jars, neither of which could hold more than half a gallon of wine, though it was claimed that they were the authentic jars used by Jesus to turn water into wine, the boy was more amused than ever to see us wandering about the church, which was rarely visited. From time to time he would peer inside his shirt and smile broadly at the chameleon.

With the air of a young prince escorting foreign ambassadors through his city, the boy led us to the Catholic Church, which also claims to be the site of the miracle of turning water into wine. He pattered around in his bare feet, pointing to the Victorian paintings of the Marriage at Cana, the dark crypt where the marriage feast was perhaps held, the two stone pitchers for which no claims are made: they had simply been placed there to show the kind of pitchers used in the time of Jesus. The church has an imposing façade, but the interior is disappointing. Once a great basilica covered the site. It was built by Count Joseph of Tiberias and survived well into the eighteenth century. A visitor in A.D. 1654 spoke of it as an immense ruin, though the columns were still standing. On a large stone three pitchers had been carved, and there was an inscription proclaiming that it was on this stone that the miracle was performed. The stone has vanished. In time the basilica became a mosque. On its ruins the Franciscans in 1881 built the present church, occupying about a third of the space of the basilica. Some small traces of the ancient basilica remain: a fragment of a mosaic pavement, an inscription in Aramaic, the bases of marble columns and a collection of dusty earthenware lamps which are kept in a cupboard.

The truth is that Cana is not very rewarding. The buses loaded with pilgrims and tourists roar past it on their way to the Sea of Galilee. The guide says, "There is nothing in Cana," and shrugs his shoulders. Perhaps he is right. There are heavy grapes ripening in the courtyards; the mud huts rest on Crusader arches; and in every house there is an ancient water jar which may, for all we know, be as old as Jesus. But now it is scarcely more than a quiet village sunning itself on the slope of a hill, with the red dome of the Greek church rising above honey-colored walls and jungles of pomegranates.

The Arab boy patted his shirt and smiled gaily, his quick eager face alive with pleasure. Soon he would find another animal, and all the boys of Cana would come running after him.

Some days later, in the gray dusk, I passed through Cana again. A girl in a tattered red gown with gold coins tinkling on her headdress was riding on a donkey beside the road, and women balancing gasoline tins full of water were making their way up the steep slope. An old man with a white beard was sitting cross-legged outside his house, smoking a water pipe and looking across the valley. Like the old man, the little village was lost in its dreams.

Tíberías

When only eighty years ago the English traveler John Newman rode down from Mount Tabor to make his way to Tiberias, he found more excitement than he expected. It was one of those bright gusty days when the air is invigorating and transparently pure, and he had enjoyed the spectacle of the blue lake set among the yellow mountains, and most of all he was drunk with the knowledge that he had stood on the rocks where the Transfiguration took place. But the descent was dangerous, his horse stumbled on the rocks, and when he passed through an Arab village at the foot of the mountain three mounted Bedouin armed with swords, pistols and twenty-foot lances wheeled past with blood-curdling cries and then charged him, the sharp points of their lances aimed at his breast. Faith upheld him, and the Bedouin, seeing that he was indifferent to death, left him severely alone, riding off discomfited to their miserable hovels.

As a bishop of the Methodist Church John Newman was accustomed to such occasional miracles. He was a small, sandy-haired man with a long beard and enormous eyes, and he was enjoying his visit to Palestine. He trusted everyone, and was especially fond of the Arabs. On Mount Tabor he had asked the way to Tiberias from a friendly Arab, and it never occurred to him that he was falling into a trap. For the rest of the afternoon he found himself plunging from

138

one wild, uninhabited gorge to another, climbing up mountains, descending into the gorges again. He was hopelessly lost. By midafternoon the skies were black with the coming storm, and by evening in the darkness, without knowing it, he was somewhere near the northern tip of the lake. He came upon two Arabs in a barley field, who told him Tiberias was half an hour to the north. The storm roared overhead. The rain was coming down, he had no more food, every torrent had become a flood, and he was already exhausted by the long journey when through some unknown valley, near midnight, he saw the Sea of Galilee. There in the early hours of the morning he pitched a tent and looked across the water at the glimmering lights of Tiberias, untroubled by anything except the sudden leap of a jackal or the startled flight of a stork. The next morning, after a short sleep, he entered Tiberias.

In those days Tiberias was still a walled city. It was a heavy wall of black basalt, nearly four times the height of a man, with some thirty watchtowers, arranged in a great square along the shores of the lake. From a distance it gave an impression of power and purposefulness, but once inside the gates he found winding lanes of muddy hovels, most of them crumbling away, and half of them untenanted. The Turkish pasha had a fine house, and the mosque was kept in good repair. Ten thousand people could have lived comfortably within the walls, but there were barely two thousand, and of these perhaps eight hundred were Jews living in a small walled ghetto on the lake shore. He was puzzled by the air of desolation, and he might have been less puzzled if he had known that fifty years before Tiberias had been leveled by an earthquake. He was especially struck by the appearance of the Jews. Though they lived under Turkish rule, they held themselves proudly, the boys being manly and athletic, and the girls surprisingly beautiful. The sky had cleared by the time he reached the city gate, and the first sight that greeted him was a crowd of "white-veiled Jewesses and of venerable Jews, with long gray beards, slowly winding their way up the mountains that rise steeply behind the city, to offer their prayers at the sepulchres of Rabbis Johanan, Akiba, Maimonides, and others of their ancestors."

He noted in his diary that the Jews firmly believed the Messiah would make His first appearance on the lake, then step forth into Tiberias to proclaim Himself before establishing His throne at Safed.

John Newman was an observant traveler who thoroughly enjoyed his blundering progress in Palestine. He rarely got anywhere on time, he was always losing his way, and he seems to have been one of those people who prefer to rely on their instincts rather than on maps. Until he reached Tiberias, he had no very great respect for Jews. Then, quite suddenly, seeing that small handsome community devoted to their ancient traditions, fervently believing that the Messiah would step through the rubble of their streets, he fell in love with them. The bearded elders and the white-veiled Jewesses climbing the mountain in the sunlit morning were to haunt him for the rest of his life.

Today there is little left of the city he saw. The great black walls have fallen down, leaving only a few decorative towers behind. The pasha's house has vanished, and the mosque is in ruins. The huddled streets of the old Turkish city were torn down long ago, and there is nowhere any sign of the small ghetto where the Jews were locked in each night. Today on the site of the ghetto there are open-air cafés under the flame-of-the-forest trees, gardens, wide streets. They have let the air in, and the most imposing building is the bus station.

Of ancient Tiberias only the tombs of the rabbis remain to remind you that this is one of the four sacred cities of the Jews. And what rabbis they were! The most stupendous names in rabbinical history are congregated in Tiberias. There is Johanan ben Zakkei, the founder of the great academy at Yavne, who at the time of the destruction of Jerusalem by the Romans in A.D. 70 was smuggled out of the city in a coffin. There is the great Akiba, who almost singlehandedly put together the vast commentaries of the Mishna and died a martyr's death in Caesarea after giving his benediction to the revolt of Simon bar Kokba against the Romans, believing to the last that Simon was the appointed Messiah, the star which would lead to the rebirth of Israel. They said of Akiba that he was the laborer who went forth into the fields and filled his basket with spelt and lentils and barley during the day, and at night he carefully sorted them; and that was how the Mishna came into being. Once when he was asked what God had been doing since the day of creation, he replied smiling, "He has been arranging marriages." Then there was Rabbi Meir, known as "the miracle worker," who was regarded as a saint in his lifetime. His two sons both died suddenly during a Sabbath afternoon when he was attending the synagogue. In the evening, when he returned to the house, his wife asked him what he would do if someone, having lent him a great treasure, returned to claim it. Rabbi Meir answered, "Of course it must be given back to him." Then his wife took his hand and led him to the bed where the two boys lay, and she removed the sheet from them. The rabbi wept, but he grew silent again when his wife said, "The Lord has given and the Lord has taken away; blessed be the name of the Lord."

These were great rabbis, renowned in their time and through all succeeding generations, but they were not the only ones to be buried in Tiberias. Among the greatest was Rabbi Moshe ben Maimuni, whom we know as Maimonides, of whom it was said that "from Moses the Prophet to Moses the son of Maimuni there have arisen none like unto him." When he died in A.D. 1204, he had contrived a vast synthesis of Aristotelian philosophy and Jewish theology; and that sharp, pungent intellect, burning with a peculiarly Spanish fire—for he was born in Cordova, and there was something of the Spaniard in him to the end—has left an impress on Jewish thought which can never be effaced. At different times in his life he was a trader in precious stones and a physician: an admirable combination, for his jeweled style was tempered by his physician's humanity, and both style and humanity were tempered by an unyielding love of God. He was almost the last of the universal philosophers. He knew all the sciences of his time and possessed a special affection for astronomy, saying he learned more about God from looking at the stars than from anything else. Not the strangest thing about him was that he became the physician of Saladin, and served the Arab prince as faithfully as he served the Jews. He lies in a white tomb in a small walled garden near the center of Tiberias, with the tombs of other famous rabbis nearby. It is a very odd place indeed, for there is no grass, only rubble, and at first I thought I had come into a building yard. The bearded guardians of the tomb recite prayers on everyone who enters, but since they clamor for baksheesh with a sound like the croaking of vultures, winged reptiles flapping their heavy sleeves, it is pardonable to wonder whether their prayers are effective.

Akiba has his white shrine halfway up the hills in a place that was once desolate, though now the new Jewish town is crowding close to it. Rabbi Meir is luckier; his white marble tomb lies close to the lake shore near the hot springs in an airy, white-domed building which also serves as a Talmudic school. It is a pleasant place with wide windows, the walls painted green and white, spacious and full of light, resembling a small palace overlooking the lake, a perfect house for a saint. There is a stone pillar supporting a large bowl in one of the courtyards. There every year during the festival of Pesah Sheni, the "second Passover," a huge bonfire is lit. This year half the courtyard went up in flames, and the storerooms were reduced to charred embers. "It was a wonderful fire," one of the Talmudic students said. "But think what might have happened to Rabbi Meir!"

The great rabbi has two tombs, but since he was a miracle-worker, this is not particularly surprising. They said of him that he was an ugly man with deep-set eyes with a fierce fire glowing in them. He earned a bare living by his beautiful penmanship, copying holy texts, and he invented a new copying ink by adding copper vitriol to lampblack. They say too that he died on his feet, laughing and singing and declaring that death was the greatest of all experiences and he welcomed it gladly. What is especially remembered of him is his fierce tenderness towards all suffering things. "The divine splendor," he once wrote, "cries out in anguish whenever a man suffers punishment." So the suffering come to his tomb and pray, and the sick lie beside the tomb, waiting for him to cure them. Of the two tombs one lies in the Sephardic part of the building, and the other in the Ashkenazi part. One of the tombs is of marble, and almost as large as that of Napoleon at Les Invalides. Through wide windows you can see the lake. In this room the doves are cooing, and there is a feeling of enduring peace.

THE SENSE OF HISTORY

I came back again and again to Tiberias, for of all the towns of Israel I found it the most rewarding. It was not only that it was the most suitable center for exploring all the Christian sites around the Sea of Galilee, and had the best hotel, and the best surf-riding, but it also possessed a singular attraction of its own in those shady streets, where nothing seemed to happen and life followed an ageless ritual. It was as though there had been no wars, as though history and legend had never touched the city.

So I would read Josephus and listen to his account of the bloody wars he had fought in the neighborhood of Tiberias, and how almost singlehandedly he had arrested nearly the entire population of the city when it revolted against his authority, and how he had once torn down the great palace of Herod Antipas because of the images of animals appearing on its walls, but these stories were almost beyond belief. Then I would read how the Jewish scholars settled in Tiberias so that the city acquired a reputation for towering scholarship, and then came the Arabs and the Crusaders and the Turks, and then there was Allenby's army and the Israelis marching over the hills to capture it only a few years ago. Blood had been spilt on every stone of the city. Saladin had stood at its gates, and the bleeding heads of Crusaders had been used as footballs in its gardens. But in all the days I was there, it never showed the least sign of being conscious of its past. It defied history; it had known so much of it.

There were the pepper trees and the softly waving palms, and the boys diving into the lake, and the ocher hills of Syria in the distance, and it was enough to sit by the lakeside, to eat and drink, to watch the petals fall. The truth was that Tiberias was bathed in the magic of the lake, and at this low altitude, nearly seven hundred feet below sea level, all the normal laws of thought and behavior are held in abeyance. It was perfectly natural to believe that the Messiah would come walking across the lake, robed in jewels, wearing a crown of heavenly fire, while the lightning played from His five-sworded hands. It was even natural to believe that He would come on a clear day, and no one would pay very much attention: the carpenters would go on with their work, and the scholars would continue to debate the absorbing problem of the coming of the Messiah, while He rose into the air above their heads. There was something wonderfully hallucinatory about that lakeside. I do not know what it is like in winter, but I know that in summer a man can get drunk simply by looking at it.

Tiberias rides the lake like a ship at anchor, a small white city, scarcely more than a village, floating in the shallows. Like Peking, it is drowned in trees, and like Peking, too, it possesses large acres which are barren and unprofitable. There are new jerry-built shops. There is the huge and preposterously ugly bus station. A creamy white mosque sheltered by flame-of-the-forest trees stands by the lake shore; it has been converted into a museum which is rarely opened. If you succeed in opening it, you will find three or four tablets filled with Greek inscriptions and a rack of fly-spotted postcards, thus proving, if any proof were needed, that Tiberias is indifferent to her history.

The truth is that the real history of Tiberias has little enough to do with wars or the great palace built by Herod Antipas in A.D. 19. The palace was destroyed less than forty years later, and it would be a waste of time to search for a thing that had so short a life. No, the real history is in the legends and anecdotes told about the city: the footsteps of the Messiah on the waters, the sayings of the Jewish sages, the old pronouncements of Arab travelers, the traditions invented out of the whole cloth by medieval pilgrims. "In this city," wrote Sir John Mandeville, "a man cast a burning dart in wrath after our Lord, and the head smote into the earth, and waxed green, and it grew to a great tree; and it grows still, and the bark thereof is all like coals." Tiberias is a place where legends grow effortlessly. "Who is the ruler of Tiberias?" asked a Jewish sage, and answered: "Why, who else but Beelzebub, the lord of flies?"

The tradition that Tiberias possessed some uncanny connection with Beelzebub is long-standing. It must have been a fairly insalubrious city a thousand years ago. Mukaddasi, the Arab geographer, visited it about A.D. 985, and it amused him to recite a kind of lexicon of the popular pastimes:

Of the people of Tiberias it is said that for two months they dance, and for two more they gorge, and for the next two months they beat the air, and for two more they go about naked, and then for the following two months they play the flute, and for two more months they wallow.

The explanation of all this is that they dance from the number of fleas, and then they gorge off the fruit of the lotus, and then they beat the air with fly-whisks to chase away the wasps from the meat and the fruit, and then they go naked from the heat, and then they suck the sugar-canes, and then they wallow in the muddy streets.

Mud, flies, fleas, wasps, none of these were in evidence during those summer days. The fishing boats were at anchor, the lake was a liquid sapphire, the air was pure and sweet. Once a day a small steamship crossed the lake to the *kibbuts* at Ein Gev on the eastern shore. Sometimes a speedboat would flash across the lake and then vanish. Everything was clean, quiet, unhurried. Only with difficulty could one bring oneself to believe that a war was being fought around the lake. On one of the leafy lanes of Tiberias, parked under a eucalyptus tree, there was a white U.N. car belonging to the Armistice Commission. Occasionally an armed patrol boat belonging to Israel would streak out towards the opposite shore. You would open a newspaper and read that a tractor belonging to the settlement at Ein Gev had been fired at from a Syrian outpost. It was like reading something that was happening a thousand miles away, but in fact the war was being fought six miles away. The fire was low, but at any moment it would burst into flame again.

So in time the lake acquires even to the occasional traveler a mythical character. War and peace, history and legend, the Messiah who has arrived and the Messiah who is yet to come, the traditions of the sages and of the apostles, all come together here in the radiance of the lake. There is no escaping from that radiance. Once you have seen it you will be its slave forever. It will haunt your dreams. In the bustle of a New York street, or in the subway, or when telephones are jangling, you will find yourself magically transported to the lake, and life will be sweet again.

THE FISHERMEN OF THE LAKE

I had spent the afternoon wandering over the Horns of Hittin, trying to make out the course of the battle which took place there in the hot summer of A.D. 1187 between the Moslem armies under Saladin and the Crusaders under Guy de Lusignan, King of Jerusalem. It was a decisive battle, and the Crusaders never recovered from their defeat. But on those windswept heights overlooking the Sea of Galilee, among the high boulders and forests of dry rustling thistles, the ruins of a synagogue and of an ancient Canaanite city, it was not easy to make out where the armies met, and by what trails the surviving Crusaders made their way to the coast. All over the mountain there were skirmishes, and the most important seem to have taken place in the hollow between the horns, where there are two or three acres of level ground. Here the Moslems had set fire to the scrub, and the Crusaders vanished among the heavy clouds of smoke and the golden flames. Here, or very close by, the True Cross had been erected for the first and last time within sight of the Sea of Galilee, while the Crusaders were butchered all round. Saladin went on to conquer most of the Holy Land.

The battle of the Horns of Hittin was one of the great decisive battles of the world, but there was no memorial of the battle, nothing to suggest that centuries of history came to an end on those barren heights. There were trenches here and there, with parapets built of great boulders, and littered in the dry grass were fragments of marble, perhaps from the ancient synagogue. No roads, not even sheep tracks, wandered across the mountain: only the barrenness, and the dry rustle of grasses underfoot. So I went down the mountain in the gathering dusk, and it was dark when I reached the small port of Minya near Tiberias, a stone's throw away from a ruined Moslem caravanserai. The fishermen were preparing for the night's fishing.

There was a time not long ago when white-sailed fishing boats hovered gracefully over the lake, and the fishermen simply threw their nets overboard and waited for God's bounty. Those times are changed. Today the fishermen on the Sea of Galilee are equipped with boats which run on diesel engines, and they do not scan the sea for signs of fish: they watch the electronic echo-sounding machines which record in brown ink on a revolving drum the presence or absence of shoals of fish. Now, as in the past, they fish mostly at night, with bright flares to attract the fish. The best fishing grounds are near the Syrian border, and the flares sometimes attract the attention of Syrian machine gunners in the hills.

There was no moon when we steamed out of the small harbor. The small pilot boat with the echo-sounding machine led three rowing boats in tow, each with its acetylene flare hanging over the stern: they were like silver pools of fire bobbing in the inky darkness: and far away, with red and green lights flashing, came the boat with the derricks and winches for hauling in the nets. There was only the dark lake and the low mountains, and here and there the ghostly glimmering of lights along the coast. The wind was whipping across the lake, and the stars were very clear.

In the pilot boat Franz Cohen stood at the wheel. He was a lean, sunburned man with quick movements and large capable hands. He was about forty, but there were already deep lines on his face. He smiled easily, and for some reason it amused him to have a passenger on that small pilot boat where there was no room to move about. He had to shout above the fierce rattling of the diesel engines to make himself heard.

From time to time he threw a bright light on the revolving drum of the echo-sounding machine.

"There won't be much of a catch tonight," he said. "It's something to do with the drought—we've had five months of drought. Sardines, yes, but not many catfish or comb fish. You know the comb fish. They are called St. Peter's fish and they are mouthbreeders. They are a strange fish and are found in the Sea of Galilee and in the Nile as far south as Tanganyika, but nowhere else, so far as I know. Carp, too. They spill over into the lake from the ponds where they are specially cultivated." He shook his head sadly. "It has been a bad year, though."

"You'll have a good catch tonight," I said.

He looked up sharply. "How do you know?"

"I don't know, but I'm sure you'll have a good catch."

He shrugged his shoulders and stared at the recorder where there were only a few faint brown pencil lines indicating the presence of very small concentrations of fish. Behind us the three rowing boats were waving in the darkness of the lake, the bright acetylene flares blazing. We had lost sight of the boat with the derricks and the green nets heaped neatly on the deck. We passed Tabgha and Capernaum, and very faintly we could see the nearby cliffs of Syria.

He said without any bitterness, "They've used cannon to shell our fishing boats. They have come out on their launches, machine-gunned our men and then made off with the catch. Only three months ago they killed one of our fishermen, and he had a wife and five children."

"Why do you go on fishing if it is so dangerous?"

"Because someone has to fish in the lake, and because the lake belongs to us."

He had turned off the engine. We were coasting now along the Syrian shore. The brown pencil lines were growing thicker, and he had decided to anchor one of the rowing boats: the bright acetylene flare would keep the fish from swimming away, and later in the night they would throw the net around the rowing boat. So the pattern of the night's fishing was established: first the anchoring of the rowing boat and then the long wait until the nets were dropped and speedily gathered in. For the next hour the small pilot boat zigzagged across the lake, searching for concentrations of fish, for a place to anchor the remaining rowing boats with their dazzling flares. The wind was coming up and the lake seemed immense. Far away we could see the lights of Tiberias climbing up the side of a mountain.

By midnight he had found three widely separated places in the lake where the echo-sounding machine recorded small concentrations of fish. He said mockingly, "You say one thing and the machine says another. Do you still think there is going to be a good catch?"

"Yes."

He said, "I trust the machine. It's a German one and cost only $300, but it has never made a mistake. What do the Gloucester fishermen use?"

"Radarscopes that cost $5,000."

He whistled under his breath.

"Do they work well—do they get good catches?"

"Yes, they get good catches."

He sighed, and then turned on the headlights to signal to the boat with the derricks. We were just off Capernaum now, and we could see the monastery faintly through the trees.

"We do pretty well with what we have," he said, grinning. "We make a living. Probably not much of a living by the standards of American fishermen, but each of us makes about $2,000 a year, and that's all right. We are all members of a cooperative, and we share what we get. But for months we have had very little from the lake —but the new season is starting."

"How many seasons are there?"

"None, really. We fish all the year round, and so there are no seasons. We find some fish every night, even if it is only a few sardines. But it is best in the middle of summer and the middle of winter. So we talk of the winter and summer seasons. We make a living, and we ask for no more."

By this time the last of the rowing boats had been anchored, and it was time to return to the first. It was strange to be steaming across the lake without having those brilliantly lit boats in tow, to be free of them. Also, it was good to be alone in the dark with only the small pilot lights showing, no longer a target for the Syrians in the hills. The stars were paling in the night mists, and the lake seemed to be growing darker every minute.

Then far away we saw the first rowing boat and heard very faintly the humming of the acetylene lamp. The boat with the derricks had come up and already the fishermen were paying out the enormous green net with the orange floats, so that it formed a circle around the blazing lamp. So there was a pool of intense bluish-silver light rimmed with the orange floats, and within this circle everything was clear as on a sunny day, and beyond lay the thick darkness of the lake. I slipped off the pilot boat and spent the rest of the night on the boat with the derricks.

These fishermen came from all around the lake. They worked silently, for they knew each other so well that there was little reason to speak. The winches rattled, and then grew silent, and the men stood there in the brilliant incandescent light, unmoving, waiting for the net to fill with its load of fish, gazing into the silver pool around the rowboat rocking gently in the waves; and there was something sculptural in their unmoving silence as they waited. Far away we could see the lights of the pilot boat zigzagging across the lake, making its electronic soundings.

It struck me that for perhaps three thousand years men had fished in the Sea of Galilee by simply casting their nets overboard. Now electric impulses were searching out the presence of the fish, and there were derricks and winches to haul the nets in and out of the water, and even the shape of the nets had changed in the past few years. The nets were purse seines developed on Yugoslav models some ten years ago, when the Israelis and the Yugoslavs were closer to one another than they are now. So Yugoslav fishermen and German engineers were affecting the destiny of the lake.

So they waited, watching the brilliant circle of light while the wind rose, and at last the winches were set in motion and the net was hauled up until it was mast-high, forming a green tent spangled with small silver fish caught in the meshes, and afterwards came the swollen purse, all silver, crammed with small slithering fish, and these were spilled into the rowing boat. There were a few catfish, dark silver and menacing, but mostly they were very small fish. The catfish died quickly, but the sardines continued to leap about the rowing boat for three or four minutes.

For the rest of the night the boat with the derricks went in search of the small illuminated rowing boats. Again and again the purse seines were payed into the water and the fish were pulled in. About midnight came the first big hauls, and thereafter there seemed to be nothing but huge, ugly catfish filling the rowing boats. In the gray dawn, with the best catch of the season, we sailed into the harbor of Minya.

A few days later, when I had left Israel, I read in the newspaper that another fisherman had been killed by Syrians while fishing in the northeast corner of the Sea of Galilee.

THE NIGHT OF TIBERIAS

The sun was curving to the crest of the dark ridge, and the lake was changing to the color of molten lead. It was one of those evenings when you expected a storm to arise, for the day had been unbearably hot, and suddenly the temperature had dropped, and there was a hush in the air. But there was no storm, only the fresh wind blowing across the lake, and the shadows falling. I thought the air would gradually grow darker, but it did not. As the sun dipped behind the hills, a strange orange glow lit the whole lake, the mountains became incandescent, and rose-red streamers were spinning across the sky. The air, the mountains and the lake were all on fire.

I have seen sunsets on the Hungarian plains and off the seas of Java which were like cascades of jeweled angels flinging themselves across the sky, but the sunsets of Tiberias were quieter, softer, altogether more gentle. There was no seething and boiling over of light, no stupendous bonfire. The whole lake and all the mountains around opened like a rose, and remained open. The orange glow melted into white and gold, and then scarlet, and then a fiery purple lit with scarlet ribbons, but even then there was no sense of turmoil. The light seemed to well up from the earth and the lake. Long after the sun set, the glow remained.

It was the same, night after summer night: that calm glow in the sky, the shimmering radiance over the lake, the sense of a stupendous drama being performed silently, peacefully. One came to expect it. It was in the nature of things that the curtain should rise every evening on this calm fire. And afterwards, until the moon rose, this golden-red glow seemed to hover over the dark city, which was built on an ancient graveyard by Herod Antipas and was haunted by innumerable ghosts.

But wandering through the shuttered streets at night, you are not aware of the ghosts. You hear the whispering of the willows and the eucalyptus leaves, and the laughter coming from the alleyways which run down to the lake. I had thought there would be innumerable fishing boats with bright acetylene lamps shining on the lake, but usually the only lights came from Ein Gev on the opposite shore, very faint in the distance. There came the scent of jasmine, filling the cool night air, and from somewhere in the hills came the low barking of jackals. The city was quiet, but there was a quivering excitement everywhere.

When the moon rose, the dogs barked, and it was almost daylight again. The curved white domes of abandoned mosques sprang out of the darkness, and the broken columns south of the city soaked in the moonlight. The lake became the color of milk. Mysterious by day, Tiberias was even more mysterious by night. When an automobile appeared, driving along the coastal road, it resembled a visitor from another planet. What was an automobile doing among ruined mosques beside a lake of milk?

Night and day Tiberias seemed to be a city which belonged to legend, outside history altogether. Tiberias was a Druse in white robes wandering along a deserted street at night, his face hidden in the folds of his keffiyeh. Tiberias was a cloud of wild doves hovering over the lake in the dawn. Tiberias was the olive-skinned girl in the red-flowered dress who calmly jumped into the lake when the sun was raging through the pepper trees, letting her dark hair flow and ripple over the water. Tiberias was the Messiah walking across the lake every morning and every evening.

The only surprising thing about Tiberias was that it was marked on the maps.

The Sea of Galilee

In ancient times all the hills around the Sea of Galilee must have been thickly wooded. "The whole region excels in crops and cattle," Josephus tells us, "and there is an abundance of forests of every kind." He speaks of the great forests of "winter-loving" walnut trees, the great clumps of palms, the vast acres covered by figs and olives, and how every inch of Galilee was cultivated by peasants who were so determined to safeguard their rich lands from invaders that they acquired the reputation of being rebels. According to Josephus there was so much natural abundance that the smallest towns had a population of fifteen thousand people. The modern commentators raise their eyebrows, and assure us that he was boasting, for he was himself a Galilean, and became governor of Galilee, and was inclined to praise his own land above others.

But was he boasting? Others beside Josephus have spoken of the fabulous richness of the soil. There must have been forests above Magdala, for Vespasian found enough timber there to build a flotilla of warships, and we know of the ilex and myrtle jungles from the poems of Meleager, who was all the more Greek for being a Galilean. Today, there is scarcely a thornbush on the rocky slopes above Magdala, and wherever you look there are only the barren reddish-colored hills. There are deserts near Galilee which are more awful than the Negev or the wilderness of Judea. Arculf, in the

153

seventh century, echoes Josephus and speaks of the woods coming down to the lake. Today, here and there, you come upon fig trees and pomegranates, walnuts, almonds, apricots, peaches, apple and lemon trees which perfume the air. The soil is still rich, though centuries of misuse have destroyed the trees. Now all around the lake the sprinklers are at work, gradually bringing health back to the soil. Only the Syrian hills rise bleakly gray and ocher in the distance, barren and burned out like a lunar landscape.

With the woods coming down to the lake on all sides, it must have been even more magical. We know how much men loved the lake from the names they gave it. It was the Bride, the Silver Woman, the Handmaiden of the Hills, the Blue Harp. Many other names were given to the lake. The Sea of Gennesaret, the Sea of Ginnesar, the Sea of Kinneret, the Sea of Tiberias which became Bahr Tubariyeh in Arabic, and the Sea of Taricheae, which is only the Greek name of Magdala, and means "the place where the fish is smoked." Probably all the big towns along the coast regarded the lake as their own, and gave it their own name. And there is an old Jewish legend that God also regarded the lake as His own, for "God created the seven seas, but the Sea of Galilee was His special delight."

Over the lake the swallows fly, white breasts and red throats flashing in the sun, and the jeweled kingfishers skim the surface, and the painted crabs, emerald and rose and purple and indigo, scurry out of their tunnels and glide among the pebbles, being themselves pebbles with the power of motion; and some are spotted with gold, others with silver. Then there are oleanders covered with pink blossoms, and every blossom has a candle inside it, for it is a more luminous pink than you see elsewhere. In winter the rains come. Then in the space of a few hours the hills are covered with silky anemones, about the size of buttercups, in all the colors of the rainbow. There are lilies and thornbush thickets, and dom trees which give little enough shade to the black goats huddled beneath them. Sometimes it seems that the Sea of Galilee is the nearest thing to Paradise on earth.

CAPERNAUM

From Tiberias it is only a short ride to Capernaum along the shore. In a grove of eucalyptus trees stands the spectacular synagogue with pure white columns and Corinthian capitals, with wide steps leading up to it, and all the forecourt littered with the debris of more fluted Hellenistic columns lying where they fell after an earthquake. Graven on the stones are olive branches and vine clusters, pomegranates, the Star of David and the seven-branched candlestick; there are even swastikas. There is no doubt that it is a synagogue, but as you come to it, you wonder what that small Greek temple is doing beside the lake. The superb façade would be even more wonderful if there were no high wall cutting it off from the lake: then you would see the flashing of the lake water mirrored on the columns.

Still, the synagogue exists, thanks to the German archaeologists who excavated it and put the pieces together, but is it the synagogue of Capernaum? It is pleasant to imagine that it is the synagogue built by the Roman centurion, where Jesus taught and prayed and cured the sick, and there is no harm in imagining that the circle of stones in the courtyard represents the foundations of Peter's house, though it is odd that the house should stand so abruptly between the synagogue and the lake. Unfortunately, the synagogue by its general design cannot be earlier than the second century A.D., and Peter's house is a circle of stones, and nothing more. As for Capernaum, no one is quite sure where it was, though there is some reason for believing it must have been somewhere near. Somewhere along that shore, buried under a shallow layer of gray crumbling soil, is Capernaum. But where?

The German archaeologists were quite sure they had found Capernaum, and they pointed to a passage in an account written by St. Sylvia in the fourth century as demonstrative proof of their discovery. St. Sylvia wrote that she had seen in Capernaum the ruined walls of an ancient church which had been built over Peter's house. "Here also," she added, "can be seen the synagogue where Jesus cured the demoniac: it is built of cut stone, and reached by many steps." The archaeologists wrote in their report: "We have no doubt that this pilgrim visited Capernaum; for of all the synagogues discovered in Galilee, that of Capernaum is the only one to which one ascends by a flight of steps."

The truth is, of course, that all synagogues in the second century were built on Hellenistic models, and were usually provided with steps. Synagogues took the form of Greek temples, subtly modified, with mosaics and columns and rich entablatures, and nothing at all can be deduced from the fact that there are steps leading up to the columns at Capernaum.

We can guess at the wealth of the towns along the lake shore from those four imposing columns with their delicate Corinthian capitals. They are neither high nor powerful; they are impressive as elaborate jewelry is impressive; and they are clearly the work of metropolitan craftsmen employed by a rich mercantile community. It has been suggested that they may have been built by the masons who had previously built Hadrian's Aelia Capitolina, and it is difficult to know where else they could have come from. Everything about that courtyard suggests a sumptuous elegance.

Today the synagogue stands in a bed of quietness, at the end of the road. The wind moves in the tamarisks and the eucalyptus trees, and the lake water laps the shore, and the courtyard sleeps. From time to time busloads of pilgrims descend, and for a few minutes there is a wild scrambling for positions and the high-pitched voice of a guide announces that this is indeed the synagogue where Jesus preached, and here or hereabouts He raised the child of Jairus from the dead, and St. Peter's house is truly over there. Then the pilgrims scuttle away, and the courtyard resumes its sleep, to the relief of the barefoot Franciscan monk who puffs on a cigarette and smiles happily to have the place to himself again. He lives alone in a vast monastery which could hold a hundred monks, and sometimes he seemed the most enviable of all the enviable people who live on the shores of the lake.

His black gown flapping among the ruins, he would point quietly to this or that stone, explaining which was authentic, which had been reworked, which was a product of German imagination. He thought St. Peter's house might have been the hut of a twelfth-century fisherman, and he marveled at the assurance of the guides.

"They know it all," he smiled, "and I—I who live here—know so little."

We walked in silence for a while until we came to a high stone wall. With some difficulty it was possible to climb on the wall and look out over fields of wild waving grass towards the red dome of a Greek church lost beyond the walls of the synagogue.

I was standing on the wall and photographing the church when the priest put his arms round my legs.

"Better come down," he said. "You don't know how dangerous it is!"

I came down.

"Why is it dangerous?"

"Because the Syrians are only a few hundred yards away. Those fields are no-man's land. Besides, the Syrians like to shoot, and they are only too good at it. Only a few weeks ago an American woman wandered out over those fields. The Syrians killed her in broad daylight."

He shook his head and made the sign of the cross. He had one of those lean, sculptured faces which you see sometimes on Roman coins; and the face crumpled with the agony of that memory.

"They go on shooting all the time," he said a little later. "Why do they have to kill in the place where Jesus promised eternal life?"

As we wandered among the ruins he talked about the pilgrims: how they were always trying to invade his monastery, and how he was always having to shoo them away; and like St. Gregory of Nyssa, who inveighed against the habits of pilgrims in the fourth century, he was uncertain whether any high degree of merit accrued to them. On the whole he thought pilgrimages did more good than harm, but not much more. He was especially annoyed by the women who came in shorts. "And what a terrible noise they make! Oh, the noise!"

I am not sure that he is justified in complaining about the noise. It must have been much noisier in Jesus's time: those crowded seashore towns filled with fishermen and traders, the market places alive with half a dozen tongues, with Romans on military service, Greeks from the prosperous cities of the Decapolis, merchants from Persia and Anatolia, Bedouin from the desert. What an uproar there was on market days! The screaming and the shouting, the cries of the vendors, the clanking of armor, the creaking of chariot wheels! In Athens the fishmongers were the noisiest, the most abusive, the most determined to cheat their customers, and no doubt it was the same on the Sea of Galilee. Jesus did not walk through silent and ghostly towns. He came from quiet Nazareth to the tumult of the lake.

THE MOUNT OF THE BEATITUDES

One evening at the Galei Kinneret Hotel we were discussing the best vantage point for seeing the lake. Someone said he had seen it from the heights of Arbel one day when the lake was the same color as the sky, and sky and lake together seemed to embrace the whole universe. Someone said that Tiberias offered the best view, because from Tiberias you can see the broadest expanse of the lake, and it was for this reason no doubt that Herod Antipas chose it for his capital. Another said there were no good places to see the lake from the land; the best place was a speedboat circling furiously in the middle of the lake. But I still think the best view is from the Mount of the Beatitudes.

The lake of course gets smaller and smaller as you climb that thousand-foot hill, until it becomes no more than a small quivering pool enclosed within a circle of ocher mountains, but here at least it comes into clear focus. From this height everything is sharp and brilliantly outlined. Patches of silver flow across the ripening blue where the winds from the mountains touch the surface, and somehow those ghostly silver ripples give a more abundant life to the lake. Down, down below lies the lake so quiet and serene that it seems not to belong to any landscape; it exists for itself in worlds of its own.

It is the blue lake of dreams and auguries, of premonitions and prophecies and unfathomable movements of the soul. From this height it is inconceivable that the lake has any depth, or that fish swim below the surface, or that storms can ever rise to throw it into turmoil. The lake is all: the mountains are only a frame. Always, as the wind flows, there is the sense of gently stirring life on the lake. The sky opens its arms to the lake, and so clearly are the clouds reflected in it that you can look down and think you are gazing at the sky.

The Italian nuns have built a hospice on the mountainside; it is such a building as you might find in northern Italy, with green shutters and spacious rooms, the wooden boards smelling of soap. The gardens are a blaze of flowers sheltering under the palms. They offered us grapefruit juice, and gave us letters to post in Tiberias, for they rarely leave the mountain. The Mother Superior's cheeks were the color of ripe apples. There was a wild gaiety in her, partially subdued by her heavy white vestments. She chattered away in four or five languages about how she had been at the hospice for fifteen years and never felt the least desire to leave it. She had heard the gunfire and seen Tiberias in flames, but no one had ever harmed her, neither Arab nor Israeli had knocked on the door of the hospice, but if they had she would have welcomed them with open arms. Saying this, she threw her arms wide open. All were welcome in the hospice. Anyone could come and stay as long as he liked. It cost little, scarcely more than the cost of food; and surely it was good for body and soul to live above a shining lake.

From the hospice there is a garden path leading to the Sanctuary of the Beatitudes, the traditional site where Jesus delivered the sermon reversing all existing values and announcing the coming of a new age. The sanctuary is not altogether pleasing. It resembles a blue and white salt shaker designed by a happy and improvident child. Inevitably there are eight walls corresponding to the eight Beatitudes, and inevitably the Beatitudes are spelled out in Latin beneath the golden dome. There is an altar of white Carrara marble, very florid, with a marble canopy over it. Everything about that small gilded chamber wears an air of exquisite bad taste: an ice-cream sundae refashioned in gold mosaics and white tiles. The mourners, the merciful, the peacemakers and the pure in heart have no place in this sumptuous, overdecorated chapel. One wonders why.

The explanation is not hard to find, for there are clues in abundance, written in large letters across the marble floor. Surprisingly—for they have little enough to do with the Beatitudes—the seven virtues are printed in mosaic characters all round the altar. Justice has her scales,

Prudence her wand, Fortitude his stout Roman castle, and all the rest of the virtues are decked out with their appropriate symbols. These commendable and irrelevant virtues are only a foretaste of what is to come. A bewildering inscription, inserted among the virtues, reads:

A.D.

MCMXXXVII

XV

ITALICA GENS

Even in one's wildest dreams one would scarcely expect to find such an inscription in the Sanctuary of the Beatitudes. The name of Adolf Hitler inscribed in gold in the Church of the Holy Sepulcher would be no more surprising. There are astonishing implications in the two letters "XV," announcing a new dispensation of time. Spelled out in full the brief inscription reads: "In the year of our Lord 1937, and in the fifteenth year of the rule of Benito Mussolini, the Italian race . . ."

What kind of madness led the Italian Fascist State to believe that it was justified in endowing the Sanctuary of the Beatitudes? What on earth, one asks oneself, has Fascism to do with the Beatitudes?

Blessed are the poor in spirit: for theirs is the kingdom of heaven.
Blessed are they that mourn: for they shall be comforted.
Blessed are the meek: for they shall inherit the earth.
Blessed are they which do hunger and thirst after righteousness: for they shall be filled.
Blessed are the merciful: for they shall obtain mercy.
Blessed are the pure in heart: for they shall see God.
Blessed are the peacemakers: for they shall be called the children of God.
Blessed are they which are persecuted for righteousness' sake: for theirs is the kingdom of heaven.

One imagines Mussolini calling for the plans of the sanctuary while sitting at his great desk in the Palazzo Venetia. "How charming," he says. "All this is in complete agreement with my philosophy, and I am especially in agreement with the third, fourth and fifth of these principles. In time, when the Italian race has mastered the world, we shall build these sanctuaries everywhere. They perfectly represent the ideals of Fascism, which we shall unfortunately not be able to approach in my lifetime."

The Tremore at Nazareth

A goddess from the Painted Tomb of Ashkelon

Bread and Fishes mosaic from Tabgha

A nymph from the Painted Tomb at Ashkelon

Peacock mosaic from Tabgha

The Cenaculum on Mount Zion

Courtyard in the Church of John the Baptist at Ain Karem

Mount Tabor

The Sea of Galilee

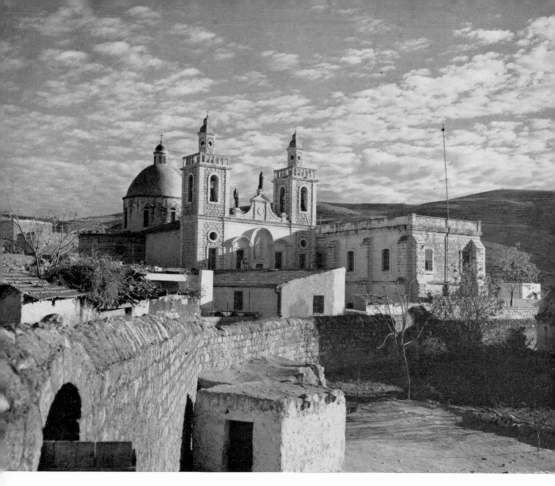

Cana

Saying this he scrawls his signature on the plans, and passes on to more pressing affairs.

On the site of this neo-Fascist sanctuary, or on some mountain nearby, Jesus spoke the words which lie at the heart of the mystery, foretelling the end of the earthly kingdoms and the coming of the Kingdom of Heaven. He proclaimed the absolute unimportance of the iron-booted state with all its panoply of power, and the absolute importance in the eyes of God of the poor and the lowly, the merciful, the peacemakers. He celebrated all that was gentle and pure. He envisaged a world where everyone lived together in quietness and gentleness, without rancor, without any raising of the voice, in an eternal brotherhood. "Rejoice, and be exceedingly glad: for great is your reward in heaven." The Fascists found little comfort in this vision, and envisaged a world where the harsh Roman laws were revived, and all who opposed them were to be crushed against the wall. That Fascism should have sought to render tribute to the Beatitudes testifies to the continuing power of Jesus to move the hearts and souls of men. It testifies, too, to an inordinate presumption.

The sanctuary on the Mount of the Beatitudes stands at the other end of the scale from the Tremore at Nazareth, for all human meaning has been abstracted from it. Strangely, no sanctuary was ever built there before. For centuries the site was occupied by two enormous terebinth trees, but these have perished. There is no need for a memorial to the Beatitudes. It is enough to stand there on the golden mountain, in the golden air, and to look down on the blue lake, the wellspring of blessings. There, if anywhere, there springs the certainty that the meek will inherit the earth. In the gentleness and perfect beauty of that landscape there is the promise that the Kingdom of Heaven will appear on earth.

THE SEVEN SPRINGS

There are not many places which appear today as Jesus saw them. The spring at Nazareth is one, and the rocky inlet at Tabgha must be another. This was the richest fishing ground, with seven springs pouring into the lake from the surrounding hills. Josephus believed one of these springs was a distant offshoot of the Nile "for here there is a fish resembling the *korakinos* which is also found in the marshes of Alexandria." His theory of an underground tunnel leading from Tabgha to Alexandria is not completely convincing, but in fact fish like those found off Alexandria are found in the Sea of Galilee. Today there are only churches along the shore. In the time of Jesus there were two towns, Kinneret and Beersheba, facing the rocky inlet. "Beersheba" means "seven springs" in Hebrew. The Greek for "seven springs" is "Heptapegon," and in Arabic this became "Tabgha."

From very early times Tabgha has been associated with the miracle of the multiplication of the loaves and fishes. St. Sylvia of Aquitaine in the fourth century speaks of "a plain covered with grass and palms, and in the midst of it seven springs arise, each with a great abundance of water. It was on this plain that our Lord fed the multitude with five loaves and two fishes. They have built a church above the stone where He placed the loaves, and those who visit it carry away part of the stone as a remedy."

The ruins of a fourth-century Byzantine church, perhaps the same one seen by St. Sylvia, were uncovered in the 1930s by German archaeologists, who brought to light a magnificent mosaic floor. No human figures appear, only birds and oleander bushes and reeds and lotuses. We see a snake attacking a heron, winding its tail round the heron's leg, and no harm is done. Fat ducks waddle, cormorants tread delicately among the lotuses, peacocks with brilliant purple feathers prance royally along the borders. All the birds are roughly the same size, the doves as large as the cormorants. There is no continuity. Each bird is alone in its own world, joyfully flaunting its own existence, and the reeds, too, grow where they please, magnificently alone. There are two immense stretches of these mosaics, and they culminate in the small mosaic of two fishes and a basket of loaves which lies behind the small stone altar. The two fishes are spinning on their tails, and they are evidently the succulent comb fish which still breed in the lake. Everything about these wonderful mosaics is joyful, artless and spontaneous.

The old Benedictine priest from the Abbey of Mount Zion, robed in white, smiles dreamily and points to the tap and the sponge. The wet sponge is necessary to bring the colors out. So, taking off your shoes, you wander over the mosaics and sponge them. The pink and dusty beaks turn to flaming scarlet, the heron engaged in a charming battle with a snake turns out to have brilliant orange wings. Ruby-red and bottle-green appear where there were only dusty grays. The lotuses are a brilliant pink, a small castle is royal purple. The mosaic floor becomes a scattering of jewels. We see these stones shining as brilliantly as they shone in the fourth century.

Not far away, in a grove of willows, stands the Sanctuary of the Primacy, a new church built by the Franciscans in 1934, in honor of the Risen Christ who was seen by the apostles as He stood on the lake shore, cooking fish on a fire of coals. Here Jesus conferred the primacy on St. Peter, and was seen for the last time on earth. Half the yellow rock is inside the church. It is a small whitewash and plaster church, not very impressive. But on what remains of the rock outside the church, lapped by the lake, there are steps leading to a rocky platform. There perhaps He cooked the fish and talked to the apostles for the last time.

THE FACE OF JESUS

Nearly twenty centuries have passed since Jesus walked along these shores, but His presence can still be felt. In the noisy cities crowding the lake shore, He spent nearly two years ministering to the sick and delivering the sermons which announced the coming of a new age. Sometimes He spoke from a fishing boat anchored in the lake, but more often on the hillsides near Capernaum. We do not know why He chose Capernaum, but we know why He chose Galilee: fertile with men, with ideas, with trade, teeming with fertility. Mostly He preached near the Plain of Gennesaret, where the mountains draw back from the lake and the earth is sweet. He wandered from city to city along the plain, sometimes withdrawing into the hills, but always coming back again.

So we imagine Him, a Galilean among Galileans, speaking the language of the lake, equally at home among fishermen and merchants, wearing a white robe, bearded and ruddy, with long hair falling to His shoulders, following the practice of the time. We imagine Him tall and with a commanding presence, with strong features and a carpenter's powerful hands, but whenever we try to look closer there is always a mystery. We never come close enough to see Him clearly.

There is a strange and awe-inspiring passage in the apocryphal Acts of John, written at Ephesus during the second century, which tells how Jesus first appeared to the two disciples John and James, the sons of Zebedee, as they were sitting in their fishing boat near the shore of the lake. Suddenly James saw Jesus beckoning to them:

> "What does this youth want with us? Why is he calling us from the shore?" said my brother James to me. And I said, "What youth?" He answered, "He that is beckoning to us." I said, "My brother James, your eyes must be dimmed by the many sleepless nights we have spent on the lake. Do you not see that the man standing on the shore is a tall man with a joyful face of great beauty?" My brother said, "I do not see him like that, but let us row ashore and then we shall know."
>
> When we hauled up the boat, Jesus himself helped us to make it fast. When we left the place to follow him, he appeared to me as an old, bald man with a thick flowing beard, while to my brother James he seemed a youth with but a faint down on his cheeks. And we could not understand and were amazed. And so it often happened, and he would appear to us in forms even more marvelous, sometimes small of stature, with crooked limbs, sometimes as a giant, reaching to the heavens.

There is something strangely convincing in this portrait of Jesus, which may well derive from an authentic tradition reported by the disciples. Like the author of the Acts of John, Origen believed that Jesus did not always have the same appearance, but continually changed his countenance according to the needs of the onlooker. Many of the early Fathers believed that Jesus was small and frail, with a long face and eyebrows that were joined together, dark-skinned, red-haired, and a hunchback. According to the Acts of Peter He was both beautiful and ugly—"*formosus et foedus.*" It may have been so. Tertullian placed in the mouth of Jesus the words of the Psalm, "But I am a worm, and no man, a reproach of men, and despised of the people." Clement said He had "no comeliness or beauty, but His appearance was insignificant, inferior to the beauty of men, a man of stripes and toil, who knew how to endure pain; his face was turned away, he was dishonored and discountenanced." Irenaeus said more simply that He was weak and inglorious—*"infirmus et ingloriosus."* In the East no one would have been amazed at the sight of His infirmities, for prophets and saints habitually suffered from strange sicknesses, their bodies breaking under vast spiritual pressures.

Although St. Augustine was to say categorically that no man knew the appearance of Jesus, the early tradition survived in an attenuated form. A remarkable number of chroniclers speak of His head being bent forward. In the eighth century Andrew of Crete relates that he saw a portrait painted by St. Luke in which Jesus is shown with "a long face, the eyebrows meeting, the head bent forward, the figure well-proportioned." John of Damascus in the same century says that "Jesus resembled his mother and was slightly stooping, with beautiful eyes, red hair which was long and curly, and he had a pale olive complexion and long fingers." Epiphanius, a monk who lived about A.D. 1150, seems to have reported an ancient tradition when he spoke of Jesus being "six feet tall, red-haired, with dark eyebrows, a ruddy complexion, cheeks full but not so round as his mother's, his neck inclining a little so that the posture of his body was not too upright." Nicephorus Callistus in the fourteenth century follows the same tradition when he speaks of Jesus having "fair, curly hair with dark eyebrows, eyes shining with inexpressible compassion, shoulders stooping a little." Common to nearly all these descriptions are the brilliant eyes, the long curling hair, the dark eyebrows, the stooping shoulders. Always the stooping shoulders!

Yet, a little surprisingly, in spite of all these detailed descriptions, the early Roman and Byzantine paintings portray Him differently. In the Roman catacombs He is the young beardless shepherd, the brother of Apollo or Orpheus, with a lamb over His shoulders or a lyre in His hands. Suddenly in Byzantium he wears the look of majesty. The portrait seems to have been modeled on the powerful figure of Zeus carved by Phidias for his temple at Olympia, and we know that at some early period in Byzantine history this statue was removed to Constantinople; and the tradition established by the early Christian emperors has survived to our own day. Only sometimes, in early

Italian paintings, do we see Him in the form of a slight stooping figure, the lips pursed in pain, as He walks beside the lake.

There are, of course, many other traditional representations of the face of Jesus. There is the agonizing portrait which appears on the Shroud at Milan, somber and menacing, heavy with mortality. There is the oddly unconvincing portrait in *The Letter of Lentulus to the Roman Senate*, which was first found in a manuscript copy of the writings of Anselm of Canterbury and dates from the twelfth century:

> His hair is the color of wine, and golden at the root, straight and without luster, but from the level of the ears curling and glossy, and divided down the center after the fashion of the Nazarenes. His forehead is even and smooth, His face without wrinkle or blemish, and glowing with a delicate bloom. His beard is full, of the same hazel color as his hair, not long, but forked. His eyes are deep blue and extremely brilliant. He is terrible in anger, but gentle and amiable in speech. Sometimes he weeps, but he has never been known to laugh.

The Letter of Lentulus is not to be dismissed lightly; there are passages in it which may derive from ancient tradition. If many of the details are suspect, there are others that ring true. As we have it now, the portrait smells of the lamp, with too many scholars amending and correcting an original text. But it is still possible that the original will be found among the papyri embedded in the Egyptian sands.

There is a passage in the Talmud where Jesus is described as "cloud-like." It is perhaps the best of all adjectives to describe Him as He moved silently across the land, always escaping from His pursuers, belonging more to the air than to the earth, shining with a mysterious light. Cloud-like, He escapes us to the very end.

So I thought, until I came to the shores of the lake. There one day, between Magdala and Capernaum, seeing the shimmering blue waters framed in the yellow hills, I discovered what many other travelers have already discovered. The face of Jesus is the face of the lake.

Ashkelon

The guidebooks with indisputable authority announce that the city of Ashkelon was founded by South African Jews in A.D. 1953, and they very properly add that it was already old when the Israelites were in bondage in Egypt.

Ashkelon must be one of the oldest cities on earth, but it wears its age lightly. The long white beaches and the low green hills remind you of California. The sea is intensely blue, the air sparkles, the warm winds flow from Africa, everywhere the new housing estates are coming up, and in the market place the girls wander about in bathing suits. Within the town there is an air of prodigious activity: trucks loading and unloading, workmen clambering up ladders, roads torn up for sewage pipes. To go to Ashkelon is to see a city rising before one's eyes.

Once it was one of the five cities of the Philistines, standing guard over the frontier between Egypt and Palestine. Here, according to the legend, Semiramis was born of a mother who was half-fish, half-woman, and Herodotus records that there was a temple to the Celestial Aphrodite, "which was the oldest of all the temples to the goddess." When the Scythians plundered the temple, Aphrodite very sensibly afflicted them with sexual impotence. Under her many names she seems to have ruled the city from the beginning, and it is possible that Ashkelon rather than Cyprus is her original home, her first dwelling place after she rose from the sea.

The Philistines were Greeks from the island of Crete. No one knows when these early sea lords conquered southwestern Palestine and built the five cities of Gaza, Ashkelon, Ashdod, Ekron and Gath. These were not the only cities they ruled, for at different times they penetrated deep into Palestine and established themselves in places as far away from the coast as Beth Shean. But while Gaza, Ashkelon and Ashdod have survived after a fashion, even the sites of Ekron and Gath remain unknown. The history of the Philistines is still buried beneath the sands.

Very occasionally we find clues, odd fragments of evidence about the Philistines. About 1280 B.C. Ramses II captured Ashkelon "when it was wicked," and the capture is recorded on the walls of the great Hypostyle Hall at Karnak. We see the double gates being attacked by Egyptians armed with axes, while the swordsmen approach behind their shields, and the defenders on the city walls are shown in attitudes of supplication, kneeling and wringing their hands. One of the defenders, the leader, is holding up a seven-branched candlestick, the ancestor perhaps of the Menorah. This candlestick is evidently a sacred object, intended to ward off the threatened evil, for it is held aloft and given remarkable prominence. But all we can say for certain is that Ramses occupied the city until the Philistines revolted again. Either as free men or as tributaries on the frontiers of Egypt, they continued to occupy southwest Palestine. Ashdod, which stands near Ashkelon, was attacked about 650 B.C. by the Egyptian king Psammetichos, and the siege lasted for twenty-nine years. "Of all the cities we know," wrote Herodotus, "none ever stood so long a siege."

Against the well-armed Philistines the Hebrews fought a war which lasted for three hundred years. When King Saul was killed by the Philistines in Lower Galilee, David mourned him and gave way to fears that the news would encourage the people of far-off Gaza and Ashkelon. The death of King Saul occurred about 1000 B.C. As late as the seventh century B.C. the Hebrews were still deploring the power of the Philistines, and Zephaniah was busily heaping curses on their heads: "For Gaza shall be forsaken, and Ashkelon a desolation: they shall drive out Ashdod at the noon day, and Ekron shall be rooted up." Amos, too, inveighed bitterly against the Philistine cities:

"I will send a fire on the wall of Gaza, which shall devour the palaces thereof, and I will cut off the inhabitant from Ashdod, and him that holdeth the sceptre from Ashkelon, and I will turn my hand against Ekron; and the remnant of the Philistines shall perish, saith the Lord God." Yet many years passed before the Philistines perished. They survived the Egyptians, Assyrians and Persians, and only under the Ptolemies did they vanish as a people, becoming assimilated with all the races surrounding them.

Herod the Great had family connections with Ashkelon. According to Julius Africanus, his father when a child was abducted by Idumaean brigands from the temple of Apollo at Ashkelon. The boy grew up among the Arabs, and became in time chief minister to Hyrcanus, placing his own sons in positions of importance. To one of his sons he gave the Greek name of Herodes, meaning "the heroic." For more than thirty years Herod ruled as absolute master of Judea.

Herod paid to Ashkelon the same tribute he paid to all the other cities he loved: he rebuilt it in marble and granite. He gave it baths, fountains and colonnades, and built a palace for himself. After his death Augustus gave the palace to Salome. At vast expense Herod imported granite from Assuan, which was worked into columns. Finally, he declared Ashkelon a free city.

Why exactly he chose to pay so much honor to Ashkelon is one of the many mysteries attached to his reign. The most satisfactory theory suggests that his mother was born there. What is certain is that his mother was named after the sweet camphire, a herb which grew most abundantly near Ashkelon. In those days Ashkelon was famous for its camphires, its sycamores and its onions, *ascaloniae*, which we know as shallots.

Ashkelon flourished under Herod and under the Romans, and came to no harm when the Arabs conquered Palestine. They called it "the Bride of the East," and Benjamin of Tudela speaks of the great market places attended by merchants from all the nations of the earth. In August, 1099, the Crusaders under Godfrey of Bouillon marched out of conquered Jerusalem and made a sudden attack on Ashkelon. The battle began at dawn, and was soon over. The Egyptian emir fled, leaving behind his jeweled sword and silver standard surmounted by a golden apple; the slaughter was terrible, and a vast booty fell into the hands of the Crusaders, who quarreled so violently among themselves that they failed to take possession of the undefended city, which remained in Moslem hands for more than fifty years. Finally, in A.D. 1270, the city was destroyed by the Mameluke Sultan Baybars. Then the long history of Ashkelon came to an end.

Today, almost nothing remains. A few columns, a few statues, a painted tomb, fragments of the Herodian wall, thousands of sherds lying in the white sand, nothing else. Under a mound near the cliffs lies the Philistine city, still unexplored. The Herodian city has been luckier. In 1920-21 Professor John Garstang excavated part of the city under the auspices of the British Palestine Exploration Fund. Some of the columns and sculptured figures he discovered now stand within a sunken ring of stone in the public park, among huge drums of creamy marble and giant capitals carved with acanthus leaves. There stands the goddess Isis, wearing her high crown, with the infant Horus beside her; it is a Roman work, with a characteristic Roman heaviness. More impressive is the winged Victory standing on a globe which is supported on the shoulders of a diminutive Atlas. Though headless, the Victory is regal; she has only just descended from the heavens, and her garments billow about her. Even more impressive are the luxuriously carved capitals from Herod's "Stoa of a Hundred Columns." In this sunlight, these florid and exotic capitals are strangely moving. They speak of Herod's wild, athletic taste for luxury, his desire to fashion his own majestic impulses in stone. Almost they are abstract portraits of a king.

Wandering through the park, you catch glimpses through the trees of crumbling walls thirty feet high, looming dark against the sunlight. They too are his monuments to himself.

THE PAINTED TOMB

In the early afternoon we went down to the sea, to the sands white as snow drifting along the coast. Grass waved in the sand hills, and the sky was a deep purple-blue, no longer the sky of northern Israel, but richer and more luminous with an Oriental ripeness. Most of the coast of Israel suggests southern Europe, but by the time you have reached Ashkelon you are already in the Orient.

Somewhere among these sand hills we knew we would find a painted tomb. It was said to be Roman, but in fact no one knew very much about it. There it was in the guidebook: *The painted tomb, Roman, of uncertain date*. And when we stumbled upon it at last, almost lost among the dunes, we hardly cared about the date or whether it was Roman or Greek. Israel has more tombs than it can cope with, but this was the gentlest and the most beautiful of all.

It stands within twenty feet of the sea on the edge of the motor road, very low and small, nestling in the sand. There is a small green door and four steps leading down into a vaulted chamber. On all the walls there are paintings, here and there obscured by time and salt spray, and all of them gradually flaking away, so that it is unlikely that they will survive for more than twenty years. A restorer has been at work, outlining vanished shapes, but enough remains to suggest the quiet magnificence of the original composition.

One would give a good deal to know who the artist was and who was buried there, but the paintings are unsigned and the bones have long ago crumbled and melted into the sands. Yet the character of the artist and the family he served are clearly indicated. The paintings represent an eternal springtime. The colors are the reddish-ocher and the succulent green of spring. On the lunette facing the door two naked nymphs recline, holding pitchers from which the water flows into pools where the marsh birds nest and fat fishes glide. The flowers are blossoming, the plump fruit hang from the trees. Everywhere reeds and lotuses wave in the wind.

All this is pleasant enough, but it is merely the invitation to the feast. The dead cannot be expected to see the two nymphs who preside over them, but they can be expected to look up at the vaulted ceiling where the vines hang from trellises in heavy luxuriance, tempting them back to life. A naked boy reaches on tiptoe to pick a cluster of grapes, and a naked girl bends over a brimming basket. Pan plays on his flute. A greyhound goes coursing after a gazelle, birds are singing, the sunlight pours down through the leaves. It was not the intention of the artist to provide simply a picture of luxuriant life in the afterworld, for suddenly through the vine leaves there appear the beckoning faces of the gods, Apollo and Demeter. The calm beautiful face of Demeter, goddess of earth and fruitfulness, peers down from the ceiling with an expression of brooding sweetness and sympathy. She is majestically crowned, and she has broad shoulders; she could easily carry the dead in her arms. The artist seems to be saying that death is no more than a lying down in the shade, and soon the sunlight will come again and the faces of the gods and goddesses will appear among the leaves, summoning them to eternal life.

There are other paintings in the tomb. There are painted shields along the wall and mourning women near the entrance, but none of these rival the extraordinary richness of the ceiling, still preserving much of its original color. There is nothing funereal; it is gay, vibrant with color, curiously convincing. "This is death," the artist seems to be saying, "and look, it is neither difficult nor dangerous. I bring you the promise of the vineyard. Demeter shall have you in her keeping."

It is an oddly exhilarating tomb, and one could spend a day happily examining the paintings, lying at full length on the sandy floor to see them better. I suspect they are Greek, of the second century B.C., for there are mosaics found recently at Pella in Macedonia belonging to that time which bear a family resemblance to these paintings, but we shall know more when the excavators go to work; there must be more tombs nearby, for there are suspicious-looking humps in the sand all along the coast.

So there it is, and you will have to hurry if you want to see it. The promise of eternal life will soon be fading from the walls.

Beersheba

Very soon after leaving Ashkelon you come to the desert. The ripe fields and the palms fall away, and there is only the empty wasteland, tawny and brown and orange, treeless and leafless, stretching as far as the eye can see. The desert has a look of expectancy. It lies there quietly, like an animal ready to spring, and seems to be pondering the fate of all those who come near. "I shall devour you all," it says. "I shall blow down the houses and eat up the roads, and no living thing shall come near me." So it has happened many times in the past. The great military roads have sunk under the sands, the churches have crumbled until there is nothing left but a few stones, whole cities have vanished. The war between the desert and the sown has been going on since the beginning of recorded time.

In the bone-dry Negev sprawling across the whole of southern Israel, the war between the desert and the sown has been joined. For once it would seem that the desert will be defeated.

Here and there along the road from Ashkelon to Beersheba there are sudden splashes and squares of succulent green occupying only a few acres, but these are only the forerunners. Occasionally there are orchards, and it is odd to see the fruit trees ending in a sharp line and the desert beginning again. So far there is only this brief beginning. The eagles wheel in the empty sky, the rocks glisten, time is running out. You can see the enemy of the desert on almost every railroad in

Israel; it has the shape of a white reinforced-concrete cylinder 108 inches in diameter, so heavy that a railroad car usually carries no more than a single cylinder. When all these cylinders are joined together and the water pours down into the Negev from the Sea of Galilee, then the desert will die. It does not know how close it is to its death.

For a few more months the desert will reign over a barren empire. Then by 1964 the pipeline will have been installed, and whole regions which are now sand and stones will turn green. The enemies of Israel have threatened to make war on her as soon as the Sea of Galilee starts flowing south. The normal Israeli response is to take the threat seriously, while continuing to build the pipelines. Ever since Moses struck the rock they have known that water is life.

But today, and for a little while longer, the Negev is still largely desert, the home of snakes and jackals, and the wandering Bedouin whose black tents tremble in the waves of heat rising from the burnt-out land. Even the beautifully graded asphalt highways seem to lose themselves in the desert. Walk fifty feet off the road and the highway vanishes; you might be in the middle of the Sahara. I have seen tanks and armored cars lumbering across the desert south of Beersheba; within five minutes they too had vanished, for the desert drowns everything in its own color.

Meanwhile the desert contends as best it can with its most potent enemy, the highways which link Beersheba to the Mediterranean coast, the Dead Sea and the Gulf of Elath. These thin threads, pushing out more threads, are beginning to strangle the desert. At Beersheba the knot is being tied.

The casual visitor comparing the bustle at Ashkelon with the bustle at Beersheba would be hard put to see any difference. Houses go up overnight; the bulldozers are hard at work; there is an incessant noise of hammering and pneumatic drills. The houses very often have the curious bombed-out look which goes with bare shells of buildings before the streets have been laid, and water and electricity are brought in. Factories are mushrooming. They have the look of being set down in some lost corner of the desert, far from roads, far from houses. The roads and houses are still on the drawing board, while the factory is already turning out its products. Beersheba is a town that cannot wait.

There are two Beershebas, the old and the new. The old Beersheba will soon be swallowed up in the new, and may perish altogether in a few years. It will be no very great loss, for it was never more than a sprawling Turkish market town, scarcely more than a large village, with only its antiquity to commend it. Abraham dug a well here; the Philistines filled it with rocks and stones; Isaac opened up the well again. The credulous are asked to believe that Abraham's original well has remained in existence for nearly four thousand years; it is the one which stands in the main street. Beersheba owes everything to its wells, and therefore whether it is Abraham's or not, it is treated with proper respect.

Around these wells there must have been a settlement from very early times, for Beersheba stands at the crossroads of the desert, and there is good grazing land all round it. Long before Abraham made a gift of seven sheep to Abimelech, the Philistine king of Gerar, and received the grazing rights, the tribes must have gathered there. Abraham planted tamarisks at Beersheba, and in their shade he built an altar to Jehovah, and here he remained for many years, and Isaac lingered. Isaac's son, Jacob, also dwelt there before setting out on his weary journey beyond the Jordan to Mesopotamia, and on his return struggled with the angel face to face, receiving the name of Israel for his fortitude, "for as a Prince thou hast power with God." Around Beersheba falls the light of the patriarchal age. Once in the blinding light of that legendary age God spoke from the heavens.

In the desert, not far from Beersheba, beside the winding road which leads down to the Dead Sea, the Israeli government has built a legendary building. Seen from the road, it resembles a temple with a shining silvery blue dome; and indeed in its general proportions it has much in common with the Dome of the Rock. It stands there low on the skyline, surrounded by the endless desolation of the desert, with high-tension wires running in long straight lines around it. It is the new holy of holies, which no one may enter on pain of death. It is the new "power with God," a nuclear power plant. It looks beautiful and harmless enough, shining there in the yellow wasteland, but in Jerusalem there were heady debates about the danger of erecting an atomic plant in the Middle East, where there are so many stored hatreds. The usual government reply was that Israel must deal from strength, while the intellectuals shake their heads in despair, not so much because the power plant has been built, but because its consequences were unforeseeable and always ominous. That silvery blue temple might become, with roads and water, the means of destroying the desert, turning it into fertile land, or it might have the effect of turning the whole Middle East into atomic flame.

When Elijah was fleeing to escape the vengeance of Jezebel, he came to Beersheba, where he left his servant, and then wandered across the desert for the space of a day's journey until he found a juniper tree and slept beneath it. He may have slept on the very site where the power plant rises. All this land is bathed in prophecy. Abraham and Elijah walked hand in hand across the wilderness, Isaac and Jacob still lead their flocks to pasture in the hills above Beersheba, and there are still altars beneath the tamarisks. For a little while longer there will be the sense of living under the shadow of God's wings; then the modern age will take over and the light of the patriarchs will go out.

It is a somber thought, and the Israelis are well aware of its implications. They answer that risks must be taken whenever a desert is reclaimed, and the greater the risks, the more honor there is in the endeavor.

SHEIK SULEIMAN

All over the Negev you come upon small Arab encampments. The long black goat-hair tents lie among the hills, and the camels stand impressively against the skyline; from the road these encampments always seem dark and a little sinister as they proclaim the permanence of the ancient past over our temporary preoccupations. The Arabs live as they lived in the time of Abraham. They raise camels, horses and goats, and this is their whole life. They have owned these grazing grounds since time immemorial, and they see no reason to leave now that the Israelis are in possession.

So they remain, wandering over the desert as they please, their faces burned black by the sun, aimless and carefree, too ragged and verminous to be entirely enviable. T. E. Lawrence said of these wandering tribesmen that they were the last of the earth's people to enjoy perfect freedom, but he learned during his travels among them that this primitive form of freedom can be bought at too high a price. Most of the Arab children I saw were suffering from some disease. Too often their women looked sickly. But like their Arab horses, the men possessed a wonderful arrogance and quivered with vitality. They were the lords of the desert still, and they knew it.

We used to drive over the sands to their encampments on the excuse of bargaining for silver-hilted daggers encrusted with semiprecious stones. Some they make for themselves, and others they sell in the market place at Beersheba; the best are the ones they wear at their waists. In time I accumulated a small collection of daggers. Unsheathed, they have an ugly, merciless look about them. Sheathed, they are wonderfully decorative. But the bargaining for daggers was only an excuse to be among them, the only way we knew of entering the encampments with honor. The children would come running out, screaming for baksheesh, while the women hid from us, only to emerge later from the tents when their curiosity was too much for them. Only the camels paid no attention to us, standing there quiet against the skyline.

I never saw an Arab encampment which did not look as though they were in the process of moving off to new grazing grounds. There was always an air of makeshift, of hurried improvisation. The very shapes of the tents suggested impermanence. They were like circus tents, and you expected them to be pulled down tomorrow. And usually the camps were dirty and evil-smelling, and too many of the people there should have been lying in hospital beds. But what was especially pleasing was the fine, taut outline of an Arab face, the dark insolence, the way they carried themselves, moving with an easy grace and solemnity which was sometimes unnerving, so that there were moments when we would have cheerfully surrendered our complicated intellectual lives for theirs, since they are closer to the earth and more instinctive.

One day, west of Beersheba, we decided to call on the ruling Sheik whose decisions were law among the nomadic tribesmen. He lived in a small fortress shaded by feathery tamarisks not far from the main highway, on a slope overlooking the endless stretches of the desert. His name was Sheik Suleiman el Hezuel, and ever since men can remember the Hezuel tribesmen have inhabited the desert around Beersheba.

When we found him, he was sitting at his ease under an awning, an old man with a weather-beaten face of great dignity and power. He wore a golden-brown cloak over his white robe, and he carried a revolver in a leather holster, and there was a gold dagger at his waist. He sat on a wooden bench heaped with cushions, while the old men of the tribe crouched round the coffeepot near his feet.

They were wonderful old men, dark and wiry, with jagged wrinkles in their shadowed faces. The coffeepot stood on a small circle of stones and sometimes they would blow on the glowing embers or pass the little cups of bitter coffee around. They rarely spoke. Sometimes they would rise in a flurry of dust-stained skirts and kiss the hands and elbow of the Sheik before whispering something in his ear; then, smiling, they would crouch down again beside the fire which gave no smoke. There was only the Sheik and the small circle of old men, companions of his youth, under the awning.

There was a time when Sheik Suleiman was a name to conjure with. No one knows how many raiding parties he led, how many caravans fell into his possession when the desert was free only to men of his his own choosing and everyone who entered it became his hostage. He had fought with Allenby when the British tide rolled up from Beersheba and drowned the Turks. Thirty years later he made his peace with Israel to become one of the few Arab sheiks remaining in a land conquered by the Jews. They said he had had fifty wives, but that may be an understatement. Once, coming upon a beautiful Bedouin girl when he was out riding, he told her he would make her his wife, until she shook her head smiling and said, "It is not lawful," and when he insisted she whispered, "How can it be, since you are my father?" Long ago he had lost count of the number of his children.

Now he was an old man nearing seventy, though he sometimes claimed to be in his fifties, and sometimes his eyelids would droop heavily and he would fall asleep for a few moments, while his thickly veined hands remained watchful over the curving dagger at his waist. Asleep or awake, he gave an impression of profound serenity.

We talked by signs, for I knew no Arabic except the ordinary words of greeting. The old men gave me coffee; it was so bitter that its very bitterness became a kind of sweetness. Once I mentioned the name of Lawrence of Arabia. The name set the old men twittering and exchanging glances, and the Sheik nodded and smiled, his gold teeth flashing. My companion knew a little Arabic and pressed him for his recollections of the fair-haired Englishman who had led the Arab revolt, but he only smiled again and waved his hands, and soon a sleeping spell came over him.

While he slept, we were taken to his guest room, a large dimly lit room crammed with Victorian furniture and ancient carpets, so shadowy and obscure that at first we could see nothing at all except a cracked blue mirror over the mantel shelf. Then, as we grew accustomed to the light, we could make out the portraits propped on the shelf. He had a special affection for Mrs. Eleanor Roosevelt, and her portrait was given pride of place, together with letters from her thanking him for gifts he had sent her. He had once proposed marriage to her; she had refused his offer gracefully, and he bore her no grudge. Queen Elizabeth, President Truman and Prime Minister Ben-Gurion gazed down from the shelf, all fly-spotted, all crumbling away.

We could make nothing of the guest room. It was solid and well built, but everything inside it—the velvet hangings, the ormolu clocks, the cracked chamberpots and the heavy mahogany funiture—seemed to be out of keeping with his character. It was such a room as might have belonged to an aging and impoverished courtesan in Paris during the last years of the nineteenth century, and heaven only knows what it was doing there in the sandy wastes around Beersheba or what guests had slept there. Over the whole room there hung the rank smell of goat hair.

He was awake when we returned—awake, and the blood was flowing vigorously through his veins, his cheeks ruddy, the fringe of white beard bristling again, the heavy hands resting on the beautiful golden dagger. The old men were still whispering by the fire, and sometimes they would gaze up at him with strange looks of adoration, nodding and smiling to one another. He asked how we had enjoyed the guest room; and we said we had enjoyed it greatly, and he was pleased. We were his guests, and we could stay in it as long as we desired.

I took some movie photographs of him, insisting that it should be in the open, for there was too much shadow under the awning. This pleased him, but he was soon tired. One of his grandsons, a bright-eyed boy of about twelve, clung to his robes, hiding behind him, then appearing as soon as the movie camera made its humming noise. The Sheik cuffed him. He wanted to be taken alone, in all his panoply. And then heavily, wearily, exhausted by the sunlight, he returned to his wooden throne.

Nothing happened; nothing of any importance. There was the crumbling fortress and the old men brooding over the coffeepot and a white stallion standing in the shade of a tamarisk tree and far away, almost lost in the sands, the black tents of the tribesmen with the camels like dark specks on the endless plains. It was a scene which must have taken place every day in the life of the old Sheik: the quiet talk, the long silences in the shade. And yet how precious it was! They were like old peasants sitting there, full of years and wisdom, wanting nothing except to be in each other's company, sipping coffee and enjoying the open air. In a year or two none of them will be left, and that too is as it must be. In their enjoyment there was the knowledge that it would not last much longer.

We were wondering how we could tear ourselves away when a surprising thing happened. An old green Buick suddenly appeared out of nowhere. It must have come down the long road from the highway, but we were not aware of its coming. For a few more minutes the quiet communion over the coffeepot continued, and suddenly the old Sheik, who had been dozing, sprang to life again. Once again the old men kissed his hand and his elbow, and then he was off driving at breakneck speed, leaving a great yellow cloud behind him.

We stayed a little while longer, and then we followed him down the dusty road to Beersheba.

Massada

The gray viper lay in the shadows, slowly dying. There was no color
in its eyes, no strength in it. Sometimes it would lift its bony head and
look at us coldly, and then the vast mouth would open wide, gasping
for air, and there would be a flicker of blue fangs until the mouth
closed again in horror and hopelessness. The mouth was pure white,
and ugly, and sometimes as it moved its head the scales shone with
an iridescent light, and they were beautiful. There was a wound five
inches behind the eyes; only the head moved; the rest was paralyzed.

All morning and half the previous night the viper had been lying
there, and no one had wanted to put it out of its misery. They were
all squatting round it, keeping at a safe distance, afraid it would come
to life again, afraid of the poison which could kill a man in three
seconds; and the viper seemed to know they were afraid. It was waiting
patiently, hoping someone would come in reach of its fangs, hoping
for vengeance. Strangely, as the blood ebbed from the wound, it
seemed to be growing darker until it was the color of the shadows.

"It came in the middle of the night," the boy said. "I slashed at it
with a stick and broke its back, and thought that was the end of it. It's
not dead yet."

"Why don't you kill it?"

He shook his head.

"No sense in killing it outright. We've had six of them in a single week. We reckon it's best for them to die slowly."

So we watched and waited, while the viper suffered its slow death, heavily, wearily, with drooping head, lying where it had been flung down on the wooden floor of the long veranda facing the Dead Sea, while the sun blazed outside and the sea sparkled like emeralds. It was one of those life-giving days when the skies are high and the air is transparently pure, a bad day to die in.

Someone pushed a forked stick close to the viper; the white mouth opened quickly, yearning for the stick, yearning for something to bite on, the bony head waving a little, following the stick, not sure of itself any more. The light was fading from the iridescent scales, and the boys were still squatting there, whispering to one another. Vipers are usually very small, and this one was no more than thirty inches long, but seemed smaller, for only five inches of it were alive. Yet we watched the viper as we would watch a dying tiger: coldly, without remorse or any sympathy.

It was strange how the small viper filled the whole veranda with its presence. There were long trestle tables and benches, and I suppose two hundred people could sit down to a meal there. Through the windows we could look out on the majestic reddish cliffs of Massada in the west and the blue mountains of Moab in the east, with the Dead Sea lying between. But nothing on the sea or the mountains or the vast veranda had any attraction for us. There was only the dark viper in the shadows, the terrible stillness, the coiled and broken body, the slow ebbing of life. Even now we kept away from the viper. We were still afraid of it.

"There's a war on between us and the vipers," the boy was saying, prodding it with the forked stick.

But it did not look like a war; it looked like a little coil of rope thrown down by someone who had nothing better to do, until the white mouth suddenly flew open for the last time, snapping at the stick with a queer vicious intensity. The snake's head rose from the floor a good two inches, but afterwards there was no more movement. The head sank down, and seemed to grow smaller, darker, as the life ebbed away. Half an hour later someone came with a bucket and took it away.

We had thought of climbing Massada, but with this heat, and with so many vipers about, we decided it would be foolhardy. The local guide refused to go with us. He said one should climb Massada at dawn, when the air is still cool, and return in the evening. It is a difficult climb, not to be undertaken except with an expert guide, and preferably in a large company. When the archaeologists were excavating the ruins on the mountain, they organized the climb as though it were a military campaign, with the help of the Chief of Staff and the Israeli Air Force. So, sadly, we remained in the foothills.

There were some advantages in remaining in the foothills. The sheer power of the mountain, darkly brooding, with its massive red buttresses and cliffs driving up from the deep gorges, the summit breaking into a kind of rocky foam, all this is seen to best advantage from below. There is energy in it, a wild purposefulness, a gaunt ugliness. Coming unawares upon this mountain and knowing nothing of its history, you would say, "Here is a fortress, here men have died." It is a serpent's head, venomous and brutal, magnified to the size of a mountain seventeen hundred feet high.

Massada is Herod's mountain, and to this day bears the traces of his megalomaniac genius, his astonishing power to shape everything he touched with his own characteristic imprint. Who else but Herod, or perhaps Tiberius, would have thought of building a palace with Corinthian columns and mosaic floors high up on those jagged cliffs? Between 37 and 30 B.C. he built a massive wall surrounding the plateau on top of the mountain, dug deep into the rock to produce vast cisterns for storing rain water, built his fantastic palace, and on the forbidding and almost inaccessible cliffs carved mysterious stairways which continue to puzzle modern archaeologists.

According to Josephus, Cleopatra was partly responsible for the building of the fortress. "Herod built this fortress as a refuge for himself," Josephus wrote, "in view of a twofold danger: peril on the one hand from the Jewish people, lest they should depose him and restore their former dynasty to power; the greater and more serious danger came from Cleopatra, Queen of Egypt." Cleopatra had been prevailing upon Mark Antony to conquer Herod and to add Judea to her own empire. By the time Herod had finished building his fortress and palace, Mark Antony and Cleopatra were in full flight before the armies of Augustus Caesar, and the Mediterranean had become a Roman lake. Herod went to Rhodes to make his peace with Augustus, and was confirmed in his rule over Judea.

Massada gives the impression of having been fortified against all eventualities: Herod feared more than the Jews, more than Cleopatra. He built for eternity. The heavy limestone wall surrounding the top of the mountain was eighteen feet high and twelve feet wide, with thirty-seven towers each seventy-five feet high, and there were four more enormous towers guarding the palace. The watchmen looked down from more than forty towers; any enemy, coming from any direction, would have been observed. There were underground passageways, roads that seemed to disappear completely, a path which "in its narrowness and perpetual windings resembles a snake, and those who would dare to walk along this path must first go on one leg and then on the other, and if they should slip, then destruction faces them, for on both sides of the path there are vast chasms." There was a lingering feeling that Josephus, to heighten the romantic story, had exaggerated the dangers of the snake path, but some young amateur archaeologists discovered it in 1954. It was worn and eroded, and they very carefully restored it.

Herod's fortress belongs more properly to the Gothic tales of the early nineteenth century. No Castle of Otranto can have been more menacing. Most menacing of all, because it was so improbable and so well defended and so remote from human contacts, was the palace which he built dangerously, and with enormous daring, on the cliffs at the northern end of the mountain. The palace was built in three tiers, clinging close to the mountain, white and gleaming, resembling the profile of a wedding cake. There was a banqueting hall with living rooms opening out from it; on the middle terrace there was a bathing pool, an astonishing luxury in a place so high and remote; and modern archaeologists have taken some comfort from the fact that there were limits to Herodian luxury. The banqueting hall, for example, was faced with stone and plaster painted to resemble marble. With its soaring white columns the palace must have been a dreadful thing to contemplate at a distance. At a closer view it had a ramshackle Hollywood quality in keeping with the ramshackle rule of Herod and his dynasty.

In this palace, defended by an immense fortress, Herod was prepared, if necessary, to live for many years. He built great storehouses and filled them with wheat, sufficient for many years, plenty of wine and oil, quantities of dates and pulses. In the armament stores were enough weapons to arm ten thousand men, together with ingots of iron, brass and lead for the forging of even more weapons. Not satisfied with his forty towers he built another on the summit of the fortress which was fifteen hundred feet high, according to Josephus, whose detailed description reads like an eyewitness account. It is always dangerous to disbelieve Josephus. He is nearly always right, even on matters where he seems to be outrageously wrong. And though that tower as high as a ten-story building would seem to be a preposterous exaggeration, archaeologists are inclined to believe it actually existed.

Herod never had to defend himself in this remote fastness. From time to time he visited it, but seems never to have lived in it for very long. After his death it was held for his son Archelaus, and when the Romans deposed him, they sent their own garrison to occupy it. For seventy years the Romans kept watch from the fortress walls. Then in A.D. 66 the Jews rose in revolt, and Massada was attacked by a small army led by Menahem, the son of Judah the Galilean, who broke open the royal storehouses and distributed the arms to his followers. The Roman garrison was butchered. With the captured arms Judah marched on Jerusalem.

Now for the first time Massada was beginning to exert its full strength. It became a rebel base of operations, the strongest fortress left in Jewish hands. Even when Jerusalem was sacked by Titus, Massada remained a powerful base, under Eleazar ben Yair, Menahem's nephew, who rallied a desperate band of rebels on the mountaintop. In A.D. 72, two years after the fall of Jerusalem, the Roman governor

Flavius Silva marched against the fortress at the head of his Tenth Legion together with tens of thousands of Jewish prisoners of war pressed into service as laborers. The Roman governor was determined to break the revolt at whatever the cost. Siege engines were brought up, a great wall was built around the mountain, and at strategic places permanent military camps were set up on the slopes. Flavius Silva gave orders that none of the defenders must be permitted to escape. He was a close lieutenant of Titus, and completely merciless. A ninety-foot siege tower bound and strengthened with iron crossties was somehow lifted bodily up the mountain; missiles fired from the top of the tower cleared the rebels from their guard posts along the Herodian wall. Then a battering ram broke through the wall. The rebels built another wall when the outer wall was breached, and this new wall, consisting of earth heaped between wooden fences, was well calculated to defeat the ram, which succeeded only in pounding the packed earth within the wooden fences. Flavius Silva decided to set fire to the fences.

For almost a year the Romans and their countless prisoners hammered at the fortress. Now summer was coming on, and they decided to break through and put an end to it. Eleazar ben Yair had 960 men, women and children under his command. The Roman army together with the auxiliaries had swelled to ten thousand men accommodated in stone-walled camps in the valley and on the mountainside, and now it was only a question of time before resistance came to an end.

Josephus, who was living in Rome when the final attack was made, reports the last stages of the battle in great detail. His report reads like an account learned from an eyewitness telling the story many months later, for though occasional scenes are seen clearly, there is a sense of remoteness, as of events happening far away, in another country, in another age. He tells how flaming torches were put to the wooden walls, and at first the south wind blew the flames back in their faces, and then the wind veered, and soon the defenders were caught in a circle of fire. Then the Romans, seeing the fortress defenseless, retired for the night. On the next day, in their own time, they would storm the Jewish camp.

That night Eleazar ben Yair summoned his followers to an extraordinary meeting. He reminded them that God had abandoned them, no mercy could be expected from the Romans, everything had worked to the advantage of the enemy, and now there remained only one last decision—in what manner would they die. They could die in slavery or they could die as free men. It would be better to die, for in this way their souls would rise immediately to heaven where no calamities would ever befall them. Their bodies would be destroyed, but their souls would endure forever, "for whatever the soul touches lives and blossoms, and whatever the soul abandons withers and perishes, for has not the soul a superabundance of immortality?"

On this high intellectual level Eleazar ben Yair summoned them to die, reminding them that the Hindus cheerfully accepted death at a time of their own choosing, and surely the Jews could do likewise! Not the Romans, but God, had appointed a term to their existence, for had not God decreed that Jerusalem should perish? Therefore it was best to abandon everything to God's mercy, to die quickly and quietly, offering no hostages to fortune, and removing from the Romans the task of killing them. All, or nearly all, of the defenders agreed to die. They threw their personal possessions into the flames, but carefully preserved the food stores in order to show the Romans that it was not for want of anything that they were driven to suicide. Then followed the last act of the strange drama on the mountaintop:

> They chose ten men by lot to be the executioners of all the rest, and then every man lay down beside his wife and children, threw his arms around them, and offered their necks to those who must perform the melancholy office of executioners. And when these ten had unflinchingly carried out their duty, they cast lots among themselves to determine which one of them should kill the other nine, and then kill himself, and all had such perfect confidence in one another that neither in doing or in suffering was there any disagreement among them. So each of the nine offered his throat, and the last man looked out over the rows of the dead to see whether there was anyone who had further need of his services, and seeing that all were dead he set fire to the palace, and summoning all his strength drove his sword through his own body and fell dead beside his family.

> So they died, believing they had left no living soul to fall into the hands of the Romans; but an old woman escaped, and another who was related to Eleazar, an intelligent and well-educated woman, and five

little children. They had hidden in the subterranean aqueducts, while the rest were arranging the mass suicide. Altogether they numbered 960 persons, women and children included. All this took place on May 2nd.

So ended Jewish resistance in Palestine, and though there were to be more revolts later, none were so fearful as this. The Romans entered the camp expecting to have to fight every inch of the way; instead, they found the bodies lying in their quiet rows. "And they did not exult over them as enemies, but wondered at the courage of their resolution, and the way in which so many of them had shown their utter contempt of death, dying without trembling." Flavius Silva left a Roman garrison in the fortress, and then marched his army back to Caesarea.

Today, at the foot of the mountain, we can still see the Roman headquarters. Heavy walls, eight feet high, surround the ancient command post, and two other camps on the mountainside are visible from below. The trail winds down into the gorge and then up again. In the heavy sun glare the trail looks like a thin vein of silver in the red rock. Soon the trail vanishes, lost in the immensity of the mountain.

Once seen, Massada can haunt you for the rest of your life; and indeed the entire landscape around the Dead Sea has a haunting, hallucinatory quality. I had imagined the Dead Sea was the color of lead. Instead, it gleams like emeralds, the light seeming to glow fiercely below the surface of the water, with here and there brilliant white patches rising from the salt beds. The potash works only occupy a small corner of the lake. The twisted salt spires, the small hills which assume the shapes of people running madly before a threatened doom, are all contained within a mile's journey along the shore. They are not in the least overwhelming, but resemble delicate improvisations on a convulsive theme; for all that shore, all those high mountains ringing the lake, reddish-yellow and smoky gray, seems to be still in a process of convulsion. Some mountains are leaping in the air, others are crouching low, still others seem to be turning and twisting in perpetual agony. The grandeur is in the dying mountains and the living lake.

The medieval chroniclers were troubled by the strange habits of the lake. Sir John Mandeville said it was known as the Sea of Devils, and that it cast out asphalt "in pieces as large as a horse" every day and on all its shores. He said that a feather dropped on the surface would fall to the bottom, but iron would float on it. "Neither man, beast, nor anything that hath life, may die in that sea," he wrote, "for it utterly rejecteth anything that breatheth life." Beautiful apples were found along the shores, but when they were opened they were seen to contain only ashes and cinders. Some strange deathly presence haunted the ghostly lake.

But in the interval between Sir John Mandeville's times and our own, the Dead Sea has come to life. Ringed by those mountains which are the result of a tremendous rending of the earth's crust millions of years ago, it gives an appearance of glittering and incandescent health, with all its wealth waiting to be harvested. Where now there are only occasional hostels, soon there will be white towns along the shores, as more and more wealth pours out of the emerald lake. Potash, bromine, chloride are all necessary for modern industry, and the lake offers them in abundance. Soon there will be only the violent and dramatic mountains to remind men that it was haunted for centuries.

THE ARCHAEOLOGIST

He was, I suppose, the last man one expected to see occupying the chair of archaeology at Hebrew University. After all, he was a war hero of towering eminence, and all the high offices in the government were open to him. In 1948, at the age of thirty-three, he was Chief of Staff of the Israeli Army, and in a series of daring forays and campaigns he had led it to victory. Afterwards he reorganized the army and shaped it into a powerful fighting force capable of attacking any coalition of enemies. Then, abruptly, he stepped down from his high position and entered the university. General Yadin became Professor Yadin, and to all Ben-Gurion's pleas that he should return to government service, he answered quietly and firmly that he had found his vocation. His father had been an archaeologist, and he was determined to follow in his father's footsteps.

They said of him that he attacked archaeological problems with the same awesome intensity with which he attacked military problems. He enjoyed applying military techniques. He liked to use mine detectors to discover buried treasure, and he liked to have well-disciplined soldiers with him on archaeological expeditions. He would borrow helicopters and walkie-talkies from the army, which rarely refused a request from the former Chief of Staff. In this way he had advantages over most archaeologists, who grub away with spades and toothpicks and whose contact with the army is generally limited to the rusty swords they discover buried deep in the earth. But neither military equipment nor military skill explains his great achievements as an archaeologist. He uncovered Hazor, spending four years in the field and another four years in studying and publishing his finds, and went on to discover the authentic letters of the revolutionary leader Simon bar Kokba in a cave near En Gedi overlooking the Dead Sea. Both discoveries were vitally important to the understanding of ancient Jewish history.

He sat in his study in Jerusalem, a tall, lean, hard-muscled man with a clipped mustache and a long narrow face. He did not look like a soldier or an archaeologist, or even like a potential Prime Minister. In slacks and an open-neck shirt he looked like a student, absurdly young to have achieved so many victories. He smoked a pipe which was always going out so that it had to be constantly relit, and he had difficulty in keeping still even for a moment. He gestured with his whole body, continually in movement like a spring coiling and uncoiling, his mind moving with the same impetuous excitement as his body. He was talking about the discovery of the Simon bar Kokba letters.

"Archaeologists had been to that cave before, and they were fairly certain that Simon bar Kokba had been there, though they had discovered nothing of any great importance. It looked like a dead end, a place where nothing more could be found, but I was puzzled by the fact that there was a Roman camp on the mountain above the cave. The camp was a clue to something—I was not sure what. I found myself arguing that if there was a camp there, there must have been a purpose for it, and the only purpose I could think of was that the Romans were prepared to go to extraordinary lengths to capture or starve out the people in the cave. Why all that expenditure of money and effort? They had to bring water and food up to the camp on top of the mountain, and that isn't easy. They were bringing equipment up, and standing guard day and night, and they were doing all this simply because there were a handful of people in a cave. Why? The only reason I could possibly think of was that the Romans knew full well that the cave was the headquarters of the Jewish resistance movement, and if this were true, then I felt certain that this was the cave of Simon bar Kokba and that important relics would be found.

"As it happened, we found the relics with the help of mine detectors, which had not been used by the previous archaeological expedition. We found some copper pans and sacred vessels, and underneath them were the letters written by Simon bar Kokba. What had evidently happened was that the Jews, facing defeat and with no hope of occupying the cave any longer, had buried their treasure and a part of their archives in the belief that they would one day return and recover them. They knew the Romans would search the cave, and so they avoided all the obvious hiding places. Despair gave them cunning, and they became masters at the art of hiding things. We never found anything in a likely hiding place. It was always in the unexpected, the undreamed of place, and we would never have discovered them without the use of the mine detector.

"We learned a great deal from En Gedi, and some of that knowledge we hope to put to use next year at Massada. We want to map out the Herodian fortress, but above all we hope to find treasures and archives left behind by Eleazar ben Yair. I do not believe they were given to the flames. I believe they were buried in the knowledge that one day the Jews would return to the mountain and take possession of them. For a long time they must have known they were doomed. They had time to think out a safe hiding place, many safe when we find Roman and Byzantine remains. It is a sign, I suppose, that we are becoming mature."

As much as any man he has contributed to the maturity of archaeology in Israel, and sometimes I wondered which was the more enviable, the youthful professor or his young students.

hiding places. I rather suspect they made the decision about t
weeks before the end. It was not a decision taken at the last mome
when they were caught up in a frenzy of self-destruction, but wl
they were still calm and capable of making plans for the futu
even for the very distant future. Somewhere on top of the mount
we hope to find letters written by Eleazar ben Yair.

"There have been many expeditions to Massada, but they were
short ones. We have reconnoitered the mountain, we have :
really dug into it. This time we plan to make a survey in depth wh
will last three seasons. We shall establish a permanent camp on :
mountain, and we shall use helicopters to bring in supplies. Qu
simply we shall live on the mountain until, with luck, we have for
it to reveal its secrets.

"But the main problem does not lie in supplies and equipme
The main problem is a psychological one. We shall have to th
ourselves into the minds of the Jews who were fighting for th
freedom in A.D. 72. Much of the work has been done for us
Josephus, who has proved to be astoundingly accurate. Already
have verified about eighty per cent, perhaps more, of his descripti
What we have to do is to give life to the mountain, to see it as
was, to find the psychological solution. In three years we should kn
those long-dead revolutionaries almost as well as we know ourselve

So he spoke, weaving in his chair, waving his arms to the low c
ing, while the traffic roared in the street outside, and sometimes
would pause long enough to take a book from the shelves and p
der photographs and maps of Hazor, En Gedi and Massada, th
places which already represented his major conquests. He wo
take down one of the volumes of his work on Hazor and open
with a kind of quick affection, almost caressing the colortype plat
for he enjoyed book-making and collecting photographs, selecti
them and putting them in their proper order.

"We are growing up," he said once. "After our independence,
went about deliberately searching for Jewish remains, as though
wanted to assure ourselves that we had been here before. Now
has changed. We are so excited by our land that we are pleas

Elath

There are many ways of going to Elath on the Red Sea, and the easiest way is by the airplane which leaves the small airport at Ramat Aviv. You can go by truck or by bus from Beersheba over the desert highway, and this is regarded as the more honorable way. Until quite recently that journey took ten or eleven hours, but a new road built by the military engineers has considerably shortened it. By airplane it takes less than an hour. There is no discomfort, no dust, no sun glare, no grinding of gears, almost no sense of being over one of the most ferocious deserts in the world. Calmly, idly, you peer out of the airplane windows at a savagely eroded land so violently contorted and convulsed that it seems to be one immense volcano permanently erupting. Then you draw the curtains and shut the desert out.

The trouble about flying to Elath is that the journey is oddly unconvincing, and you are left with the feeling of having performed a fraudulent act. In the old days caravans took three or four weeks to make the same journey eastward through the Scorpion Pass and then south along the Wadi 'Arabah, stopping for the night wherever there were wells. Marauding Arabs were always a danger, and sometimes the wells dried up. Snakes and scorpions lay underfoot, and leopards haunted the hills. A man had to have strong nerves if he was to bring a caravan safely through the wilderness.

195

From the airplane the desert looks pleasant enough: pleasant, and wholly unimaginable. One does not believe in those wounds caked with yellow blood, those scars with broken crusts. There are mountains which have the shapes of grasping hands, ready to pluck anything as improbable as an airplane out of the sky. Sometimes the earth cracks open and white flesh appears under the yellow rind. For endless mile upon endless mile there is only the earth showing you in how many ways it can be broken. The guidebook announces that the fossils of giant lizards with the necks of giraffes fifteen feet long have been discovered in those burned-out mountains, and looking out from the airplane you find yourself reflecting calmly that those lizards are probably living there still. The airplane is already circling over the blue waters of the Gulf of Aqaba before you can fully realize how dangerous the desert is.

Elath lives up to the travel posters. The sun shines every day of the year, the sea is the rich glittering blue of the Orient, there are two or three gleaming white hotels on the seafront, and the girls wear bikinis. You cannot swim very far because there are tiger sharks in the Red Sea, and so there are small swimming pools staked out with blue nylon netting. The heat is merciless, and so it is the custom to take a chair into the sea and sit down on it. Egypt is a mile away on one side, Jordan a mile away on the other side. Best of all is the wide valley sweeping back into the hinterland, with the mountains looking like purple lions in endless procession.

KING SOLOMON'S MINES

When Nelson Glueck of the American School of Oriental Research set out down the Wadi 'Arabah in 1936, carrying a Bible in one hand and a spade in the other, he was continually reminded of events that happened thousands of years ago. His guide was a local Arab with fine features who looked as though he had stepped out of the ranks of the children of the Exodus. He could have been one of the Israelite chieftains or tribal leaders who had led their people through the Wadi 'Arabah before the Israelites turned eastward around Edom and Moab to reach the Promised Land. The landscape, to anyone familiar with the Bible, seemed strangely familiar. That burning valley, forming part of the Jordan rift between the Dead Sea and the Gulf of Aqaba, had remained unchanged through the centuries, and sometimes he would find cooking pots of the time of Solomon lying where they had been abandoned.

Even today the valley is little changed. Two motor roads have been carved through it, there are occasional gas stations and pumping stations, there is a copper mine, and there is Elath at the very end of it. For the rest there is only the wild treeless wilderness, the purple mountains, the wide flat valley strewn with thornbushes.

Nelson Glueck rode down the valley on camelback, halting at every spring and water hole, making a crisscross progress from one side of the valley to the other. Many weeks passed, and he was near the end of his journey when he discovered at the foot of some red hills what seemed at first to be a heap of black cinders within a strongly walled enclosure. Here the raw ore dug out of the nearby mountains was treated in small furnaces. The black cinders were slag, and the strong walls were presumably built to prevent the slaves working at the furnaces from escaping. Then at last the mystery of the wars between Judah and Edom was cleared up; they were wars for the possession of copper in the mountains near the Red Sea. And other mysteries, too, were explained. Commentators had always been puzzled by the declaration of Moses: "The Lord thy God bringeth thee into a good land, a land whose stones are iron, and out of whose hills thou mayest dig brass." In those fierce red hills there was both iron and copper.

A bus from Elath takes you along the Wadi 'Arabah to the famous slag heap of burned and shining black stones, not far from the great cliffs with their five red thunderheads which Nelson Glueck called the Pillars of Solomon. They are magnificent cliffs, strangely virile, colored a deep reddish-purple with glints of black and green; they resemble five columns of an unimaginably large temple. They suggest Solomon in all his glory.

At nearby Timnah the mines are being worked again after an interval of nearly two thousand years. From Elath the copper ore is shipped to Japan to be refined. The copper in our transistor sets comes from King Solomon's mines.

THE GLASS-BOTTOMED BOAT

There are times when Elath seems like the dead end of the world, when the light beating up from the 'Arabah is almost unbearable in its intensity, and there is no more joy to be found in swimming in the blinding sea. At such times it is best to go out in the glass-bottomed boat and to rest in the quietness of the submarine world.

There is only one glass-bottomed boat in Elath, and it seems to have been glued together from plate glass, old timbers, old nails and a donkey engine. There is a canopy, which is a welcome protection from the sun. The donkey engine rattles unpleasantly, but the chief defect is that the bluish plate glass, two inches thick, is smeared with dust, which is hardly fair to the opalescent fish. When the boat is motionless or coasting silently in the shallows, when the engine is cut off and the guide has stopped talking about the wonders of the deep, the Red Sea comes into its own. Then we are like children pressing our noses against the shop windows at Christmas, seeing more gilt and gingerbread than we ever knew existed.

The Red Sea is not red but a deep purple-blue, not soft like the waters around the islands of Greece, wine-dark and imperial, but glowing with a diamond-hard brilliance. It is fiercely purple and relentlessly blue except in the shallows, where it is the color of cool green jade. And just as the water is hard and brilliant, so too are the fishes, which look as though they had been carved out of jewels. There is nothing so ordinary as a silver fish. There are fishes composed of sapphires and rubies and others of emeralds and turquoises with large diamond circles around their agate eyes. They move in and out of coral caves gleaming rose-pink and crimson in the green depths. How those heavily jeweled objects can move so lightly is a mystery, but move they do. Imagine an entire jeweler's window poured into a fishbowl, and you have some idea of the Red Sea as seen from a glass-bottomed boat.

There are long stretches where nothing happens, nothing moves, only the wiry gray sea-grass sways languorously according to the rhythm of the tides, so slowly that it is beyond comprehension that the grasses have any real life of their own; and beyond the grasses are the empty spaces of the sea, where only the sharks glide. Each colony of fish seems to inhabit only a small space of the sea. They gleam like jeweled butterflies, but they are held within a narrow space as in an invisible cage.

The landscape at the bottom of the sea is as obscure and intricate as a large-scale map. There are sea mountains capped with clusters of green and yellow apples. They are rotten apples, creased and wrinkled, and you feel that if you touched them they would disintegrate into powder; and the fishes swarm around them and vanish into the apple caves. For some unknown reason these apple trees are only on the sea's hills; there are none in the long, sloping plains and valleys.

In the shadowless, silent roads of the sea there are cities and empires, nations and tribes on the march. It is true that the cities are very small, and the tribes only march over a few inches of territory. But the impression of a bustling, brilliant, incandescent world, with every tribe obeying its own laws, with the boundaries clearly marked, and the social organisms well established, is inescapable. Those electric-blue fish shaped like arrowheads seem to be darting about in all directions, but in fact there is a deliberate plan and purpose in their wanderings. The long purple fish like a winged serpent glides over the smooth bottom; this is his territory, he will not move into the upper reaches where the sharks and minnows wander. The fish that resemble pink spiky puffballs inhabit the mountains of scarlet coral; the fish that look like multicolored ribbons belong to the gray roots of the apple trees. All have their separate worlds, their tiny universes.

The anemones wave in the crystalline depths; the pink buds of coral grow to an immense height over the years. Here and there melons and cucumbers grow incongruously on the sea bottom, trailing their dusky foliage. But it is the apple trees, those solemn windfalls, which chiefly attract attention: apple piled on apple, and through the thin lanes between them the fish move in continual procession. Not all the apples are green or yellow. Sometimes they are purple, or touched with scarlet, and some are white like eggs. The unpredictable is always happening. A snub-nosed shark appears, but the blue arrowheads do not hurry any faster. If a crocodile studded with gems suddenly appeared and started thrashing its tail, we would not have been surprised.

For half an hour or more we watched through the cloudy plate glass, lost in this glittering dreamlike Oriental world where nothing happened according to rule. Strangely, these scarlet, yellow, purple and emerald-green fish were never predatory while we watched them; they never attacked one another; they were continually, assertively going about their own mysterious affairs. We were returning to harbor when we came upon the first signs of human habitation. How welcome they were! There was a sunken boat, very white and frail, and a coil of rope which had the same frail whiteness. Then came a discarded motor engine and a fish trap, with the fish swimming about urgently within the silver meshes—it was like a silver beehive, with all that feverish activity. Here was evidence of human handiwork, of man's empire over the sea; but it was pathetic evidence, for one felt that a trick was being played on those brilliant fish which had been running so freely among their apple trees. They were so colorful, so gay and so careless that it seemed an effrontery to capture them at all.

We were in two or three fathoms, coming towards the harbor, when we saw something I never expected to see. Down below, on the yellow sands, glittering like salt, was a shroud. It had the shape and form of a man, but no man was within it. The cloth rippled exactly as cloth ripples in the wind, and the ripples gave life to it. It was living and dead, and had the same frail whiteness as the sunken boat, so quiet and lost, so palpably human, that for some reason it sent the mind spinning backwards to an empty tomb and all the star-clustered, storm-swept legends of the Resurrection. Only this shroud was so quiet and lonely at the bottom of the sea.

Then we went back to Elath along the pebbly beach to the nylon swimming pools and the girls sitting so oddly in chairs with the sea up to their waists. One of the English ships was moving out into the bay, beginning its long journey to the copper ore refineries in Japan, but otherwise nothing had changed. All morning and all afternoon it was the same: the steady glare of the sun, the blinding sea and the empty hills.

swimming pools and the girls sitting so quiet in their chairs with the sea up to their waists. One of the English ships was moving out into the bay, beginning its long journey to the copper ore refineries in Japan, but otherwise nothing had changed. All morning and all afternoon it was the same: the steady glare of the sun, the blinding sea and the empty hills.

Jerusalem

Jerusalem is a place worth leaving for the pure pleasure of coming back to it. The golden walls, the broad streets and alleyways seem to belong to some half-finished, abandoned capital which quite suddenly has been populated with all the races of the earth. You come upon Jews from Kurdistan in swollen turbans and striped purple gowns, burly Jews from Morocco, hawk-faced Jews from Persia, Yemenites with faces of burnished copper, gold-bearded Hasidim, dark-skinned Cochin women who still wore the saris they had worn in India. The faces of the European Jews were equally distinctive. The Sephardic Jews had an olive tint and faintly Spanish features; they moved more gracefully than the more urgent Ashkenazi Jews from Central and Eastern Europe. In Jerusalem people stand out. They are not lost in the crowds as they are in Tel Aviv, which breeds a kind of anonymity. In Jerusalem every man is a king and every woman a queen.

How well the faces stand out against the color of the golden stone! The ancient walls provide a backcloth against which they work out the drama of their lives, very conscious of the drama, and therefore standing close to the footlights. There is always a sense of remoteness between the people of the new city and the silent walls of the old city, which no longer has power to menace. If one day the Israelis of Jerusalem woke to find the old city swallowed up in an earthquake, they would not be surprised. Life would go on, and they would continue to build the new Jerusalem of their heart's desire, only this new city would be less dramatic than that ancient imperial setting. Like Peking, like Moscow, like Paris, Jerusalem provides ancient dimensions by which the people can be measured, and they are determined not to be found wanting. They know they are walking in the shadow of the eagles' wings.

So one wanders around Jerusalem looking at faces rather than ruins, seeing in the smile of a child or the gaze of an old man some portion of the blessedness which is being in Jerusalem. Faces looming up in the crowded streets tell their histories. This man with the pinched cheeks and the furrowed brow has survived the concentration camps and will carry the poisons of Germany with him to the grave. That Yemenite girl has never thought of Europe, never even suspected its existence. The Rumanian scholar limps a little; he was shot at while escaping over the frontier before it became commonplace for Jews to leave Rumania. This young bald Lithuanian, who can split theological hairs in three ways, is the only survivor from a large family of merchants. So it goes on; all have their stories to tell. So many of them have been imprisoned and within an inch of massacre that their faces still wear the dawning light of relief. All have had adventures, and all are surprised at being alive.

But when you leave Jerusalem, this intensity vanishes. The faces of Tel Aviv are silent, almost expressionless. I rarely saw a face that stood out from the crowd in Tel Aviv or in Haifa. All that was best seemed to be concentrated in Jerusalem and on the shores of the Sea of Galilee. In Galilee the landscape is everything. In Jerusalem the landscape is so brutal and majestic that people somehow contrive to be equal to it. They were the two poles of the land—Jerusalem high among the hills, Tiberias deep in its submarine world like a legendary kingdom below the sea.

It was always hard to leave Jerusalem. Why leave the heights? Why go down into the world? The little train, creaking through the Judean foothills, travels for half an hour through stony and broken land, and this is still Jerusalem, but when you come to the fertile plains, you have the feeling of being cheated. The majesty has gone. The golden-blue light has been washed from the sky, and there are no longer any gold walls. So you make plans to return to Jerusalem as soon as possible and stay there forever, until in the evening light you see the Sea of Galilee spreading out before you beneath the yellow hills. Then you wonder how you will ever leave Galilee.

Usually I returned to Jerusalem at night from Tel Aviv, having left Galilee in the afternoon. These night journeys had their own dramas, because the taxi drivers were hounded by devils and liked to take corners on two wheels. The headlights picked out Arabs moving like ghosts through the trees, and they would settle like a blaze of incandescence on the smashed armored cars in the Judean hills. Then, after a few hours' sleep, there was always the light dawning over Jerusalem again.

THE HORSE CHESTNUTS

We had been wandering through the Mea Shearim district of Jerusalem on the Sabbath, on one of those blistering hot days when the air was like a flame. There were four of us, myself, an American student at Hebrew University, a young Jewish agricultural student from Rehovoth, and a girl who had lived all her life in Jerusalem. The girl was the liveliest, and she said she never walked through those narrow cobbled streets without a feeling of horror.

I asked her what was horrible. She was Jewish and so were they, and surely that was a bond between them.

"You don't understand," she said. "They are so intolerant, so stuck up, so certain they are in the right and all the rest of the world is wrong, that they have become hidebound. They are crippled by their beliefs. They are not interested in the Jewish state, won't lift a finger to help it unless they are forced, and they despise our leaders. They are waiting for the Messiah. When the Messiah appears, they will bow down and worship Him, and somehow they will all sit on His right side, and they will look pityingly at the rest of us. They know, and they give us no credit for knowing anything."

But the people of Mea Shearim strolling about on the Sabbath, bowing to one another, did not look like religious zealots. All the men wore long curling beards and enormous pinwheel astrakhan hats, usually of a brilliant reddish-brown fur. They wore white socks and long kaftans of patterned silk, and their earlocks dangled like kiss curls. Many of them wore prayer shawls with the twelve tails representing the twelve tribes of Israel. The men and the boys dressed in the same way, and looked superb, but the wives all wore ugly red wigs, and the wigs were often askew. One felt sorry for the wives, who looked worried and hesitant, hanging on the lips of their husbands, and always deferring to their sons; but no doubt male arrogance is common throughout the world. It seemed strange that on a day of such feverish heat the men and boys should be wearing fur hats and those voluminous garments.

I said something about the pageantry they brought to Jerusalem. They did no harm by their eternal studying of the Torah, and no doubt they did some good. After all they were a very small group and would probably die out in a generation or two; why should one object to them?

"Do you know what is most horrible about them?" the girl went on. "It's the intolerable mingling of mysticism and aristocracy, of religion and feudal elegance. The clothes they wear are those worn by rich merchants and aristocrats in Poland in the Middle Ages. What on earth has the long-dead Polish aristocracy to do with modern Jerusalem? Even the Poles did not cut off the hair of their women. There's barbarism for you—cutting off the hair of women!"

"Why do they do it?"

"To keep women in their places—that's why!" she said, shaking her heavy auburn curls which reached down to her shoulders. "That's the old Judaism, but it won't work any more. There will have to be new laws—'Thou shalt not tell women what to do. Thou shalt not keep them in subjection. Thou shalt not forbid them anything.'"

She laughed gaily, and was off on one of her happy diatribes against the Jewish males, who still in their subconsciousness seem to believe they were superior to women.

"Oh, it will have to stop!" she said, brooding and shaking her head. "Soon enough we shall have to fight for our rights! We'll have to have half of everything—half the positions in the government, in industry, in finance, in everything!"

"You won't want it when you get it," said the Rehovoth student.

"I'll wait till we get it before I decide whether I want it," she said sensibly.

We took a taxi and went out to the new Hebrew University campus, which has replaced the University on Mount Scopus, now in Jordanian territory. On the wind-swept height near Mount Herzl, with the walls of old Jerusalem in the distance, new buildings are springing up at a furious pace. They are in the modern style, which is to say that they have very large windows and almost no character at all. The new synagogue resembles an egg. These buildings had the advantage of being light and airy, but they might have been set down in Los Angeles or Acapulco. There is nothing distinctively Jewish about them, and this is a pity.

"Why do you object to them?" the girl asked.

"Because this is Jerusalem," I said, and it still seems to me a sufficient answer.

I do not know how the problem can be solved; perhaps it was beyond solving. There is probably no architecture which possesses sufficient strength to crown the massive weight of one of those bare Judean mountains; even the crenelated fortress walls of old Jerusalem are scarcely adequate. The one advantage of modern architecture is that it lets the light in.

We were sitting in the university bookshop, which excels all other bookshops I know because it is provided with comfortable chairs and low tables and ashtrays and because the atmosphere is conducive to quiet reading, when the American student said, "Well, what are you doing in Jerusalem anyway?"

There are no simple answers to questions like that. I had dreamed about Jerusalem for fifty years, but what I had dreamed had no relation to reality. I had seen the golden stone, and the skies which were royal blue shot through with gold light, and no one had ever mentioned this in the history books. I had come to find out how much substance there was in my dreams.

"Is that why you came here?" the American asked relentlessly.

"Oh, that, and many other reasons. I wanted to take some photographs, and to see people. The best was Jerusalem and the Sea of Galilee, and surely one doesn't have to have any reason for seeing them? The people are good, and Israel is here to stay. I learned that, and I wouldn't have known it if I hadn't come here."

The American was relentless. He wanted some concrete explanation, some rigid four-by-four statement of purpose, until I remembered that long ago I had played a very small role in the beginning of Israel. In 1917, without knowing it, I had been in at the birth of Israel.

"It happened in this way," I explained. "There was a lecturer in chemistry at the University of Manchester called Chaim Weizmann. He was a friend of Lord Balfour, and one evening Balfour came to him and told him that acetone, a solvent in the manufacture of cordite, was unprocurable in England. It was needed desperately for the war effort. Dr. Weizmann set to work, devised a process for procuring acetone from horse chestnuts, and soon the factories were producing as much acetone as anyone could want. Millions of horse chestnuts were gathered by children. In gratitude for this discovery came the Balfour Declaration, which laid the foundation for the Jewish state in Palestine."

"Where do you come into it?" the American asked.

"I was one of the children who collected horse chestnuts."

It was not a final answer, but it kept the American at bay for a little while.

Soon we drove to Ain Karem, where John the Baptist was born somewhere among the red terraced hills. There are two churches— the Church of the Baptist and the Church of the Visitation, both gleaming whitely, both curiously empty. The Tremore at Nazareth and the Upper Room on Mount Zion could move one to tears, but these churches in Ain Karem seemed to have lost their numinous qualities. They had their grottoes, the little caves labeled in marble and gold. There were priests who spoke learnedly of the ancient traditions, and there was an atmosphere of respectful reverence, but there was no John the Baptist. Only in the quiet sunlit courtyard of the Church of the Baptist, among the ruins of old walls and enormous earthenware pots filled with flowers, was there some hint of the past, the sense of an unalloyed perfection.

I only saw one building which successfully crowned a Judean

mountaintop. That was the huge Hadassah Medical School above Ain Karem, towering powerfully like a vast fortress over all the neighboring mountains, dark against the skyline, guarding the approaches to Jerusalem. These new buildings had been constructed at a cost of thirty million dollars, mostly contributed from America. Among those buildings stood the small synagogue with Chagall's blazing windows. More than anything else that fortress against those royal skies symbolized the new Jerusalem.

THE MEMBER OF THE KNESSET

He was a tall man with a shock of thick wavy hair, heavy eyebrows, a face of red leather carved into a million wrinkles. He was one of the youngest, if not the very youngest, member of the Knesset, the house of parliament now installed at a busy corner of King George V Avenue. He wore no tie, and there was about him as he moved an irrepressible air of gaiety, but when he was still his face assumed a masklike gravity. He had more worries than most men: wounds that had not healed, a sick wife, a child in hospital. He was thirty-five, but there were times when he looked sixty, and there were other times when he looked twenty. That morning he radiated youthful good humor and health.

We made slow progress down Ben Yehuda Street, for people were always stopping him to pump his hand. There would be jokes and a good deal of backslapping, and very soon he was taking out his notebook and writing down a name and address; someone had to be helped, some problem had to be inquired into, something had to be done. He was a man without impatience, or so it seemed, until a sharp cutting edge broke through his soft Sephardic accent, and the anger flared over an injustice committed, a favor asked too smoothly. There were moments, as we went down the crowded street, when it occurred to me that he was a young prince walking in procession through his own city.

We went to a coffee shop near the bottom of the street, not far from the Russian church. The waitresses flocked round him and he kissed two of them on the cheek before collapsing in a cane-bottom chair. He said wryly, "Now you know what it is like to be a member of the Knesset."

He ordered an espresso and leaned forward, his face cupped in his hands, his elbows firmly planted on the marble table top.

"What can I do for you?"

"Tell me about modern Israel."

He laughed and mopped his forehead with a red handkerchief.

"Which one?"

"Are there many of them?"

He sighed and said, "Yes, over two million of them."

"Then tell me about the essential one—the one that cuts through all the two million."

"There isn't an essential one. I'm being perfectly truthful when I say that every Israeli has his own concept of Israel. There are Jews who hate Israel, who regard the state as an abomination before the Lord, and they are living here in Jerusalem. Then there are the Jews, mercifully very few, who hate Israel because they believe Jerusalem should be ruled from Moscow. Between the two extremes are the varying opinions and beliefs of the two million. In the *kibbutsim* they believe in the communal life—no money, everything belongs to the community. In the *moshavim* they believe in money but still live the communal life. There are some gentlemen in Tel Aviv who believe in money and nothing else. There are six or seven different forms of social life going on simultaneously, and there is nothing quite like it anywhere else in the world. At least we have proved that we don't have to have a single social system. We are perfectly happy with our plural economy. We have found that it works. You can have capitalism, and you can have the communalism of the *kibbutsim*, and there is no antagonism between them. We are a state in the process of social experiment on six or seven different fronts—"

I was writing this down furiously on the back of an envelope.

"Why write it down?" he laughed. "Social experiment is not very important, not nearly so important as we thought it was. It is the easiest thing in the world to start a social experiment, to make people live according to whatever social rules you care to invent. All social rules are valid except those which reduce the individual to insignificance. What is much more important is what goes on in the hearts of people: whether they have faith in themselves, whether they know where they are going, their relationships to one another and with God. We have faith in ourselves—that is certain. But we are not sure where we are going."

"Where do you think you are going?"

"Sometimes I think we are going to the bottommost pit of hell. I mean this quite seriously, and at the same time metaphorically. Every Jew in Israel above the age of forty is tormented by his memories. He bears a heavy load of guilt if he has not suffered, and if he suffered in the concentration camps he is tormented by nightmares, and he, too, bears a load of guilt for having survived. We feel we are guilty before the Lord; not outwardly, not to the world, but in ourselves, in our hearts. We are ridden with fear, agonies, exaltations, all kinds of psychoses. We are closer to Belsen and Auschwitz than we know. The smoke of the exterminators hangs over Jerusalem, and colors our thoughts. We returned, each with his load of guilt, and we thought that when we laid the guilt down on the Holy Land it would vanish. Instead, it is heavier than before."

There was a long pause. The espresso had been served, and the waitresses hovered around him. They were Yemenite girls and knew no English.

"A little while ago you said you have faith in yourselves," I said, "and now you say there is this oppressive burden of guilt. How can you have faith and guilt?"

"Then you don't know the Jews," he said, half-smiling. "Faith and guilt go hand in hand. Perhaps guilt is only another form of faith. Perhaps what we need is a new faith. We need a new Moses, a new Sinai, a new tablet of the Law."

"Will you get them?"

"No, we'll do without them. Sometimes I think the best thing that has happened is that we have produced no great leaders—no Moses, no Joshua, no David, no Uzziah. Our greatest men do not have the resonance of a Churchill or a Roosevelt. The more I think of it, the more I come to believe that the land is our Moses, our Sinai, our tablets of the Law. This was our greatest discovery—the land of Israel. It is something we never knew until we came here, although we had dreamed about it for twenty centuries. We belong to the land, and that is why we shall never leave it. For the Jews there will always be the sense of closeness to God, of being in some way chosen by God, but now for the first time in many centuries we have the conviction of being chosen by the land."

He thought this over for a while, and then he said, "I suppose it is the same everywhere—this love of the land deep down within us—but for us it is something new. That is why we fought so hard to protect it. Through the ages the pact made by God to Abraham was repeated and renewed, and now at long last we have the feeling that we understand it. We understand it now in all its dimensions of history and theology and poetry, but it is the earth, the very earth, that we love. So in time, working on the earth, we shall forget the burden of horror and guilt which accompanied us in our long wanderings. We have come home."

So he spoke in his quiet voice, wrestling with the angel, saying sometimes things that contradicted other things he had said, but always charging his words with human emotion, never explaining away the exaltations which came from oppression and despair, but accepting them as a part of life, perhaps the most important part. He had a mind like a battering ram, intellectual, sensual, earthy, capable of fine distinctions, but more capable of generating the intellectual power which breaks through all obstacles.

"That's what it comes to," he said at last. "It is the simplest thing imaginable. We have discovered that we are the children of the land of Israel, and nothing else is so important to us."

He left a little while later, looking as he walked up Ben Yehuda Street more than ever like a young prince in his own city.

It was my last day in Jerusalem. I wandered through all the familiar places, to the university and back again to Mount Zion, and down by the Mandelbaum Gate, where there was the silence of the grave. I went to Ramat Rahel, and looked again towards Bethlehem and the ghostly ash-white Herodium rising out of the parched, eroded land. Then for the last time I went to the Department of Antiquities on

King Solomon Street, that small and crowded museum where so many of the great archaeological discoveries of Israel are kept. There, standing against a wall, was a mosaic discovered near Rehovoth, showing the seven-branched candlestick and the implements of Jewish worship. In brilliant colors were depicted the ram's horn, the snuff-shovel, the citron and the palm branch. This fifth-century mosaic had a life of its own, vigorous and clean. The seven-branched candlestick was depicted in little lozenges of scarlet and yellow, with red flames pouring from the black candles: it resembled a tree in flower, but even more remarkable than the delicately balanced design was the inscription written in Greek. It read: "May there be blessings upon this people."

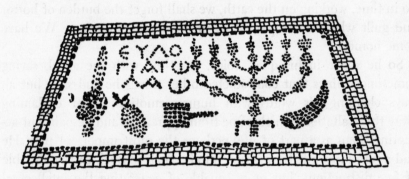

Index

Index

Index

215

Format by Gayle A. Jaeger
Set in Linotype Electra
Composed, printed and bound by The Haddon Craftsmen, Inc.
HARPER & ROW, PUBLISHERS, INCORPORATED

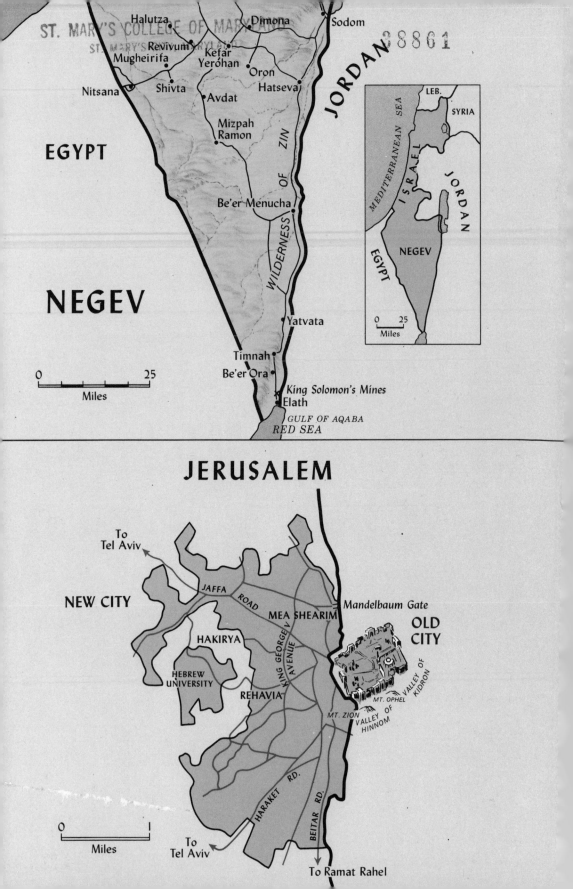

Halutza
Dimona
Sodom

Revivum
Mugheirifa
Kefar
Yeróhan
Oron
Hatseva

Nitsana
Shivta
Avdat

EGYPT

Mizpah
Ramon

WILDERNESS OF ZIN

JORDAN

Be'er Menucha

NEGEV

Yatvata

Timnah
Be'er Ora

King Solomon's Mines
Elath
GULF OF AQABA
RED SEA

0   25
Miles

MEDITERRANEAN SEA

LEB.
SYRIA

ISRAEL

JORDAN

EGYPT

NEGEV

0   25
Miles

JERUSALEM

To
Tel Aviv

NEW CITY

JAFFA   ROAD

MEA SHEARIM

Mandelbaum Gate

**OLD
CITY**

HAKIRYA

KING GEORGE V AVENUE

VALLEY OF KIDRON

HEBREW
UNIVERSITY

REHAVIA

MT. OPHEL

MT. ZION
VALLEY OF
HINNOM

HARAKET RD.

BEITAR RD.

To
Tel Aviv

To Ramat Rahel

0   1
Miles